The Ethics of Generating Posthumans

The Ethics of Generating Posthumans

Philosophical and Theological Reflections on Bringing New Persons into Existence

Edited by
Calum MacKellar and Trevor Stammers

BLOOMSBURY ACADEMIC
LONDON • NEW YORK • OXFORD • NEW DELHI • SYDNEY

BLOOMSBURY ACADEMIC
Bloomsbury Publishing Plc
50 Bedford Square, London, WC1B 3DP, UK
1385 Broadway, New York, NY 10018, USA
29 Earlsfort Terrace, Dublin 2, Ireland

BLOOMSBURY, BLOOMSBURY ACADEMIC and the Diana logo are trademarks
of Bloomsbury Publishing Plc

First published in Great Britain 2022
This paperback edition published 2023

Copyright © Calum MacKellar, Trevor Stammers and contributors, 2022

Ryan McInerney has asserted his right under the Copyright, Designs and
Patents Act, 1988, to be identified as Author of this work.

Cover design by Ben Anslow
Image © CHRISTOPH BURGSTEDT/SCIENCE PHOTO LIBRARY / Getty Images

All rights reserved. No part of this publication may be reproduced or transmitted
in any form or by any means, electronic or mechanical, including photocopying,
recording, or any information storage or retrieval system, without prior
permission in writing from the publishers.

Bloomsbury Publishing Plc does not have any control over, or responsibility for, any
third-party websites referred to or in this book. All internet addresses given in this
book were correct at the time of going to press. The author and publisher regret any
inconvenience caused if addresses have changed or sites have ceased to exist,
but can accept no responsibility for any such changes.

A catalogue record for this book is available from the British Library.

Library of Congress Cataloging-in-Publication Data
Names: MacKellar, Calum (Engineer), editor. | Stammers, Trevor, editor.
Title: The ethics of generating posthumans: philosophical and theological reflections on
bringing new persons into existence / edited by Calum MacKellar and Trevor Stammers.
Description: London, UK; New York, NY, USA: Bloomsbury Academic, 2022. | Includes
bibliographical references and index.
Identifiers: LCCN 2021036128 | ISBN 9781350216549 (hb) | ISBN 9781350216556 (epdf) |
ISBN 9781350216563 (ebook)
Subjects: LCSH: Humanism. | Human beings. | Posthumanism. | Transhumanism. |
Theological anthropology. | Ethics.
Classification: LCC B821 .E84 2022 | DDC 144–dc23
LC record available at https://lccn.loc.gov/2021036128

ISBN: HB: 9781-3502-1654-9
PB: 9781-3502-1658-7
ePDF: 9781-3502-1655-6
eBook: 9781-3502-1656-3

Typeset by Deanta Global Publishing Services, Chennai, India

To find out more about our authors and books visit www.bloomsbury.com and
sign up for our newsletters.

Contents

A note on the text   vii
List of contributors   viii
Faith perspectives   x

Introduction   *Calum MacKellar and Trevor Stammers*   1

Part I   Who is a transhuman and posthuman person?

1. The concept of a 'person' and its history   *Michael Fuchs*   19
2. One of us: Humans, transhumans and posthumans   *Richard Playford*   32
3. Remaining human: The philosophy of Charles Taylor aimed at the ethics of generating trans- and posthuman persons   *Gregory Parker Jr.*   47
4. Being somebody: Towards a categorical imperative for the age of transhumanism   *Christian Hölzchen*   62

Part II   How can transhuman and posthuman persons be generated?

5. On the scientific plausibility of transhumanism   *Chris Willmott*   77

Part III   Philosophical aspects in generating transhuman and posthuman persons

6. Domination and vulnerability: Herman Bavinck and posthumanism in the shadow of Friedrich Nietzsche   *James Eglinton*   93
7. The question of technology and relationships: How might Martin Heidegger's idea of enframing shape how posthuman persons and their generators relate to one another?   *Matthew James*   106
8. Deliver us from (artificial) evil: Are the generators of Artificial Intelligences morally accountable for the actions of those they generate?   *Trevor Stammers*   118

Part IV   Theological aspects in generating transhuman and posthuman persons

9. A Jewish outlook: A Jewish case study in creating transhuman and posthuman persons   *Deborah Blausten*   133
10. A Christian outlook: The rational body: A Thomistic perspective on parenthood and posthumanism   *Michael Wee*   145
11. An Islamic outlook: Islamic perspectives on the ethics of bringing transhuman and posthuman persons into existence   *Mehrunisha Suleman*   159

Part V Ethical aspects in generating transhuman and posthuman persons

12 Procreating transhuman and posthuman persons *Calum MacKellar* 181
13 Posthuman children: Questions of identity *Gillian Wright* 196

Conclusion *Calum MacKellar and Trevor Stammers* 207
Appendix: Scottish Council on Human Bioethics recommendations on the
    generation of transhuman and posthuman persons 227

Index 231

A note on the text

This book was prepared in collaboration between the Scottish Council on Human Bioethics (SCHB) in Edinburgh and the Centre for Bioethics and Emerging Technologies (CBET) at St Mary's University in London. As such, it represents the collective work of many individuals and is edited by Calum MacKellar from the SCHB and Trevor Stammers from the CBET.

The SCHB was formed in 1997 as an independent, non-partisan, non-religious body made up of physicians, lawyers, ethicists and other professionals from disciplines associated with medical ethics. The principles to which the SCHB subscribes are set out in the United Nations Universal Declaration of Human Rights, which was adopted and proclaimed by the UN General Assembly by resolution 217A (III) on 10 December 1948.

The CBET was created in 2009 as part of St Mary's University and focuses on the ethical and social implications of biomedicine and other new technologies. It coordinates postgraduate research, while organizing conferences and regular series of public seminars on major issues in bioethics.

Contributors

Deborah Blausten is Rabbi at Finchley Reform Synagogue in London. She holds an MA in education and technology and a degree in medicine from University College London as well as an MA in applied Rabbinic theology from Leo Baeck College, where she was ordained. She serves as a member of the World Union for Progressive Judaism's Executive Board and in several other roles within the international Reform movement and writes and teaches frequently on subjects of Jewish interest.

James Eglinton is Meldrum Senior Lecturer in reformed theology at the University of Edinburgh. He previously served as Senior Researcher in systematic and historical theology at the Theological University of Kampen in the Netherlands. He holds a doctorate in theology from the University of Edinburgh as well as undergraduate degrees in law (University of Aberdeen) and theology (University of Glasgow).

Michael Fuchs is Professor of practical philosophy and ethics at the Catholic Private University of Linz in Austria, where he is also Deputy Rector of Education and Research. He studied philosophy, Catholic theology and Germanistic in Toulouse (France) as well as in Bonn and Köln (Germany).

Christian Hölzchen was a research assistant at the Institute for Ethics at the University of Tübingen. He is currently serving as a Lutheran pastor in training near Stuttgart in Germany while finishing his dissertation on the ethics of philosophical anthropology.

Matthew James is Associate Professor of bioethics and medical law at St Mary's University, Twickenham and Adjunct Associate Professor in the School of Law of the University of Notre Dame in Australia. He has worked in the UK Westminster Parliament as a parliamentary researcher for a Member of Parliament and shadow minister before working as a senior researcher for several Westminster-based think tanks. He holds postgraduate degrees in bioethics and academic practice and is Fellow of the Royal Society for Arts (FRSA) and Senior Fellow of the Higher Education Academy. He is the Director of the Centre for Bioethics and Emerging Technologies at St Mary's University and a member of the Scottish Council on Human Bioethics in Edinburgh.

Calum MacKellar is Director of Research of the Scottish Council on Human Bioethics and a member of the Centre for Bioethics and Emerging Technologies at St Mary's University, having worked for a number of years in industry, academia and the Bioethics Division of the Council of Europe in Strasbourg (France). He holds a postgraduate degree in chemical engineering from the European High Institute of

Chemistry of Strasbourg and a doctorate in Biological Chemistry from the University of Stuttgart in Germany.

Gregory Parker Jr. is a researcher in systematic theology at the University of Edinburgh, specializing in the relationship between dogmatics and ethics in the theology of Herman Bavinck. Having graduated from Gordon-Conwell Theological Seminary in the United States, he is also a member of the Scottish Council on Human Bioethics in Edinburgh.

Richard Playford is Lecturer in religious studies at St Mary's University Twickenham, having completed a doctorate in philosophy at the University of Reading and a master's in the same discipline at the University of Birmingham. He is a member of the Centre for Bioethics and Emerging Technologies at St Mary's University as well as a fellow of the Royal Society of Arts and a fellow of the Higher Education Academy.

Trevor Stammers is the editor of *The New Bioethics*. He was a medical doctor for thirty years before becoming an associate professor of bioethics and medical law at St Mary's University, Twickenham, during which time he took part in the research for, and editing of, this book. He is also a member of the Scottish Council on Human Bioethics in Edinburgh and a Fellow of the Royal Society of Medicine.

Mehrunisha Suleman holds a DPhil in population health from the University of Oxford, a degree in biomedical sciences tripos from the University of Cambridge as well as a medical degree and a master's in global health sciences from the University of Oxford. She is presently a postdoctoral researcher at the Centre of Islamic Studies at the University of Cambridge, an expert for UNESCO's Ethics Teacher Training Programme and a Council member at the Nuffield Council on Bioethics. Moreover, she is a member of the Faculty of Public Health and has an Alimiyyah degree in traditional Islamic studies, which she was given under the supervision of Shaykh Akram Nadwi at Al Salam Institute.

Michael Wee is a doctoral candidate in Philosophy at Durham University, where he is working on language, mind and ethics in the later Wittgenstein. He is also an Associate Member of the Aquinas Institute at Blackfriars Hall, Oxford and a Young Researcher Member of the Pontifical Academy for Life, the Holy See's advisory body on bioethics.

Chris Willmott is Associate Professor in the Department of Molecular and Cell Biology at the University of Leicester. Having graduate in biological sciences and undertaken a doctorate in biochemistry and a postgraduate certificate in education, all at the University of Leicester, he also has an MA in bioethics from St Mary's University College, Twickenham. He was awarded a National Teaching Fellowship in 2005.

Gillian Wright trained in medicine (University of Cambridge, Oxford and Glasgow) and medical law and ethics (University of Glasgow), and has worked as a palliative care physician for a number of years. She is a member of the Scottish Council on Human Bioethics and was a senior research associate with this Council when researching and preparing her chapter for this book.

Faith perspectives

Because theological beliefs relating to the generation of transhuman and posthuman persons are wide ranging, the chapters addressing religious perspectives only represent the views of the authors and should not be considered as any 'official' position of the relevant faiths.

Introduction

Calum MacKellar and Trevor Stammers

Bringing into existence new persons has always fascinated humanity since its very origins. The way human individuals come into being, and how they bring their own children into the world, goes to the very heart of their identity. Scientific, religious and mythological creation accounts of human beings are arguably the most important of all stories because they address the basic settings for the continued existence of humanity and the ultimate meaning and purpose of life. They also reflect and reveal deep anthropological and philosophical insights.

Until now, the new persons brought into existence (children) have always been entirely human. But with the development of modern science and technology, the generation (defined as a general, ethically agnostic, non-gradual, bringing into existence) of new kinds of persons through novel procedures is now being considered, especially in the ideologies of transhumanism and posthumanism.

Transhumanism

The prefix 'trans' (from the Latin for 'across') is generally used to describe that someone or something has moved across from, or beyond, a certain boundary. Accordingly, 'transhumanism' is an ideology reflecting a willingness to move beyond the frontier of what is considered to be human. The term itself was developed by the British biologist Julian Huxley (1887–1975),[1] who used it for the title of an influential 1957 article[2] to suggest:

> Up till now human life has generally been, as [the English philosopher] Hobbes [1588–1679] described it, 'nasty, brutish and short'; the great majority of human beings... have been afflicted with misery...
>
> [W]e can justifiably hold the belief that... the present limitations and miserable frustrations of our existence could be in large measure surmounted.... The human species can, if it wishes, transcend itself – not just sporadically... but in its entirety, as humanity.[3]

For Huxley, therefore, transhumanism refers to the use of science and technology to liberate humanity from the restrictions and limitations of human nature, such as the mortal human body.[4] How this human nature is defined, however, may be difficult to characterize. For example, it may include the totality of the physical and behavioural characteristics of all living beings who are natural descendants of the original *Homo sapiens* species or it may just include what is currently understood as human cognition and rationality.

Transhumanism also offers an ethical vision in which technological innovation is the central human achievement and thereby becomes the medium to attain authenticity, liberty and justice.[5] Thus, transhumanists (those who support transhumanism ideology)[6] believe that, for the autonomy and freedom of future persons to be fully realized, they must be liberated from the constraints and order of nature so that they can plan and choose their own existences.[7]

In more specific terms, transhumanism can be characterized as a multidisciplinary, cultural phenomenon consisting of beliefs, literatures and social practices addressing not only scientific and technological changes but also deeper existential concerns. In fact, it can be considered as an ideology of ultimate progress; it offers a vision of the moral ordering of self and society in relation to technology-driven world transformation. The Swedish philosopher Nick Bostrom indicates:

> Transhumanism is a way of thinking about the future that is based on the premise that the human species in its current form does not represent the end of our development but rather a comparatively early phase. We formally define it as follows:
>
> 1. The intellectual and cultural movement that affirms the possibility and desirability of fundamentally improving the human condition through applied reason, especially by developing and making widely available technologies to eliminate aging and to greatly enhance human intellectual, physical, and psychological capacities.
> 2. The study of the ramifications, promises, and potential dangers of technologies that will enable us to overcome fundamental human limitations, and the related study of the ethical matters involved in developing and using such technologies.[8]

However, whether certain procedures can be considered as enhancements[9] or improvements within Bostrom's definition may be controversial and a matter of perspective, since the same procedure may be seen as progress to some but as regress to others.[10] Nevertheless, by going back to Huxley's original definition of transhumanism, it is possible to simply consider the concept of 'transcending' natural human limits without evaluating the desirability of such a procedure.

One further assertion in transhumanism is a rejection of the assumption that human nature is a constant and that *nature* in general, or *human nature* in particular, should be protected and retained as an imperative. Thus, transhumanists accept an evolutionary account of human beings but are not content to remain passive and simply let biological and social influences direct the future of the human race. Instead, they intentionally seek to control evolution and direct it towards what they consider to be improved and enhanced descendants.[11,12] In so doing, they would use tools such as genetic manipulation, nanotechnology, cybernetics, robotics, informatics and computer simulation.[13] The convergence of such technologies may then enable transhumanists to implement significant enhancements and improvements of human mental and physical abilities which they deem desirable.[14]

Transhumanism also reflects a dissatisfaction with the current abilities of humanity[15] and may even see human biological embodiment as a burden and a curse.[16] It thus focuses on how human beings ought to be transformed so that they might flourish, live longer healthier lives, enjoy greater cognitive powers and have an increased capacity to experience more robust and pleasurable inner states.[17,18] However, transhumanism does not generally give a vision of the final ideal of future enhanced persons. In other words, progress is measured not by attaining some pre-set goal but by using technology to expand human choices and capacities.

In addition, transhumanists generally see themselves as the descendants of humanists. For example, Bostrom indicates: 'Transhumanism can be viewed as an extension of humanism, from which it is partially derived.'[19] With transhumanism, however, the state of being human is just a stage in the evolutionary process towards a higher 'good', though there is often no indication about what this actually represents.[20] As the American-based religious scholar Hava Tirosh-Samuelson explains, transhumanism is a 'work in progress' – 'There are many facets to transhumanism, but they all cohere into the claim that the human species is on the verge of a new phase in its evolution.'[21] However, transhumanism continues to support a scientific and naturalistic understanding of human beings together with the concept of rationality and a type of truth, thereby continuing in the Enlightenment tradition.[22]

Transhuman persons

A transhuman person is an individual who has moved across, or beyond, the distinct boundary of what is considered to be human, though some human characteristics may remain. As Bostrom explains: 'In its contemporary usage, "transhuman" refers to an intermediary form between the human and the posthuman [where nothing physically human remains].'[23] It is generally believed that one of the first persons to define and then use the specific term 'transhuman' to characterize an individual was the Iranian-American author and futurist, Fereidoun M. Esfandiary (1930–2000), also known as FM-2030, who employed the term as shorthand for 'transitional human'. In other words, for him, transhuman individuals are the earliest manifestations of new evolutionary beings.[24] Accordingly, it is possible to define transhuman persons as having bodies which transcend the boundaries of the natural human though are still, in part, recognizably human. Such beings include:

1. Entirely biological transhuman persons such as:
   - Biological synthetic humanoid persons (often defined as biological 'androids' – a term originating from the Greek *andr* meaning 'man' and *oid* expressing 'likeness').[25]

- Human-nonhuman interspecies persons.[26]
- Any other entirely biological artificial persons with body parts which resemble those of human beings, including the brain.

2. Part-machine part-biological transhuman persons (cyborgs) such as:
   - Persons with machine bodies and human or non-human biological brains.
   - Persons with biological bodies and computer brains.
   - Persons who are a combination of the above.

3. Machine transhuman persons such as:
   - Robots who look and act in a way similar to human persons (often defined as robotic androids).

Posthumanism

The prefix 'post' (from the Latin for 'after' or 'behind') is generally used to describe the reality that someone or something is coming 'after', 'later' or 'subsequent to' in time. In this context, it is generally agreed that the term 'posthumanism' was coined by the Egyptian-born American postmodern philosopher Ihab Hassan (1925–2015) in a 1977 essay 'Prometheus as Performer: Toward as Posthumanist Culture'. In this, he suggests that 500 years of humanism may be coming to an end.[27] Two understandings of posthumanism, which are related, then developed.[28]

The first suggests that conceptual, philosophical and cultural aspects of humanism should be challenged. For instance, the American author N. Katherine Hayles suggests that the way human beings even consider themselves should be questioned indicating that individuals have 'always been posthuman' since, for example, they can be considered as no more than physical substance.[29] Thus, a more theoretical perspective of posthumanism may not imply a moving beyond humanness in some biological manner but a redefinition, instead, of what is 'human'.[30] Hayles characterizes four different aspects of a posthuman ideology:[31]

- The prioritization of information patterns over material substances.
- The acceptance that consciousness is a mere product of the physical.
- The recognition that the human body is just an original form and substance of a being which can be upgraded or replaced.
- An acknowledgement that human beings can simply be considered as intelligent machines making the two interchangeable.

This form of posthumanism would also challenge humanist anthropocentrism and categorical dualisms.[32] The American science and technology scholar Donna Haraway indicates: 'Chief among these troubling dualisms are self/other, mind/body, culture/nature, male/female, civilized/primitive, reality/appearance, whole/part, agent/resource, maker/made, active/passive, right/wrong, truth/illusion, . . . God/man.'[33]

And to this list the following can be added: subject/object, fact/value, public/private, human/nonhuman, organism/machine and natural/artificial.[34]

The second form of posthumanism also challenges 'humanism' but is more physiological and material while based on technological and scientific developments. Accordingly, though transhumanism and this kind of techno-scientific posthumanism both originate in the human and agree that the 'human' of humanism may be outdated,[35] the latter builds on the aims, values and ideology of the former. The German philosopher Stefan Lorenz Sorgner indicates: 'Transhumanism affirms the use of techniques to increase the likelihood of bringing about the posthuman.'[36] Thus, this form of posthumanism continues to support the belief that humanity can take charge completely of its future evolutionary destiny by totally redesigning itself in its own way. In other words, the means and aspirations of transhumanism pioneer a future which finds its end goal in posthumanism[37] – where beings are generated and their existence is entirely beyond the human.

Accordingly, from this technological perspective of posthumanism, living beings may eventually reach a stage where nothing of what remains may be defined as human. The Canadian computer scientist and futurologist Hans Moravec postulates that machines will eventually convert the entire universe into an extended thinking entity.[38]

Tirosh-Samuelson also suggests that technology will enable humans to successfully bring about what established religions have sought for thousands of years, namely immortality.[39] In this respect, the American inventor and futurist Raymond Kurzweil indicates: 'Our mortality will be in our own hands. We will be able to live as long as we want',[40] which, interestingly, is not quite the same as immortality.

Clear differences between transhumanism and the different forms of posthumanism ideologies do exist, however, in that the former is rooted in science and technology, evolutionary theory, utilitarianism and applied ethics. Posthumanism, on the other hand, comes out of postmodernism and is more closely associated with theoretical philosophy, literary theory and cultural studies while supporting a more narrative approach to ethical discourse.[41,42] The American social philosopher Steve Fuller explains: '[T]ranshumanism . . . involves a desire to intensify and extend uniquely human properties beyond their normal physical parameters, whereas posthumanism . . . involves an indifference if not a hostility to the original humanist project.'[43] Thus, for posthumanists, 'humanity' is simply a state in the development of 'being' but has no special vantage point.[44]

However, there is still no consensus relating to the definitions of transhumanism or posthumanism and both terms are sometimes considered synonymous by some commentators, including in this volume. And even when they are distinguished, some degree of overlap remains.

Posthuman persons

A posthuman person in techno-scientific posthumanism is an individual who no longer expresses human characteristics in any significant manner. As Bostrom explains:

> It is sometimes useful to talk about possible future beings whose basic capacities so radically exceed those of the present humans as to be no longer unambiguously

human by our current standards. The standard word for such beings is 'posthuman'.[45]

Thus, posthuman beings would exist in a state that has moved completely beyond the boundary of what is considered human and would, for example, include:

1. Biological posthuman persons, such as:
   - Synthetics biological persons who no longer retain any human characteristics whatsoever.
2. Non-biological posthuman persons, such as:
   - Virtual persons living in cyber-space (who are, for example, the result of a mind upload).
3. Cyborg Posthumans
   - Persons resulting from a combination of biological and machine elements, but who no longer retain any human characteristics whatsoever.

Generally, however, it is difficult to accurately describe the posthuman individual. Hayles, for example, characterizes such a being as 'an amalgam, a collection of heterogeneous components, a material-informational entity whose boundaries undergo continuous construction and reconstruction.'[46] Adding:

> [T]he presumption that there is an agency, desire, or will belonging to the self and clearly distinguished from the 'will of others' is undercut in the posthuman, for the posthuman's collective heterogeneous quality implies a distributed cognition located in disparate parts that may be in only tenuous communication with another.[47]

Thus, it may be unclear how a specific identity can actually exist in the posthuman state.

Generating new beings in an historical context

As already mentioned, accounts of bringing persons into existence date back to antiquity and it may be useful, at this stage, to present a number of these stories to explore some of the ideas they convey. Indeed, these concepts may be useful in examining the possible ethical generation of transhuman and posthuman persons, including the associated motivations, warnings and risks.

One of the earliest creation accounts of persons is the late eighth-century BC Greek myth of Prometheus (of which many versions exist), who is one of the pre-Olympian gods known as the Titans. He is asked by Zeus, the king of the Olympian gods, to form a human being from water and earth since Prometheus is considered as an embodiment of wisdom, knowledge and the sciences. Consequently, because he is a kind of 'father' to these human beings, he also becomes their champion, helping and supporting them whenever he can. As a result, he eventually tricks the other gods by stealing one of their most special possessions, namely fire, and gives this to the humans to help them in their development. However, as a punishment for the theft, Zeus sentences Prometheus to eternal torment, whereby the immortal Titan is attached to a rock, and an eagle sent every day to eat his liver, which regenerates during the night. Eventually, Prometheus is delivered from his punishment by the demigod hero Heracles, the son of Zeus.

Interestingly, the Greek name Prometheus is composed of *pro*, which means 'for', 'before' or 'ahead', as well as *mathein*, which means to 'know' or 'understand'. Thus, a Promethean future of humanity may represent a time when human beings use scientific knowledge and technological innovation to engineer themselves for that future. As the philosopher Trijsje Franssen, from the Netherlands, explains: 'Prometheus thus symbolizes courage, mastery and transcendence of limits in order to gain knowledge, develop techniques and improve the human being.'[48] In other words, just as Prometheus stole the secret of fire from the gods, human beings may be called to steal the secret of generating new persons from biological life.

Another account of generating a living being from inanimate matter is given by the Roman poet Ovid (43 BC–17/18 AD) in his narrative poem *Metamorphoses*, where he tells the story of a sculptor, Pygmalion, who makes an ivory statue of a woman, which is so beautiful and realistic that he eventually falls in love with it. And, over time, he longs for his statue to become alive – a wish which is eventually granted by Aphrodite, the Greek goddess of love, beauty and procreation. Pygmalion then names this woman Galatea.

A further account of bringing into existence a living being takes place in the Hebraic account of the 'wizard of Samaria', Simon Magus, who was a sorcerer as well as an alchemist and whose confrontation with the Apostle Peter is recorded in the Bible in Acts 8.9–24. In some early additional accounts, Simon Magus is also portrayed as being able to generate a kind of living being from thin air, which is then turned into water, then blood, from which he finally forms physical flesh.[49] Simon of Samaria, in many ways, is the perfect example of the Promethean trickster, while at the same time challenging God by presenting himself as the Great Power (Acts 8.8) and calling himself the favoured or fortunate one (translated in Latin as *faustus*).[50] Thus, he may be one of the original characters behind the story of Faust developed, among other writers, by the German author Johann Wolfgang von Goethe (1749–1832).[51] In Goethe's story, Faust is represented as a very self-confident individual, preferring human to divine knowledge, who puts aside moral integrity and asks the Devil to give him magic power and success in exchange for his soul. The Devil accepts but Faust's irresponsible decision eventually catches up with him and his soul is eternally enslaved in retribution and regret.

Throughout history, generation stories of a homunculus (Latin for 'little person') were also recounted. One of the first was mentioned by the Islamic Persian polymath, Avicenna (c. 980–1037), who reported that a homunculus had been formed by a certain Qaliqulas, an adviser to a king named Harmanus, who lived in the Middle East around AD 300. Apparently, Harmanus, finding intercourse repugnant, did not have any children, so Qaliqulas generated an artificial child for him named Salaman.[52] The concept of a homunculus was also popularized in sixteenth-century alchemical writings, such as those attributed to the Swiss physician and alchemist, Paracelsus (1493–1541). In his *De natura rerum* (1537), he outlines a method for generating such homunculi from male sperm. With respect to the moral messages of such generation accounts, the British science writer, Philip Ball, asks:

> What, then, is the homunculus, the artificial man? Although made from human seed, he is either less than or more than human, or both at once. It is questionable whether he has a soul. He is perhaps the spawn of witchcraft and demons, and as such, is something monstrous, even if not in appearance. He has special, hidden knowledge. He may be infertile.[53]

A different account of generation takes place, as will be seen (see Chapter 9) in the Jewish tradition of the golem, which is an imperfect or incomplete living humanoid generated from the animation of raw earth. Indeed, *golem* in Hebrew means 'unformed matter'.[54] According to the anonymous *Sefer Yetzirah* (Book of Creation), an important text of Jewish religious magic, a human-made golem could be brought to life by the ritualistic use of the Hebrew language. One of the most famous golems is the one generated by Rabbi Judah Loew ben Bezalel (d. 1609) in Prague, which eventually had to be destroyed because it rebelled again its human master.[55]

A better-known example of the generation of a transhuman takes place in the novel *Frankenstein: The Modern Prometheus*, published in 1818, by the English writer Mary Shelley (1797–1851).[56] This tells the story of a scientist, Victor Frankenstein, who generates a transhuman person from a number of human cadavers. The novel describes his initial excitement in the unrestricted generation of a new kind of person but also prompts ethical reflection concerning individual and collective responsibility in caring for the resulting person.[57] In addition, the story presents what may happen when generators are eventually negatively overwhelmed by what they have generated.

Another instance of generating new transhumans is given in 1920 by the Czech writer Karel Čapek's (1890–1938) science-fiction play *R.U.R (Rossum's Universal Robot)*. This was the first time that the word *robot* (which in Czech describes a 'forced labourer') was used in order to represent a manufactured being (which, in the play, is actually biological and not mechanical). In the story, the manager of the robot factory indicates that the real aim of its founder, Mr. Rossum, was to generate new people, adding: 'He wanted to become a sort of scientific substitute for God. He was a fearful materialist, and that's why he did it all. His sole purpose was nothing more nor less than to prove that God was no longer necessary.'[58] Actually, the name 'Rossum' represents a play on words since the Czech 'Rozum' means 'Reason'. Thus R.U.R. initiates a conflict between the ability to generate (or produce) and to reason.[59] In fact, the play portrays how a lack of reasoning about possible consequences eventually gives rise to a bleak future for humanity.

More recently, an account of synthetic android persons is given in the British director Sir Ridley Scott's 1982 film *Blade Runner*, which is loosely based on the American Philip K. Dick's 1968 novel *Do Androids Dream of Electric Sheep?*, in which bioengineered humanoids, known as replicants, are generated to become labourers in space colonies. Some of them, however, escape and seek recognition as persons – something which always seemed beyond their reach. In their frustration, one the replicants eventually kills the principal engineer who initially generated them while another begins a romantic relationship with the human hero, reflecting a similar situation to Pygmalion and Galatea.

How this book was prepared

In order to examine the ethical consequences of generating new persons, it will be necessary to first seek to define certain key terms. This, however, will not be easy since trying to understand the manner in which persons are generated is often hampered by the sheer number of different words employed. For example, words such as 'reproduction', 'begetting', 'creation', 'procreation' and 'making' all have different nuances of meaning. As the American physician and bioethicist Leon Kass explains:

> Consider the views of life and the world reflected in the following different expressions to describe the process of generating new life. Ancient Israel, impressed with the phenomenon of transmission of life from father to son, used a word we translate as 'begetting' or 'siring'. The Greeks, impressed with the springing forth of new life in the cyclical processes of generation and decay, called it genesis, from a root meaning 'to come into being'. . . . The premodern, Christian English-speaking world, impressed with the world as given by a Creator, used the term 'pro-creation'. We, impressed with the machine and the gross national product (our own work of creation), employ a metaphor of the factory, 'reproduction'.[60]

In this respect, the word 'creation' usually has a specific use in theology in that only God is seen as 'creating'. Moreover, other words such as 'procreating', 'manufacturing' or 'reproducing' have, as will be seen in Chapter 12, special meanings. In the context of bringing about *artificial* life, finding an appropriate word may be even more difficult since such a prospect became realistic only relatively recently.

In this book, the word 'generating' will be used to reflect a general and ethically agnostic perspective in 'bringing into existence' new kinds of persons. However, another possible term was coined by Ball to express the generation of such persons, namely 'anthropoeia', which combines the prefix *anthropo* (meaning people in Greek) and the word *poiesis* (meaning 'the making' or 'the bringing forth' in Greek).[61] Ball indicates that the special artificial aspect of anthropoeia may then give rise to a 'real frisson' as to the excessive pride or self-confidence and even impious nature associated with the concept. At the same time, he indicates that the generation of artificial life is controversial for the three following reasons:

1. The new life did not occur of its own accord in nature, thus raising suspicions of demonic intervention. In a way, this reflects a disapproval of the means rather than the end. Ball explains that the problem may lie between ordained nature and contingent art.
2. Human life is seen as a unique and divine mystery, a gift of God or gods.
3. The generation of artificial life gives rise to uncomfortable questions about the soul.

These points may reflect, therefore, the confusions about human nature that anthropoeia initiates. As Ball indicates: 'If we can be raised from inanimate or dead matter, where does our life reside, and from which source does it spring? These issues compel us to question our privileged status in God's creation.'[62]

This all means that, at present, there is very little understanding of what it means to generate new kinds of persons from an ethical, theological and philosophical perspective, despite some of the most important faiths in the world having developed, over many centuries, the theme of generating entirely posthuman persons. Moreover, notwithstanding some of the transhuman and posthuman proposals seeming rather futuristic, the topic of the ethical generation of new kinds of persons is practically urgent as new technologies develop. For example, since human-nonhuman interspecies embryos are already being generated, those who believe that embryos can be considered as persons may already be challenged by the generation and existence of transhuman persons.[63]

The structure of the book

In this pressing context, this book is constructed into different sections. The first part, 'Who is a transhuman and posthuman person?', begins with Michael Fuchs' exploration of what it means to be a transhuman or posthuman person. Commencing and ending in an elevator, he gives a philosopher's lightning (and enlightening) tour of the historical meanings of 'persons'; from the masks of ancient Greek theatre, we travel to medieval, and then contemporary philosophers. The chapter also starts and finishes with the English philosopher and physician, John Locke's still-predominating concept of personhood centred on the self-consciousness of memories over time, and its ongoing influence in a world of transhuman and posthuman aspirations.

Richard Playford then argues that transhumans and posthumans are still basically 'human' and will always remain 'one of us' no matter how much they are modified. He suggests that human language does not make humans different in kind from other animals; instead, it is their rationality that makes them totally different from non-human species. He concludes that since transhumans will be rational animals, they should be considered as human as their generators.

Following this, Greg Parker analyses the works of Canadian philosopher Charles Taylor and surmises how he might have evaluated the generation of posthumans. He does this utilizing Taylor's concepts of two different kinds of human 'fullness' – the first, where human meaning and agency are *under* technology and the second, where human agency is engaged through technology. By applying these concepts and speculating as to how Taylor might classify the 'agency of angels', Parker assesses why Taylor would likely have had difficulty affirming the generation of transhumans and posthumans.

Christian Hölzchen then dissects the Kantian concepts of autonomy and the categorical imperative in an attempt to derive categorical imperatives that could apply to the generation of transhuman and posthuman persons. While the focus of Kantian autonomy is often on the *nomos* (rule), Hölzchen focuses on the *autos* (self) and a particular understanding of embodiment. For him, personhood cannot be separated from the fact that living beings have to negotiate their limited and individual lives in coexistence as bodies. Persons both *have* a body and *are* a body. He considers the posthuman vision as akin to 'curing a headache by cutting off the head'.

The second part, 'How can transhuman and posthuman persons be generated?', comprises Chris Willmott's concise yet comprehensive analysis of the different possible scientific procedures which could be used to generate such beings. From the biological perspective, this includes genome editing and the production of chimeric, hybrid and human admixed embryos. From 'the machine end of scale' of generation, he discusses both magnetic and direct electrical current transcranial stimulation, radio-frequency identification chip insertion, brain-machine interfaces and androids – all masterfully presented in a way easily accessible to the non-scientist.

The third part, 'Philosophical aspects in generating transhuman and posthuman persons', begins with James Eglinton, one of the biographers of the Dutch Reformed theologian, Herman Bavinck. He examines Bavinck's writings from the early 1900s, when the theologian began to discuss ethics in the light of the increasing influence of Friedrich Nietzsche and his concept of the *Übermensch*. Eglinton suggests that, concerning the generation of new kinds of persons, Bavinckian and posthuman anthropologies are 'poles apart', contrasting the two views respectively as *homo vulnerabilis* and *homo dominus*.

Using the German philosopher Martin Heidegger's concepts of the enframing of technology and 'standing reserve' – component parts of a process to accomplish some other goal – Matt James speculates how the German philosopher might have viewed the generation of posthumans. Though, at first, tranhumanist philosophy may appear to 'encapsulate everything that Heidegger warns against', James suggests an alternative pathway which 'retains something of what it means to innovate and experiment as humans and reimagines a new positive expectation from science and technology' of which Heidegger may have approved.

Trevor Stammers then explores the accountability and responsibility of the generators of posthuman Artificial Intelligences for any evil such entities may subsequently instigate. He illustrates the over-optimism of posthuman aspirations to date and critiques the reductionist nature of the 'Information Ethics' conception of 'Artificial Evil', which equates ethics with changes in entropy, albeit of a metaphysical kind. Stammers argues that embodiment and moral agency are both necessary for moral responsibility and that the generators of what are currently considered to be 'artificial autonomous agents' are likely to bear at least partial accountability for evil committed by their computerized 'children'.

In Part IV, 'Theological aspects in generating transhuman and posthuman persons', scholars from the three Abrahamic monotheistic traditions discuss their views on generating such persons through conceptual elements of their respective faiths. The part begins with the legendary golems, living beings fashioned by human generators, which are the focus of Deborah Blausten's chapter on Jewish approaches to the generation of transhuman and posthuman persons. She traces the golem legend's development over nearly two millennia, from its origins in the Talmud up to the present day. Blausten then demonstrates how the moral lessons of the golems' various manifestations in history have been used to both prohibit and permit the generation by humans of transhuman and posthuman persons, though the moral integrity in the objectives of the generators is crucial.

Following this, Michael Wee uses the Christian lens of Thomistic anthropology to present the paradoxical concept of 'rational embodiment' and argues why the sharing of biological material constitutes parenthood in a way that the sharing of inanimate matter between artefacts does not. He is, therefore, sceptical that the generation of posthuman persons could ever be analogous to biological parenthood, because though posthumanism is premised on expanding the potential of the body, it involves a complete rejection of the body as a centre of rationality and personal history.

A comprehensive analysis of Islamic texts forms the basis of Mehrunisha Suleman's assessment of how that tradition might determine whether or not the generation of posthuman persons is 'playing God'. She concludes that bringing into existence novel beings is not anathema in Islam but nevertheless raises concerns about the consequences of doing the same in connection with issues of relatedness, dependency, the notion of 'creation without care' and ideas on perfection and imperfection, need and trust. She concludes by asking whether relationships are a key part of being human, and if they are, whether posthumans will be devoid of such or whether they will develop relationships between themselves.

The final Part, 'Ethical aspects in generating transhuman and posthuman persons', commences with Calum MacKellar's examination of whether it is even possible to specifically *procreate* (in contrast to other acts of generation, such as reproduction or manufacture) transhuman and posthuman persons. He indicates that the very notion of the aspirational concept of procreation implies that two persons of complementary gender generate offspring to be unconditionally loved and accepted from their own exclusive, selfless, unconditional and faithful embodied love for one other.

Gillian Wright follows by examining how generated posthumans may regard both themselves and those who brought them into being. Through the lenses of personal identity, social identity, biological and social kinship, as well as those of moral responsibility, she emphasizes the importance of a person's identity and the relationships that help to shape it. She explores the phenomenon of 'genealogical bewilderment', which may arise through both adoption and the use of donor gametes, while suggesting that a similar situation may arise in generating posthuman persons.

The conclusion to the book then brings all these different aspects relating to the generation of transhuman and posthuman persons together to consider whether such generation can ever be done ethically.

Notes

1. Julian Huxley was the older brother of Aldous Huxley (1894–1963), the author of the 1932 book *Brave New World*.
2. It is likely that Teilhard de Chardin influenced the terminology of Julian Huxley in coining the term 'transhumanism'. The two were close friends; David Grumett, 'Transformation and the End of Enhancement: Insights from Pierre Teilhard de Chardin', in *Transhumanism and Transcendence*, ed. Ronald Cole-Turner (Washington, DC: Georgetown University Press, 2011), 38. However, the word actually derives from an earlier 1940 paper by the Canadian philosopher William Lighthall (1857–1954); Peter Harrison and Joseph Wolyniak, 'The History of "Transhumanism"', *Notes and Queries* 62, no. 3 (2015), 465–7.
3. Julian Huxley, *New Bottles for New Wine* (London: Chatto & Windus, 1957), 13–17.
4. Ted Peters, 'Markers of Human Creaturehood: Soil, Spirit and Salvation', *Science & Christian Belief* 30, no. 2 (2018), 141–2.
5. Hava Tirosh-Samuelson, 'Transhumanism as a Secularist Faith', *Zygon* 47, no. 4 (2012), 728.
6. Bostrom indicates: 'A transhumanist is simply someone who advocates transhumanism'; Nick Bostrom, 'Introduction – The Transhumanist FAQ: A General Introduction', in *Transhumanism and the Body*, eds. Calvin Mercer and Derek F. Maher (New York: Palgrave Macmillan, 2014), 1–17, 4.
7. Ronald Cole-Turner, 'Afterword – Concluding Reflections: Yearning for Enhancement', in *Transhumanism and the Body*, eds. Calvin Mercer and Derek F. Maher (New York: Palgrave Macmillan, 2014), 174–91, 177.
8. Bostrom, 'Introduction – The Transhumanist FAQ: A General Introduction', 1.
   Bostrom further explains that 'transhumanism is a loosely defined movement . . . [that] represents an interdisciplinary approach to understanding and evaluating the ethical, social and strategic issues raised by present and anticipated future technologies.' Nick Bostrom, 'Transhumanist Values' (2001) available on his website http://www.nickbostrom.com (Accessed on 8 January 2021). For a fuller treatment see idem, 'Transhumanism FAQ, A General Introduction', version 2.1, available on http://www.nickbostrom.com (Accessed on 8 January 2021).
9. Enhancement procedures can generally be distinguished between those that do not take the human individual beyond what now exists in nature, which are usually considered under eugenic procedures, and those that go beyond the limit of what now exists in nature, which would be considered as a form of transhumanism.
   The concept of 'enhancement' should also be contrasted to the concept of 'therapy' which only seeks to restore a person with a pathology to normal health.
10. For example, a procedure facilitating the reading of a person's mind may be seen as enabling better communication by some but as threatening privacy by others.
11. Steve Fuller and Calvin Mercer, 'Introduction', in *Transhumanism and the Body*, eds. Calvin Mercer and Derek F. Maher (New York: Palgrave Macmillan, 2014), iii–vi, v.
12. For a discussion about how humans may attempt to control their evolutionary future, see: Maxwell J. Mehlman, *Transhumanist Dreams and Dystopian Nightmares: The Promise and Peril of Genetic Engineering* (Baltimore, MD: Johns Hopkins University Press, 2012).

13 Michael Burdett, *Technology and the Rise of Transhumanism* (Cambridge: Gove Books Ltd, 2014), 5.
14 Fuller and Mercer, 'Introduction', i.
15 Michael Burdett and Victoria Lorrimar, 'Creatures Bound for Glory: Biotechnological Enhancement and Visions of Human Flourishing', *Studies in Christian Ethics* 32, no. 2 (2019), 241–53, 243.
16 Hava Tirosh-Samuelson, 'Religion', in *Post- and Transhumanism: An Introduction*, eds. Robert Ranisch and Stefan Lorenz Sorgner (Frankfurt am Main: Peter Lang, 2014), 49–71.
17 Burdett and Lorrimar, 'Creatures Bound for Glory: Biotechnological Enhancement and Visions of Human Flourishing', 245.
18 Bostrom, 'Introduction – The Transhumanist FAQ: A General Introduction', 3.
19 For example, Nick Bostrom, indicates: 'Transhumanism can be viewed as an extension of humanism, from which it is partially derived.' Bostrom, 'Introduction – The Transhumanist FAQ: A General Introduction', 1.
20 Brent Waters, *From Human to Posthuman* (Burlington: Ashgate, 2006), 78.
21 Hava Tirosh-Samuelson, 'In Pursuit of Perfection: The Misguided Transhumanist Vision', *Theology and Science* 16, no. 2 (2018), 200–22, 200.
22 Stefan Lorenz Sorgner, 'Pedigree', in *Post- and Transhumanism: An Introduction*, eds. Robert Ranisch and Stefan Lorenz Sorgner (Frankfurt am Main: Peter Lang, 2014), 29–47.
23 Bostrom, 'Introduction – The Transhumanist FAQ: A General Introduction', 4.
24 Robert Ranisch and Stefan Lorenz Sorgner, 'Introduction: Post- and Transhumanism', in *Post- and Transhumanism: An Introduction*, eds. Robert Ranisch and Stefan Lorenz Sorgner (Frankfurt am Main: Peter Lang, 2014), 7–28; Bostrom, 'Introduction – The Transhumanist FAQ: A General Introduction', 4.
25 See for example: Maxwell J. Mehlman, *Transhumanist Dreams and Dystopian Nightmares*.
26 Calum MacKellar and David Albert Jones, eds., *Chimera's Children: Ethical, Philosophical and Religious Perspectives on Human-nonhuman Experimentation* (London and New York: Continuum Books (Bloomsbury Publishing), 2012).
27 Ranisch and Lorenz Sorgner, 'Introduction: Post- and Transhumanism'.
28 Tirosh-Samuelson, 'Religion', 49–71.
29 M. Katherine Hayles, *How We Became Posthuman: Virtual Bodies in Cybernetics, Literature, and Informatics* (Chicago and London: University of Chicago Press, 1999), 291.
30 Andy Miah, 'A Critical History of Posthumanism', in *Medical Enhancement and Posthumanity*, eds. B. Gordijn and R. F. Chadwick (Dordrecht: Springer, 2008), 71–94, 72, Mentioned in Marcus Rockoff, 'Literature', in *Post- and Transhumanism: An Introduction*, eds. Robert Ranisch and Stefan Lorenz Sorgner (Frankfurt am Main: Peter Lang, 2014), 251–70, 253.
31 Hayles, *How We Became Posthuman*, 2–3.
32 Ranisch and Lorenz Sorgner, 'Introduction: Post- and Transhumanism'.
33 Donna Haraway, 'A Cyborg Manifesto: Science, Technology, and Socialist-Feminism in the Late Twentieth Century', in *Simians, Cyborgs and Women: The Reinvention of Nature* (New York: Routledge, 1991), 149–81.
34 Ranisch and Lorenz Sorgner, 'Introduction: Post- and Transhumanism'.
35 Ranisch and Lorenz Sorgner, 'Introduction: Post- and Transhumanism'.
36 Lorenz Sorgner, 'Pedigree', 30.

37 Tirosh-Samuelson indicates: 'Transhumanism, then, is the Process that Will Culminate in Posthumanism, its Telos'. Tirosh-Samuelson, 'In Pursuit of Perfection: The Misguided Transhumanist Vision', 203.
38 Hans Moravec, *Mind Children: The Future of Robot and Human Intelligence* (Cambridge, MA: Harvard University Press, 1988), 116.
39 Tirosh-Samuelson, 'Transhumanism as a Secularist Faith', 713-16.
40 Ray Kurzweil, *The Singularity Is Near: When Humans Transcend Biology* (New York and London: Viking Penguin, 2005), 9.
41 Stefan Lorenz Sorgner, 'Editor's Note', *Journal of Posthuman Studies* 1, no. 1 (2017), 1-8 (8 pages).
42 Francesca Ferrando, 'The Body', in *Post- and Transhumanism: An Introduction*, eds. Robert Ranisch and Stefan Lorenz Sorgner (Frankfurt am Main: Peter Lang, 2014), 213-26, 221.
43 Steve Fuller, 'Evolution', in *Post- and Transhumanism: An Introduction*, eds. Robert Ranisch and Stefan Lorenz Sorgner (Frankfurt am Main: Peter Lang, 2014), 201-11, 201.
44 Fuller, 'Evolution', 202.
45 Bostrom, 'Introduction – The Transhumanist FAQ: A General Introduction', 3.
46 Hayles, *How We Became Posthuman*, 3.
47 Hayles, *How We Became Posthuman*, 3-4.
48 Trijsje Franssen, 'Prometheus: Performer or Transformer', in *Post- and Transhumanism: An Introduction*, eds. Robert Ranisch and Stefan Lorenz Sorgner (Frankfurt am Main: Peter Lang, 2014), 73-82, 79.
49 Philip Ball, *Unnatural: The Heretical Idea of Making People* (London: The Bodley Head, 2011), 39.
50 Ball, *Unnatural*, 47.
51 The Faust character may also be based, among other sources, on Johann Georg Faust (c. 1480-1540), a magician and alchemist who lived in Württemberg (now part of Germany) who studied divinity at Heidelberg University in 1509.
52 Ball, *Unnatural*, 37-8.
53 Ball, *Unnatural*, 47.
54 Ball, *Unnatural*, 147-8.
55 Hava Tirosh-Samuelson, 'Utopianism and Eschatology: Judaism Engages Transhumanism', in *Religion and Transhumanism*, eds. Calvin Mercer and Tracy J. Trothen (Santa Barbara, CA: Praeger, 2015), 161-80, 170.
56 Interestingly, Marcus Rockoff indicates that:

> The project of Victor Frankenstein has striking parallels to transhumanism. In the tranhumanist project three elements can be identified that are already present in Shelley's Frankenstein: (1) the specific diagnosis of the current human being as a defective existence; (2) the purposeful modification and improvement of humanity to free it from disease and limitations of the human life span (immortality), but also to [amplify well-being] . . . ; (3) the belief in rationality, science and technology as the main resources to improve humankind and make the world a better place. Rockoff, 'Literature', 251-70, 257.

57 David H. Guston, Ed Finn and Jason Scott Robert, 'Editor's Preface', in *Mary Shelley, Frankenstein, Annotated for Scientists, Engineers, and Creators of All Kinds*, eds. David H. Guston, Ed Finn and Jason Scott Robert (Cambridge, MA: The MIT Press, 2017), xi-xii.
58 Karel Čapek, *R.U.R. (Rossum's Universal Robot)*, first published in 1920 (London: Gollancz, 2011), 10.
59 Adam Robert mentioned in Čapek, *R.U.R. (Rossum's Universal Robot)*, viii-ix.

60 Leon Kass, *Toward a More Natural Science* (New York: The Free Press, 1985), 48. Quoted in Gilbert Meilaender, *Bioethics: A Primer for Christians*, 3rd edn (Grand Rapids, MI: Eedermans Publishing Co, 2013), 10.
61 Ball, *Unnatural*, 2.
62 Ball, *Unnatural*, 318.
63 MacKellar and Albert Jones, eds. *Chimera's Children*.

Part I

Who is a transhuman and posthuman person?

1

The concept of a 'person' and its history

Michael Fuchs

When we enter an elevator, we often find a sign, mostly a small plate, indicating the capacity. 'Ten persons are the equivalent to 800 kg.' One person is the equivalent to a certain quantity of matter – a body weight of 80 kilograms. However, when we enter the field of philosophy and try to learn something about the notion of 'person' or 'persons', we do not learn anything about the load-bearing capacity of elevators. Instead, the discussion very much relates to the problem of the identity of persons, more specifically their identity over time. As the Belgian-born American philosopher, Amélie Oksenberg Rorty, stated: 'Disagreements about the criteria for personal identity have been persistently unresolved.'[1]

Thus, it is possible to ask what does identity mean and is there something special about the identity of persons? 'Most of us believe', as the British philosopher Derek Parfit (1942–2017) wrote in his famous 1984 book *Reasons and Persons,* 'that our own continued existence is, in several ways, unlike the continued existence of a heap of sand.'[2] When Parfit writes about identity, he is well aware of the English philosopher and physician John Locke's (1632–1704) famous chapter 27, 'Of Identity and Diversity', in his *Essay Concerning Human Understanding.* Locke added the chapter, in which he treats persons and the conditions of their persistence, to the second edition of *An Essay Concerning Human Understanding* in 1694 only after being encouraged to do so by his Irish friend William Molyneux (1656–1698). However, Locke's treatment of personal identity is one of the most discussed aspects of his entire work and it is the regular starting point of ongoing contemporary debates on the topic. To answer the question of whether something or someone stays the same requires an idea about the core of this entity, be it the core of a person or the core of a tree.[3] Judgements about personal identity over time require an answer to the question of what the person is. In this regard, for Locke:

> To find what personal identity consists in, we must consider what 'person' stands for. I think it is a thinking intelligent Being, that has reason and reflection, and can consider itself as itself, the same thinking thing in different times and places; which it does only by that consciousness, which is inseparable from thinking, and, as it seems to me, essential to it: . . . For, since consciousness always accompanies thinking, and it is that which makes everyone to be what he calls self, and thereby

distinguishes himself from all other thinking things, in this alone consists personal Identity, i.e. the sameness of a rational Being.[4]

Conditions of identity and persistence are also relevant in the discussion on the ontological and moral status of human embryos and whether they are persons. Some of the discussants, such as the Australian philosophers Helga Kuhse and Peter Singer, dismiss the notion of embryo or infant as a person:

> We must recall, however, that when we kill a new-born infant there is no person whose life has begun. When I think of myself as the person I now am, I realize that I did not come into existence until sometime after my birth. At birth I had no sense of the future, and no experiences which I can now remember as 'mine'. It is the beginning of the person, rather than of the physical organism, that is crucial so far as the right to life is concerned.[5]

In contrast, those who argue in favour of an early onset of human identity or even personhood use arguments that the stages of development are linked. The Catholic scholar Norman Ford stated in 1991:

> [T]he human person is a living individual with a human nature, i.e. a living ontological individual that has within itself the active capacity to maintain, or at least to begin, the process of the human life-cycle without loss of identity.[6]

In analysing this and other positions like it, philosophers have distinguished a species argument, an identity argument, a continuity argument and a potentiality argument, which have all been carefully discussed elsewhere.[7] But I will skip these and return to Locke's argument. In *An Essay Concerning Human Understanding* (II, XXVII § 16), he makes it clear that, for him, the identity of the subject or the person results from self-consciousness; identity of the subject is not logical prior to self-consciousness. His concept of consciousness always has the connotation of reflexivity.

Locke's thesis has a negative aspect. Consciousness and personal identity are not necessarily tied to a substance, such as a body[8] or a soul.[9] The positive part is the focus on mental connectedness – the memory criterion. British philosopher Quassim Cassam (among others) calls this a functional concept of a person: According to the functional view, 'possession of a range of specific psychological capacities is both necessary and sufficient for being a person'.[10]

But if we think in terms of ordinary language, this functional concept is not broad enough. American philosopher Arthur Danto (1924–2013) stressed this point as far back as 1967:

> Neither in common usage nor in philosophy has there been a univocal concept of 'person.' Rather, the word 'person' and its almost exact cognates in the modern Western languages, as well as in Sanskrit (purusa), have numerous uses which at best seem only to border on one another. In recent common usage, 'person' refers to any human being in a general way, much as the word 'thing' refers unspecifically to any object whatsoever.[11]

Danto has found several usages and discussed their conceptual connectivity: a person as something that is distinct from a (mere) thing and that may be regarded as an end-in-itself, a legal person and a 'person' as synonym with 'role' or 'part' in a comedy or a tragedy (cf. dramatis personae). Indeed, the concept of a person has a long history and it is not easy to understand the semantic connectivity of different meanings. In my historic outline, I will not seek to address whether something like an original meaning existed while leaving open the question of whether a core concept is present.

Ordinary Greek language and ancient philosophy

I start with some contexts where the notion of person and the Greek equivalent were used prior to a philosophical analysis of the term and then sketch some steps of the philosophical history of the notion.[12]

According to the dictionary of Liddle/Scott, the Greek word πρόσωπον (prósōpon) can be used in the sense of face, visage, countenance, front, mask or character, part in a drama or appearance or legal person or person.[13] As far as the contexts in which the notion of person are concerned, there is no clear historical order; I begin with the context of theatre, though not claiming that this was the original context.[14] Since the Greek πρόσωπον can mean 'mask' it was suggested that person (cf the Latin word 'persona') signifies the actors in dramatic performances. In ancient and medieval times, many approaches used this idea for etymological analysis. It has also been suggested that person could come from the Latin verb 'personare', which means 'sound through' or from the participium 'personando': sounding through. Although philologists do not accept this etymology, the idea that πρόσωπον could not only stand for the mask but also for an actor speaking through the mask or an individual playing a certain role in a community or society is of great importance. In Latin, for instance, in texts of the Roman poet Horace (65–8 BC), 'personatus' still means 'being masked'. Moreover, the concept of person is used in the theory of the verb in texts on grammar. This is shown by the grammar of the Greek, Dionysius of Thrax (170–90 BC) in the passage 'On the Verb' (ῥῆμα).[15]

Another context where the notion of πρόσωπον appears is in law, more precisely the teaching of the theory of law, such as the *Institutes* of the Roman jurist Gaius (130–80), an introductory textbook of legal institutions written about AD 161. These *Institutes* or commentarii of Gaius are the most important works of this literary genre. They consist of four books which may be traced back to a lecture transcript. The first is concerned with persons and their different legal status; the topic of the second is related to things and how rights over things are acquired; the third is about the law of inheritance, succession and obligations; and the fourth book treats legal actions and legal procedures.[16] The idea is that there is a complete classification of everything that can be regulated by law: 'All the law which we make use of has reference either to persons, to things, or to actions.'[17]

There is neither in grammar nor in the theory of law a formal definition of a person. In grammar, a person is an entity that is either speaking, can be addressed or something that is spoken about. In the theory of law, persons are not things and are not legal actions. All 'men' are either free or slaves. It is not clear if, or how, these ways in which the term 'person' is used are related to the idea of the mask or the idea of an actor on a stage.

In preclassical ancient philosophy, we only find short sentences about the individual human being. The Greek philosopher Heraclitus (c. 535–c. 475 BC) is not only concerned with the world-order (κόσμος) but also with his own thinking,[18] and, for him, thinking is more a general universal process than an individual attempt.[19] However, for the Greek scholar Empedocles (c. 494–c. 434 BC), the understanding of the κόσμος (cosmos) and an adequate way to live one's own life are connected. A correlation seems to exist between the perceiving subject and the material world: 'For it is by earth that we see earth, by water water, by aether divine aether, and by fire destructive fire, and fondness by fondness, and strife by baleful strife.'[20] In other words, we might say that Empedocles had some idea of the human being as a microcosm.

For the Greek medical writer and presocratic philosopher Alcmaeon of Croton (fifth century BC), as for Homer, human beings are 'mortals' and, in some sense, they are the only mortal beings. Alcmaeon notes: 'Human beings perish because they are not able to join their beginning to their end.'[21]

In classical ancient philosophy, we find many texts giving abstract descriptions of the individual human being who can be defined as a living being with rationality (ζῷον λόγον ἔχον) and who is able to discuss practical and moral issues (ζῷον πολιτικόν). But in the works of the Greek philosophers Plato and Aristotle, as in presocratic writing, there is no concept of human dignity or of a person.[22]

The idea of dignity as a concept of moral philosophy appeared with the Stoics. But unfortunately, we only have fragments of their teaching. Stoic theories came down to us by both short and long citations and reports given by others of whom one of the most important is the Roman philosopher Cicero (106–43 BC), who is also of highest importance in developing the notion of personhood. In his book, *De Officiis*, he rephrases the so-called Four-personae theory,[23] which was allegedly developed by the Greek philosopher, Panaetius of Rhodes (c. 185–c. 110/109 BC) – at least if we trust Cicero's own statement:

> We must realize also that we are invested by Nature with two characters, as it were: One of these is universal, arising from the fact of our being all alike endowed with reason and with the superiority which lifts us above the brute. From this all morality and propriety are derived, and upon it depends the rational method of ascertaining our duty. [. . .] To the two above-mentioned characters is added a third, which some chance or some circumstance imposes, and a fourth also, which we assume by our own deliberate choice. Regal powers and military commands, nobility of birth and political office, wealth and influence, and their opposites depend upon chance and are, therefore, controlled by circumstances. But what role we ourselves may choose to sustain is decided by our own free choice. And so some turn to philosophy, others to the civil law, and still others to oratory, while in case of the virtues themselves one man prefers to excel in one, another in another.[24]

For Cicero, moral excellence or *arête* is a question of if and how we succeed in coordinating the different roles the four personae represent: our general rational nature, our specific character, our social situation and our social role. In other words, excellence is a question of coherence or, as one might say, of authenticity.[25] Cicero does not focus on the second role or the second person. He has no strong concept of individuality in the sense that a single human being is irreplaceable.[26]

It is uncertain whether this four-personae theory had a strong impact on our modern thinking about persons. Maybe the second person could be the starting point to reflect on singularity, individuality and personality. Cicero himself seems to be more interested in balancing the four personae and especially human nature, individual difference and social role.

However, the theological doctrine of the holy trinity, to which we will now turn, was even more influential than the Ciceronian theory. Indeed, the central ancient philosophical definition of persona was developed in this theological context whereby the concept of person was influenced by reflections on Christ and his incarnation.

Boethius: Theological contexts and philosophical distinctions

It was in the context of theology that Christological and Trinitarian argumentation required an analytical approach to find clear distinctions and definitions for the terms used. These problems had a long history. The Greek Christian scholar Eutyches (born in Constantinople in 378) declared that Christ was a fusion of human and divine elements; two natures becoming one nature. This contrasts with the view of the other Greek theologian Nestorius (386–450), who emphasized that Christ has two natures and probably two personhoods.

Generally, the concept of person in theology and in the teaching of the Church serves as an attempt to describe the three divine instances in relation to one another, a relation which is not just a gradation but also to describe Christ (as both God and human) as a kind of unity or wholeness.

However, the definition I will discuss here was given by the Roman politician and philosopher Boethius (c. 477–524 AD). Before doing so, however, and just to illustrate the difficulties that theologians who were educated in philosophy could have with the notion of a person, it is helpful to look at the Roman theologian St Augustine (354–430 AD). In his *De trinitate* (On trinity), he expresses considerable doubts that the notion of person could be used as a panacea to resolve the controversy on the doctrine of trinity. He states:

> Yet, when the question is asked, What three? human language labors altogether under great poverty of speech. The answer, however, is given, three 'persons', not that it might be [completely] spoken, but that it might not be left [wholly] unspoken.[27]

Nevertheless, the concept of person was used to strongly reject the Sabellianistic (modalistic) interpretation of the trinity,[28] namely that the three divine persons are only three modes of appearance of an undifferentiated one God.

With Boethius, the Latin word persona, which corresponded to the Greek πρόσωπον (prósōpon), also includes the content of the Greek word ὑπόστασις (hypóstasis)[29], 'that which stands beneath'.[30] Thus, for Boethius, the question of Trinity is: three hypostases or three persons with one being or one essence. The formula for Christ then became: two natures, one person. Thus, it is Boethius who tried to give a philosophically sound explanation of the concepts. The notion of 'person', according to his famous definition, 'is the individual substance of a rational nature' (*'persona est naturae rationabilis individua substantia'*[31]). This definition has four elements: naturae, substantia, individua and rationabilis.[32] Thus, trees, horses or cows are not described as persons, but Boethius indicates that we define god, angels and human beings as persons.[33]

Boethius does not discuss if nonhuman primates or other animals could be 'rationabilis'. Language is the strongest argument for him to decide the conceptual question. Neither does he discuss whether human beings exist who are not individuals or not 'rationabilis'. He does not reflect about a possible existence of thinking entities, which are artefacts.[34] However, one of the elements of Boethius' definition, individual, is explained in his Commentary to the Isagoge of Porphyrius:

> Individual is called what cannot at all be divided, such as unity or intellect; individual is called what, because of its solidity, cannot be divided, like a diamond; individual is defined that whose predicate does not accord with other similar individuals, like Socrates.[35]

Boethius' concept of individuality as indivisibility had a significant impact, not least because of its incorporation into his definition of the term 'persona'. Nevertheless, it was never the only concept of individuality.[36] Indeed, 'Individuum', in medieval Latin texts, was used both as a translation for 'ἄτομον' (which can be translated as undivided or as undividable) and as a synonym for 'ens singulare', singular being. In addition to Bioethius' definition of the person, the Medieval Scottish philosopher and theologian Richard of Saint Victor (who died in 1173) was one of the most important references for scholastic philosophy and theology. Richard explained trinity in terms of loving and being loved. In his view, the term 'person' is not the substantiality, the standing in itself, but the relationship to other entities.[37]

Aquinas and Kant

The theologians of the thirteenth century were then confronted with several definitions of a person, such as that of the Italian theologian Thomas Aquinas (1225–74), who makes this fact explicit, starting with the definition of Boethius:[38]

> What is the definition of 'person'? In *De Duabus Naturis* Boethius formulates the following definition of 'person': 'A person is an individual substance with a rational nature' (rationalis naturae individua substantia).[39]

In his answer, Aquinas focuses on a special kind of individuality related to the capacity to act in a free way:

> And so among the other substances, singular substances with a rational nature likewise have a special name. And this name is 'person'. And so 'individual substance' occurs in the aforementioned definition of 'person' insofar as 'person' signifies a singular thing in the genus of substance, whereas 'with a rational nature' is added insofar as 'person' signifies a singular thing among the rational substances.[40]

The objection 5 and Thomas' reply to this objection are both of interest:

> Objection 5: A separated soul is an individual substance with a rational nature. But a separated soul is not a person. Therefore, this definition of 'person' is incorrect. [...]

> Reply to objection 5: A soul is a part of the human species, and so even if it is separated, it cannot be called an individual substance, i.e., a hypostasis or a primary substance, because it still retains the nature of a thing that can be united to something else – just as a hand, or any other part of a man, cannot be called an individual substance. And so neither the name 'person' nor its definition belongs to a separated soul.[41]

It seems that Aquinas' idea of hylemorphism, the connection of matter and form, makes him resistant, or at least hesitant, to accept a concept of person as something purely intellectual. In other words, he would likely not have called a data set a person and, similarly, the transhumanist idea of 'uploading', for him, would not describe a continuing existence of an individual personal being. Nevertheless, for the theologians of the thirteenth century, 'person' is not just applicable to human beings.

For Aquinas, it is the connection of dignity and personhood that is the basis for calling both human beings and God persons, although the etymological background of the word 'persona' does not seem to be appropriate in the context of speech about God.[42] The critique of philosophizing in terms of substance found in Richard of Saint Victor, Locke's *Essay* and the Scottish philosopher David Hume's (1711–76) *Treatise of Human Nature* had an impact on the German philosopher Immanuel Kant (1724–1804).[43] The transcendental 'I' cannot be an object of knowledge. In other words, Kant takes the negative part of Locke's argument (s.o. page 20) without making use of the positive part. Consequently, the concept of a person does not play a role in Kant's theoretical philosophy though it has a strong role in his practical philosophy. In Kant's moral and legal philosophy, it is closely related to the concept of autonomy and dignity. A person is an end in itself and cannot be used solely for other purposes.[44] Persons must not be used merely as means to someone's end. They are sources of value in their own right.[45]

Recent descriptive and revisionary metaphysics

If we look at theories on personhood from recent decades, it is quite common to mention a list of necessary conditions, most of which are mental capacities. One such list is given by the American philosopher Niklas Rescher, for whom intelligence, affectivity, agency, rationality, self-understanding, self-esteem and mutual recognizance 'are severally necessary and jointly sufficient conditions'.[46] Another list was provided by the American philosopher and cognitive scientist Daniel Dennett,[47] for whom consciousness and rationality are also central. He explicitly mentions the capability of 'verbal communication'.

Among the most interesting recent concepts of personhood is one from the English philosopher Peter Strawson (1919–2006), who derives his concept of the person from an examination of the ways in which we ordinarily talk of ourselves: 'We ascribe to ourselves actions and intentions [. . .], sensations [. . .], thoughts and feelings [. . .], perceptions and memories'[48], locations and attitudes as well as physical properties such as size, colour, shape and weight. Strawson's conclusion is that these ascriptions can be divided into two groups, namely mental properties and physical properties, or, as he first puts it, things that we also ascribe to material bodies and things that we 'should not dream of ascribing'[49] to other material bodies. For Strawson persons are basic particulars as material bodies are basic particulars. We can identify and re-identify persons because we can identify and re-identify material bodies. However, when we talk of ourselves, we do not just talk about material bodies. Moreover, we are not a fusion of consciousness and body, or feelings and cognition. That is why Strawson insists that the concept of a person is 'primitive'.

Similarly to Aquinas, 'person' for Strawson describes the intimate unity of body and consciousness, though, for him, the bodily person is just an example of a particular that can be identified and re-identified while occupying a certain place in space and time. A person for Strawson is not necessarily irreplaceable or unrepeatable, as it was for some authors in the phenomenological tradition at the beginning of the twentieth century.[50] The person has no greater difference from other personal beings than other individuated bodies would have. It is not 'more unique' than a car or a horse.

With the dissociation between human being and person, explicit in Locke's essay, implicit in Kant's philosophy but already accepted by Boethius or Aquinas (who talk about angels and God or about God as persons that are not human beings), many questions arise that are even more challenging today than in Kant's or Aquinas' times. The answers to these questions have consequences for practical decisions.

In his *Essay Concerning Human Understanding*, Locke says that 'person' is 'a forensic term'[51]. But that cannot mean that the term 'person' is just practical, or normative. It is related to 'actions and their merit'[52] but with actions of real entities. It is a theoretical term with normative consequences. Most of the philosophers cited here make use of ordinary language, which reflects the different dimensions of the term 'person' very well. The use of ordinary language for his philosophical starting point is obvious for Strawson but is also important in Boethius' philosophical argumentation as it might be for others.

However, it is true that analysis of ordinary language is only one tool. Sometimes discussion on criteria of personhood or personal identity might conclude that the way we use ordinary language should be changed. But, as far as I know, nobody has yet claimed that we should change the wording on our elevator signs. Nevertheless, we have neither consensus about the extension and the meaning of the concept of a person nor agreement on the methods and requirements to change ordinary language and its normative implications.

Notes

1 Rorty, Amélie Oksenberg, 'Introduction', in *The Identities of Persons*, ed. A. O. Rorty (Berkeley, Los Angeles: University of California Press, 1976), 1-15, 1.
2 Derek Parfit, *Reasons and Persons* (Oxford: Clarendon Press, 1984), 232.
3 Locke develops his idea of continuity and identity of persons by showing or arguing in favour of a contrast to conditions of identity and persistence of atoms, oaks and horses.
4 John Locke, *An Essay Concerning Human Understanding*, ed. Peter H. Nidditch (Oxford: Clarendon, 1975), II, XXVII.
5 Helga Kuhse and Peter Singer, *Should the Baby Live?* (Oxford University Press, 1985), 133. Interestingly Kuhse and Singer call the entity at birth (which according to their view did not yet come into existence), 'I', although they want to avoid this 'I' being seen as the same person as the adult person.
6 Norman Ford, *When Did I Begin? Concept of the Human Individual in History, Philosophy and Science* (Cambridge: Cambridge University Press, 1991), 84-5.
7 Gregor Damschen and Dieter Schönecker, eds. *Der moralische Status menschlicher Embryonen: pro und contra Spezies-, Kontinuums-, Identitäts- und Potentialitätsargument* (Berlin: Deutsches Referenzzentrum für Ethik in den Biowissenschaften: In focus: Research with human embryonic stem cells, 2003).
8 As for instance for Bernard Williams or David Wiggings: Bernard Williams, 'Are Persons Bodies?', in *The Philosophy of the Body: Rejections of Cartesian Dualism*, ed. Stuart. F. Spicker (Chicago: Times Books, 1972), 137-56; David Wiggins, 'The Concern to Survive', *Midwest Studies in Philosophy* 4 (1979), 417-22; David Wiggins, *Sameness and Substance* (Oxford: Basil Blackwell, 1980).
9 Consciousness could be conceptualized as equivalent to or as property of a thinking substance as Descartes did: Descartes, 'Meditationes de prima philosophia', in *René Descartes, Oeuvres*, eds. Charles Adam and René Paul Tannery, Tome 7 (Paris: Léopold Cerf, 1904).
10 Quassim Cassam, 'Persons', in *The Oxford Companion to Philosophy*, ed. Ted Honderich (Oxford and New York: Oxford University Press, 1995), 655-6, 655.
11 Arthur C. Danto, 'Persons', in *The Encyclopedia of Philosophy*, ed. Paul Edwards (New York: Macmillan, 1967), Vol. 5, 110-14, h. 110.
12 Danto, 'Persons', 110-14; Following the article of Danto an historical and systematic overview was already given in several books and handbook articles: Manfred Fuhrmann, Brigitte Kible, Georg Scherer, Hans-Peter Schütt, Wolfgang Schild and Maximilian Scherner, 'Art. Person', in *Historisches Wörterbuch der Philosophie*, Band 7 (Basel: Schwabe, 1989), 269-338; Dieter Sturma, *Philosophie der Person: Die Selbstverhältnisse von Subjektivität und Moralität* (Paderborn: Mentis Verlag GmbH, 2008); Dieter Teichert, *Personen und Identitäten*, Quellen und Studien zur Philosophie Bd. 48 (Berlin, NY: de Gruyter, 1999).
13 Henry George Liddell and Robert Scott, *A Greek-English Lexicon, Revised and Augmented Throughout by Sir Henry Stuart Jones with the Assistance of Roderick McKenzie* (Oxford: Clarendon Press, 1940).

14 For some authors, there is no doubt that theatre is the original context: Rainer Specht, 'Stadien des Personbegriffs. Notizen beim Lesen eines Wörterbuchartikels', in *Denken der Individualität: Festschrift für Josef Simon zum 65.Geburstag*, eds. Thomas S. Hoffmann and Stefan Majetschak (Berlin, NY: de Gruyter, 1995), 27–37.

15 'περὶ ῥήματος. πρῶσοπα τρία, πρῶτον, δεύτερον, τρίτον. πρῶτον μὲν ἀφ' οὗ ὁ λόγος, δεύτερον δὲ πρὸς ὃν ὁ λόγος, τρίτον δὲ περὶ οὗ ὁ λόγος' (Dionysios Thrax, in *Grammatici Graeci* I,1, ed. G. Uhlig, Leipzig 1883).

> A Verb is an indeclinable word, indicating time, person and number, and showing activity or passivity. The verb has eight accidents: Moods, Dispositions (voices!), Species, Forms, Numbers, Tenses, Persons, Conjugations. There are five *Moods*: Indicative, Imperative, Optative, Subjunctive, and Infinitive. There are three *Dispositions*: Activity, Passivity, and Mediality – Activity, as τύπτω (I strike); Passivity, as τύπτομαι (I am struck); Mediality, marking partly activity and partly passivity, as πέποιθα (I trust), διέφθορα (I waste), ἐποιησάμην (I became), ἐγραψάμην (I registered). There are two *Species*: Primitive and Derivative – Primitive, as ἄρδω; Derivative, as ἀρδεύω. There are three *Forms*: Simple, Compound, and Super-Compound – Simple, as φρονῶ; Compound, as καταφρονῶ; Super-Compound, as ἀντιγονίζω (I Antigonize), φιλιππίζω (I Philippize). There are three *Numbers*: Singular, Dual, and Plural – Singular, as τύπτω; Dual, as τύπτετον Plural, as τύπτομεν. There are three *Persons*: First, Second, and Third. The First is the person *from* whom the assertion is; the Second, the one *to* whom it is; and the Third, the one *concerning* whom it is.

16 Gaius, 'Institutiones: The Institutes', in *Parts One and Two. Text with Critical Notes and Translation*, ed. Francis de Zulueta (Oxford: Clarendon Press, 1946), 2 vols.

17 'Omne autem ius, quo utimur, vel ad personas pertinet vel ad res vel ad actiones. Sed prius videamus de personis'. Gaius, 'Institutiones', 1, 8.

18 'I have sought for myself' Fragment 101. H. Diels and W. Kranz, *Die Fragmente der Vorsokratiker* (in three volumes), 6th edn (Dublin, Zürich: Weidmann, 1952), Greek texts of the fragments and testimonia with translations in German.

19 'Having harkened not to me but to the Word (λόγος) it is wise to agree that all things are one' (Fragment 50).

20 Empedocles, Fragment B 109, Diels and Kranz, *Die Fragmente der Vorsokratiker*, Vol. 1, Chapter 31, 164–78. Greek texts of the fragments and testimonia with translations in German.

21 Diels and Kranz, *Die Fragmente der Vorsokratiker*, Vol. 1, Chapter 24, 210–16. Greek texts of the fragments and testimonia with translations in German.

22 Christoph Horn, 'Geschichte der Menschenrechte – Antike', in *Menschenrechte. Ein interdisziplinäres Handbuch*, eds. A. Pollmann and G. Lohmann (Stuttgart and Weimar: Metzler, 2012), 1–5.

23 Christopher Gill, 'Personhood and Personality – The Four-"Personae" Theory', in *De Officiis I, Oxford Studies in Ancient Philosophy*, ed. Cicero (Oxford: Oxford University Press, 1988), 6, 169–99; Phillip'de Lacy, *The Four Stoic 'Personae', Illinois Classical Studies* (Champaign: University of Illinois Press, 1977), 2, 163–72.

24 M. Tullius Cicero, *De Officiis*. With An English Translation. Walter Miller (Cambridge, MA: Harvard University Press, 1913).

> 'Intellegendum etiam est duabus quasi nos a natura indutos esse personis; quarum una communis est ex eo, quod omnes participes sumus rationis praestantiaeque eius, qua antecellimus bestiis, a qua omne honestum decorumque trahitur et ex qua ratio inveniendi officii exquiritur, altera autem quae proprie singulis est tributa. ut enim in corporibus magnae dissimilitudines sunt, alios videmus velocitate ad cursum, alios viribus ad luctandum valere, itemque in formis

aliis dignitatem inesse, aliis venustatem, sic in animis existunt maiores etiam varietates. [115] 32. Ac duabus iis personis, quas supra dixi, tertia adiungitur, quam casus aliqui aut tempus imponit; quarta etiam, quam nobismet ipsi iudicio nostro accommodamus. Nam regna, imperia, nobilitas, honores, divitiae, opes eaque, quae sunt his contraria, in casu sita temporibus gubernantur; ipsi [p. 118] autem gerere quam personam velimus, a nostra voluntate proficiscitur. Itaque se alii ad philosophiam, alii ad ius civile, alii ad eloquentiam applicant, ipsarumque virtutum in alia alius mavult excellere.'

25 Maximilian Forschner, 'Über Person und Persönlichkeit oder wie ein Mensch authentisch wirkt. Die Antwort der Stoa', in *Zwischen Illusion und Ideal: Authentizität als Anspruch und Versprechen Interdisziplinäre Annäherungen an Wirkmacht und Deutungskraft eines strittigen Begriffs*, eds. Michael Hofer and Christian Rößner (Regensburg: Pustet, 2019), 75–93.

26 Dieter Teichert, 'Personen und Identitäten', in *Quellen und Studien zur Philosophie*, Bd. 48 (Berlin, NY: de Gruyter, 1999), 95–6.

27 Augustine of Hippo, *On The Trinity*, V, 9.

28 Robert Lachenschmid, Sabellianismus, in *Lexikon für Theologie und Kirche* (Freiburg: Herder, 1986), 2nd edn, vol. 9, 193.

29 Gerd Haeffner, 'Person und Natur', in *Die Einheit des Menschen, zur Grundfrage der philosophischen Anthropologie*, ed. L. Honnefelder (Paderborn: Schöningh, 1994), 25–40, 28.

'Ein ontologischer Begriff wurde, 'opersona' freilich erst dadurch, daß die modalistische Interpretation, es handle sich bei den drei göttlichen Personen nur um drei Erscheinungsweisen bzw. Rollen eines in sich undifferenziert einen Gottes, abgelehnt wurde. Nun nimmt das lateinische Wort persona, das dem griechischen prósopon entsprach, auch den Gehalt des griechischen Wortes hypóstasis auf. Damit ergibt sich die Bedeutung, die in der Definition des Boethius ausgesprochen ist'.

30 Liddell and Scott, *A Greek-English Lexicon*.

31 Anicius Manlius Severinus Boethius, 'Die Theologischen Traktate', ed. Michael Elsässer (Hamburg: Meiner, 1988), Tractatus V, III, p. 74. To come to this definition Boethius makes use of a Tree of Porphyry, the *Arbor Porphyriana*, a classic device for illustrating what is also called a 'scale of being'. The goal of his analysis of concepts is to distinguish 'natura' and 'persona'. Nature can either be substance or accident. Substance can either be bodily or not bodily, bodily substances can either be living or not living, living beings can either be sensible or not sensible, sensible living beings can either be rational or not rational.

32 Corinna Schlapkohl: Persona est naturae rationabilis individua substantia. Boethius und die Debatte über den Personenbegriff (Marburg: Elwert, 1999).

33 Boethius, Anicius Manlius Severinus,

'Die Theologischen Traktate', ed. Michael Elsässer (Hamburg: Meiner, 1988): 'Ex quibus omnibus neque in non uiuentibus corporibus personam posse dici manifestum est (nullus enim lapidis ullam dicit esse personam), neque rursus eorum uiuentium quae sensu carent (neque enim ulla persona est arboris), nec uero eius quae intellectu ac ratione deseritur (nulla est enim persona equi uel bouis caeterorumque animalium quae muta ac sine ratione uitam solis sensibus degunt), at hominis dicimus esse personam, dicimus dei, dicimus angeli' (tractatus V, II).

34 Robots are not living beings. Even if we could accept that they are rational and individual, Boethius may find difficulties to find an adequate place for them in his scale of beings.

35 '[D]icitur individuum, quod omnino secari non potest, ut unitas vel mens, dicitur individuum quod ob soliditatem dividi nequit, ut adamas, dicitur individuum cuius praedicatio in reliqua similia non convenit, ut Sokrates', Anicius Manlius Severinus Boethuis, *'Commentaria in Porphyrium a se translatum'*, in *Boethius Opera Omnia, Patrologia*, ed. J.-P. Migne, Series latina, 64 (Paris, 1891), 71–158, 97c.

36 Jorge Gracia gives a detailed overview about the complexity of the notion: Jorge J. E. Gracia, *Individuality: An Essay on the Foundations of Metaphysics* (New York: State University of New York Press, 1988); Jorge J. E. Gracia, 'Individuality, Individuation', in *Handbook of Metaphysics and Ontology, Vol. 1*, eds. H. Burkhardt and B. Smith (München, PA: Philosophia, 1991), 385–8.

37 *Persons in the holy trinity are related, not separated (as the word substantia could suggest). At first, however, he speaks of the person's 'incommunicable' existence: persona est intellectualis naturae incommunicabilis existentia.* Richard de Saint Victor, *De Trinitate, texte critique avec introduction, notes et tables de Jean Ribaillier* (Paris: Vrin, 1958), iv, c. 22.

38 Thomas Aquinas *Summa theologiae* I, q. 29, art. 1: What is the definition of 'person'? In De Duabus Naturis Boethius formulates the following definition of 'person': 'A person is an individual substance with a rational nature (rationalis naturae individua substantia).'

39 Thomas Aquinas, *The Summa Theologiae*, Second and revised Edition, 1920. Literally translated by Fathers of the English Dominican Province, I, q. 29, art. 1:

40 Thomas Aquinas, *Summa theologiae* I, q. 29, art. 1.

41 Thomas Aquinas, *Summa theologiae* I, q. 29, art. 1.

42 'Article 3: Should the name "person" be used in the case of God? "Person" signifies that which is most perfect in all of nature, viz., that which subsists in a rational nature. Hence, since everything that involves perfection should be attributed to God – given that His essence contains within itself every perfection – it follows that the name "person" is appropriately said of God. However, it is not said of God in exactly the same way in which it is said of creatures; rather, it is said of God in a more excellent way – just like the other names which, having been imposed by us on creatures, are attributed to God. This was explained above when we were discussing the names of God (q. 13, a. 3).'

> 'Objection 2: In De Duabus Naturis Boethius says, "The name 'person' seems to derive from those masks (personae) that were used to represent men in comedies and tragedies. For 'person' comes from 'sounding through' (personare), since a louder sound had to be shouted out through the cavity of the mask. Now the Greeks called these masks 'prosopa' from the fact that they are placed over (pros) the face (ops) and hide one's visage from the onlookers." But this cannot apply to the case of God except perhaps in accord with a metaphor. Therefore, the name "person" is said of God only metaphorically. [. . .]'

'Reply to objection 2: Even though the name 'person' does not belong to God with respect to that because of which the name was imposed, nonetheless, it especially belongs to God with respect to that which the name is imposed to signify. For because famous men were being represented in the comedies and tragedies, the name 'person' was imposed to signify those who have dignity. Hence, in the churches it was customary to use the name 'person' for those who had some sort of dignity. For this reason, some define 'person' as follows: 'A person is a hypostasis with a distinctive property pertaining to dignity'. Moreover, as has been explained (a. 1), it is because subsisting in a rational nature is a great dignity that every individual with a rational nature is called a person. But the dignity of God's nature surpasses every dignity, and, accordingly, the name 'person' belongs especially to God.'

43 Sturma, *Philosophie der Person*, 148–153; Teichert, 'Personen und Identitäten', 197–206.

44 'Da er sich aber nicht bloß als Person überhaupt, sondern auch als Mensch, d. i. als eine Person, die Pflichten auf sich hat, die ihm seine eigene Vernunft auferlegt, betrachten muß, so kann seine Geringfähigkeit als T i e r m e n s c h dem Bewußtsein seiner Würde als V e r n u n f t m e n s c h nicht Abbruch tun, und er soll die moralische Selbstschätzung in Betracht der letzteren nicht verleugnen, d. i. er soll sich um seinen Zweck, der an sich selbst Pflicht ist, nicht kriechend, nicht k n e c h t i s c h (animo servili), gleich als sich um Gunst bewerbend, bewerben, nicht seine Würde verleugnen, sondern immer mit dem Bewußtsein der Erhabenheit seiner moralischen Anlage (welches im Begriff der Tugend schon enthalten ist); und diese S e l b s t s c h ä t z u n g ist Pflicht des Menschen gegen sich selbst.': Immanuel Kant, *Die Metaphysik der Sitten*, ed. W. Weischedel (Frankfurt a.M.: Suhrkamp, 1977), 569.

45 'Allein der Mensch als Person betrachtet, d. i. als Subjekt einer moralisch-praktischen Vernunft, ist über allen Preis erhaben; denn als ein solcher (homo noumenon) ist er nicht bloß als Mittel zu anderer ihren, ja selbst seinen eigenen Zwecken, sondern als Zweck an sich selbst zu schätzen, d. i. er besitzt eine W ü r d e (einen absoluten innern Wert), wodurch er allen andern vernünftigen Weltwesen A c h t u n g für ihn abnötigt, sich mit jedem anderen dieser Art messen und auf den Fuß der Gleichheit schätzen kann. Die Menschheit in seiner Person ist das Objekt der Achtung, die er von jedem anderen Menschen fordern kann; deren er aber auch sich nicht verlustig machen muß. Er kann und soll sich also, nach einem kleinen so wohl als großen Maßstabe, schätzen, nachdem er sich als Sinnenwesen (seiner tierischen Natur nach), oder als intelligibles Wesen (seiner moralischen Anlage nach) betrachtet'. Immanuel Kant, *Die Metaphysik der Sitten*, ed. W. Weischedel (Frankfurt a.M.: Suhrkamp, 1977), 569.

46 Niklas Rescher, *A System of Pragmatic Idealism*, Vol. 2 (Princeton: Princeton University Press, 1993), 114.

47 Daniel Dennett, 'Conditions of Personhood', in *The Identities of Persons*, ed. A. O. Rorty (Berkeley, Los Angeles, 1976), 175–96, 177–8.

48 Peter F. Strawson, *Individuals: An Essay in Descriptive Metaphysics* (London: Routledge 1959), reprinted 1971, 89.

49 Strawson, *Individuals*, 89.

50 For the phenomenological conception, see: J. F. Crosby, 'The Individuality of Human Persons: A Study in the Ethical Personalism of Max Scheler', *The Review on Metaphysics* 52 (1998): 21–50. Quite similar to the concept of Scheler is the conception of Edith Stein: Edith Stein, Endliches und ewiges Sein. Versuch eines Aufstiegs zum Sinn des Seins, Edith Stein Gesamtausgab, ed. L. Gelber, Bd. 11/12 (Freiburg et al.: Herder, 2006).

51 John Locke, *An Essay Concerning Human Understanding*, ed. Peter H. Nidditch (Oxford: Clarendon, 1975), II, XXVII, § 26.

52 Ibid.

2

One of us

Humans, transhumans and posthumans

Richard Playford

Introduction

The Swedish philosopher Nick Bostrom explains:

> Transhumanism is a loosely defined movement that has developed gradually over the past two decades. It promotes an interdisciplinary approach to understanding and evaluating opportunities for enhancing the human condition and the human organism opened up by the advancement of technology. Attention is given to both present technologies, like genetic engineering and information technology, and anticipated future ones, such as molecular nanotechnology and artificial intelligence.[1]

Very roughly, a 'transhuman' is a person that looks recognizably human, but who has been modified through technology (think of cyborgs and other similar creatures). A 'posthuman' is a person who has been modified by, or united with, technology in a way which prevents them from looking recognizably human.[2]

Increasing numbers of scientists and philosophers believe that transhumans and posthumans will one day become a reality, potentially in the near future. This possibility raises a number of ethical and philosophical issues, not least of which is their relationship to us (unmodified) humans. Indeed, it seems that this question is of first importance because we cannot answer any of the subsequent questions their reality might raise (for example, legal, ethical and political questions) before we have answered this question. We need to know whether they are 'one of us'. In this chapter, I will try to shed some light on this question. Perhaps strangely, I will begin by examining the difference between nonhuman and human animals. I will do this in order to sharpen up our understanding of human nature. Having done this, I will be in a position to examine whether transhumans and posthumans[3] are 'one of us'. Once I have answered this question in the affirmative, I will then consider some of the most pressing ethical concerns that emerge out of this realisation.

You talkin' to me?

In the Psalter, the psalmist asks of God, 'What is man, that thou art mindful of him?'[4] Religious and interpretive issues aside, I think this is a good question. What is it that distinguishes us as a species from other organisms?

A common answer refers to our linguistic abilities. The Greek philosopher Aristotle (384–322 BC), for example, in the *Politics*, highlights:

> [m]an alone of the animals possesses speech. The mere voice, it is true, can indicate pain and pleasure, and therefore is possessed by the other animals as well (for their nature has been developed so far as to have sensations of what is painful and pleasant and to indicate those sensations to one another), but speech is designed to indicate the advantageous and the harmful, and therefore also the right and the wrong; for it is the special property of man in distinction from the other animals that he alone has perception of good and bad and right and wrong and the other moral qualities, and it is partnership in these things that makes a household and a city-state.[5]

This might suggest that what makes us human is the ability to use language. In and of itself, however, this is too simple. The definition of language and what is needed for a communication system to count as a language is extremely difficult to determine and is highly philosophically contentious.[6] However, modern science has shown that a variety of nonhuman animals have surprisingly sophisticated communication systems. To give a handful of examples, a number of species of birds have been found to use compositional syntax in their communication systems.[7] Trained apes are able to master vocabularies of several hundred words, comparable to human toddlers.[8] Many nonhuman animals also display context sensitivity and dependence when communicating.[9,10]

These findings risk turning the distinction between human beings and nonhuman animals into one of degree, rather than one of kind. On the one hand, we could embrace such a position. This is the conclusion of the English naturalist Charles Darwin (1809–82) based on his theory of evolution,[11] and many subsequent scholars have followed his lead. However, others are left feeling uncomfortable by this view. Nonhuman animals often do surprise us with their intelligence, sophistication and beauty. However, no such animal has ever written even a single word, let alone something of Shakespearan or Dickensian quality. Further, when we compare nonhuman animal 'tools' to the rockets that put men on the Moon there seems to be no comparison. Perhaps we should be cautious about so quickly rejecting the possibility of a difference in kind between human and nonhuman animals. I accept that we should not rule out the possibility that the difference between us and them is merely one of degree absolutely or with complete certainty. After all, we should remain open to all options and reality can often surprise us. However, this intuition, that there is something uniquely different and special about human beings, and these observations, that our art, technology and culture far outstrips even those of the most intelligent nonhuman animals, suggest we should only conclude that the difference is one of degree when all differences of kind have been ruled out.

Perhaps the difference in kind can be found in language by acknowledging that nonhuman animals can have surprisingly sophisticated communication systems while insisting that there is at least one feature, or handful of features, that clearly demarcates human languages from nonhuman animal communication systems.

The Italian philosopher Pietro Perconti[12] believes that this can be done by examining context-dependence in human languages compared to context-dependence in nonhuman animal communication systems. He distinguishes between four types of context-dependence. The first three he borrows from the American philosopher John Perry.[13] He then adds a fourth category of his own. He believes that the first two are, with certain caveats added, unique to humans. As a result, Perconti believes that, although nonhuman animal communication systems can display context-dependence (the latter two categories), human languages display it in a unique way which he labels 'indexicality'. This would render the difference between human languages and animal communication systems, and thus potentially the difference between human beings and nonhuman animals, one of kind rather than one of degree. I will now briefly summarize Perconti's argument while explaining why I do not believe this to be a fruitful avenue to pursue when trying to find a difference in kind between human beings and nonhuman animals.

The first type of context-dependence is labelled 'pre-semantic'. According to Perry, we use the context in a pre-semantic way to establish 'which meaning a word is being used, or which of several words that look or sound alike is being used, or even which language is being spoken'.[14] Perconti illustrates this with the example of the word 'bank' in English.[15] If we were walking along a river looking for a place to have a picnic and I said, 'That is a good bank!' you would know that I meant something very different than if we were walking through the centre of London past a financial institution. You know what I mean by the word 'bank' because of the context. In one context, I mean the side of the river. In another context, I mean a place or organization responsible for financial transactions. As Perconti explains: 'These uses are called pre-semantic in that recourse to the context *precedes* recognition of the meaning of the expressions and indeed serves to identify the right meaning.'[16,17]

Perconti then examines whether any animal communication system uses context in this way. He concludes: 'If we rely on the knowledge available today, we find that pre-semantic uses of the context seem to have no counterpart in the languages of other animals.'[18]

However, he then adds that 'it must be admitted that this assertion is not based on research specifically aiming to verify this possibility'.[19] As a result, it seems that basing any philosophical conclusions on this would be unwise. A philosophical theory which rests on highly contentious empirical premises seems to be obviously undesirable. Further, any conclusion based on it would have to be conditional and dependent upon future scientific findings. Due to this, I do not believe that Perconti has yet made his case.

The second form of context-dependence that Perconti appeals to are what Perry calls 'semantic uses'. These involve the use of demonstratives and indexicals. For the sake of completeness, pure indexicals have their content or referent fixed purely through their meaning and use. Standard examples include 'today' and 'I'. I can utter these words and you will know to what I am referring entirely because of their meaning, and the time and place in which I have used them. Pure indexicals are often contrasted with true demonstratives which require something additional in order to fix their content or referent. Standard examples include 'that' and 'this'. If I simply said 'that' without pointing to an object, or when it has not been made clear by the previous words in the conversation, it would be unclear to what I am referring.[20] What pure indexicals and true demonstratives have in common is that their reference changes from use to use and context to context and as a result they are all included under the banner of 'indexicals'. These terms were originally devised by the influential American philosopher David Kaplan.[21] What is interesting about indexicals is that they have what has come to be called a 'character'. As Perconti explains: 'Character is the linguistic rule associated with the demonstrative that guides us in determining the right individual in the context. For example, the character of "that" is more or less "the relevant object that is distant from the speaker".'[22] Similarly, the character of 'I' is more or less 'the speaker, unless they are directly quoting another individual in which case it is that individual' or something to this effect. Human languages clearly contain indexicals.

What about animal communication systems? Do they contain indexicals? As Perconti says: 'If we found an animal signal fixing its reference by means of a rule of application analogous to character, then we would be faced with something similar to expressions like "today", "this" and "there".'[23] Perconti explores this question in considerable detail and examines a number of examples. He ultimately concludes that although some species of animal can be *taught* to use indexicals this happens rarely and is not part of the *natural* behaviour of any species other than humans.[24]

Once again, however, problems may exist. First, as with my concern about pre-semantic uses, future empirical research may falsify Perconti's claim, and this strikes me as undesirable. Further, the fact that nonhuman animals can be taught to use indexicals strikes me as doubly worrying. If animals of a certain species can be *taught* to use indexicals, then it is clearly an inbuilt potentiality of that species to *use* indexicals. As a result, the fact that they do not currently 'naturally' use indexicals strikes me as an accidental rather than an essential feature of their nature. If a gorilla can be taught to use indexicals by human beings, then it does not seem a stretch to imagine that a gorilla could teach a gorilla to use indexicals. If a group of gorillas having been taught to use indexicals, escaped into the wild and taught other wild gorillas to use them, then we would have gorillas using them in the wild. Thus, it might become part of their *natural* behaviour. Perhaps one would object that ultimately it was human beings who taught these gorillas to use indexicals and so even then this should not count as part of their *natural* behaviour. My concern here is that if they can be taught to use them, then it only takes one gorilla genius to have a freak flash of insight to get the whole thing started entirely without human beings. I do not see how anyone could deny that this would then count as part of their *natural* behaviour. Indeed, presumably this is how our early human or pre-human ancestors invented the use of indexicals, so if it is *natural* for us then it would be *natural* for these gorillas.

I am cautious here of overstepping my bounds as a philosopher. Much of this is conjecture on my part and there may be ethological and biological reasons to rule this out. However, I believe that my basic concern still stands. We still have not categorically ruled out the possibility that some nonhuman animal species do use indexicals 'naturally' (however we understand the word 'natural'). Even if this could be done (and on practical grounds this seems unlikely), we still have instances of nonhuman animals being taught to use them. This suggests to me that, once again, we have found a difference of degree not of kind.

For the sake of completeness, I will briefly explain the two other types of context-dependence Perconti explores. The third is post-semantic uses. Perconti explains: 'Post-semantic uses of the context occur when, after the words have been identified, their standard meaning has been recognised and the situation of occurrence has been appealed to, something else is still required in order to identify the proposition expressed by a certain utterance.'[25] A standard example would involve someone uttering something like 'It is raining'. In order to fully understand what they meant, whether it is true, and what implications this has, one would need to identify (at the very least) the unarticulated time and place (and perhaps other additional factors). This is done using the context. Perconti suggests that there are animal analogues of this type of context-dependence.

The final type of context-dependence are what Perconti labels 'extra-semantic uses'. He writes: 'By "extra-semantic uses" I mean variations in meaning depending on social and psychological factors.'[26] As an example, in twenty-first-century Britain for someone under the age of twenty (at least when I was under twenty), the word 'sick' can be a term of approval, roughly synonymous with 'cool'. However, for someone over the age of forty, the word 'sick' is a term of disapproval, roughly synonymous with 'perverse'. Perconti suggests that there are animal analogues of extra-semantic context-dependence.

Due to these sorts of considerations, it seems to me that we are unlikely to find a clear difference in kind between human beings and nonhuman animals purely by comparing nonhuman animal communications systems to human language. At the same time, language is clearly an important part of what makes us human. After all, we talk about human *languages* compared to animal *communication systems*. This suggests that when we look for what makes us unique among animals, although we are not looking at language directly, we are looking for something intimately tied to language.

Being rational and rational beings

As the philosopher Matthew Boyle points out: 'According to a tradition reaching back at least as far as Aristotle, human beings are set apart from other terrestrial creatures by their rationality.'[27] Put another way, human beings are rational animals.

However, as the British philosopher Bertrand Russell (1872–1970) pointed out: 'Man is a rational animal – so at least I have been told. Throughout a long life I have looked diligently for evidence in favour of this statement, but so far I have not had the good fortune to come across it.'[28] Russell was not unique in his scepticism about the idea of man as a rational animal. Within modern psychology, there is a growing body of research suggesting that, particularly under certain circumstances, humans are prone to logical errors in reasoning, subconscious biases and so on. Some instances of this type of research include a study by the psychologists Evans, Barston and Pollard,[29] who showed that people often fare poorly when it comes to identifying valid arguments if they already have strongly held beliefs about the conclusions. As an example, test subjects will often assume that a technically invalid argument is valid as long as it has a plausible conclusion. Another piece of research which suggests that humans may, in fact, be poor reasoners was undertaken by the psychologists Johnson-Laird and Savary[30], who showed that humans often fare very poorly at certain types of probabilistic reasoning. Perhaps one conclusion that could be drawn from research like this is that we rarely form beliefs or come to decisions for (entirely) rational or logical reasons. This, so somebody could claim, shows that we are not really rational animals. If humans do not make practical decisions or form their beliefs in a rational way all or even most of the time, what sense can we make of the claim that human beings are rational animals?

As Boyle points out, rather than seeing rationality as one human property or ability among many, we need to understand that 'rationality transforms all of our principal mental powers, making our minds different *in kind* from the minds of nonrational animals'.[31] How this is possible is best illustrated, perhaps surprisingly, by looking at the difference between animals and plants. I take it as a given that there is a difference in kind between plants and animals. However, as we will see, this difference in kind cannot be identified with any single property or handful of properties. Rather, the difference between plants and animals is based on a different fundamental way of being in the world which modifies all of their principal properties and abilities. This is best illustrated by examining some concrete examples.

One of the most obvious (apparent) differences between plants and animals is that animals can move in a way that plants cannot. After all, dogs and cats can walk and run, but trees are literally rooted into the ground. This might make us conclude that the difference is one of locomotion. However, this is too quick.[32] There are a number of 'sessile' animals which are incapable of movement. Further, plants can move, most obviously towards the Sun. Sunflowers are particularly good examples of this.[33] Another feature we might point to would be the fact that animals eat whereas plants photosynthesise, but we are all familiar with the infamous Venus flytrap which captures and 'eats' its insect prey. These two examples demonstrate that isolating a single capacity, or even bundle of capacities, and simplistically using that as the cut-off point between plants and animals will not suffice. There may well often be borderline cases which refuse to fit neatly into either category if we use this method.

A difference in kind can be identified between plants and animals by looking at how they engage in their multifarious activities. As Boyle explains:

Consider what it means to talk about *activity* in the case of a plant and in the case of an animal. Many people will be tempted to say that plants do not act at all, and there is of course a sense in which that is right: they do not act in the sense in which animals act. Nevertheless, there are clearly some episodes in the lives of plants in which they figure as agents rather than mere patients.... Nevertheless, when we speak of the goal-directed acts of an animal, we are clearly speaking of agency and goal-directedness in an altogether different register. It is not merely that an animal can do *more* than a plant; it is that talk of 'doing' can apply in a whole new way to an animal.[34]

Boyle then illustrates this difference in more detail by highlighting that, unlike animals, 'descriptions of the here and now can never enter into the characterization of the "acts" of plants except in the form of triggerings, helps or hindrances'.[35] He gives the example of a tree growing round a stone compared to an animal walking round a stone.

> The root of a tree can be growing round a stone, but it would be at best sentimental to suggest that the root is growing in a certain way *in order to get round this stone*. The presence of this stone here and now does not inform the *content* of the tree's act of root-growing, that toward which it is goal-directedly tending. The tree's roots simply grow, as far as possible, according to a certain pattern: the stone enters as a hindrance to this growth, something that interferes, and hence qualifies the sense in which the shape of the resultant growth can be understood as the tree's own doing, rather than as a reflection of something done to it.[36]

Animals, however, can actively respond to the here and now, and thus a description of the present circumstances can enter into the content of what they are doing. As Boyle highlights,

> Its capacities for perception and desire transform its mode of being alive precisely because they make this possible: they open animal life, not merely to the causal influence of present circumstances in the form of triggering, hindrance, or facilitation, but to the kind of influence that enters into the constitution of what the subject is doing. Thus, an animal can try *to get that object*, or do something *in order to avoid this obstacle*.[37]

Another way of approaching this distinction is to point out that animals act as individuals in a way that plants do not. A particular oak tree can grow a particular branch, but the explanation for why this is happening has little do with that individual. Growing branches is simply what oak trees do! The individual oak tree itself has not determined what should happen. On the other hand, when we try to understand why an animal is doing what it is doing then, depending upon the act in question, we do have to look at the experiences, history and dispositions of this particular individual. To put this (far too) crudely, in some sense of the word, nonhuman animals can be said to *choose* certain things (although in a very different way to humans), whereas plants cannot *choose* anything in any sense of the word. As Boyle points out: 'It is not merely that animals can do things that plants cannot; it is that the whole language of "doing" take on a new significance, a new logical character, when we turn from plants to animals.'[38]

We are now in a position to examine the difference between non-rational animals and human beings. The distinction between human beings and non-rational animals is not simply that we are capable of doing, being and having things that they cannot do, be and have. Rather, the distinction is that human beings are capable of being the subject of ascriptions of doing, being and having in a distinctive sense. Both humans and non-rational animals (and plants) can act in a goal-directed manner and as a response to their environments and circumstances. However, only human beings, in the full sense of the word, are capable of acting *intentionally*. As Boyle explains:

> It is widely conceded that a condition of the applicability of ascriptions of doing in this distinctive sense [intentional doing] is that the creature should be doing what it is doing knowingly, in virtue of exercising its power to determine what ends are worth pursuing and how to pursue them . . . the power to act in this distinctive sense – to engage in doings whose ascription implies that the subject knows what he is doing and what for – is the special prerogative of rational creatures.[39]

Rational animals, uniquely, are capable of acting towards a specific goal while knowing it and understanding it as a goal. Non-rational animals are capable of acting towards a specific goal but will not know it and understand it as a goal. Finally, plants are capable of acting towards general goals, but not specific goals. As Boyle explains, using the language of the Italian theologian Thomas Aquinas:

> Thus Aquinas holds that although nonrational animals can be said to intend an end and act voluntarily in pursuit of it in 'an imperfect sense,' they are not capable of intention or voluntary action in 'the perfect sense,' since they do not ordain their movement to an end in virtue of knowledge of that end 'under the aspect of an end'. Rather, they merely apprehend an object they desire and act from instinct or acquired habit in pursuit of it.[40,41]

As a result, a rough (and highly flawed) litmus test for rationality, that perhaps intuitively (but imperfectly) brings out the relevant distinction, is that in order for something to be rational we need to be able to ask and it needs to be able to answer, at least in principle, the question: 'Why are you doing this?' However, even this is too much. This obviously presupposes that the rational creature speaks a language and is capable of communicating with us, and this may not be possible. As a result, even this litmus test is inadequate, although perhaps it illustrates the basic insight.

A few clarifications are now needed. First, there is not enough space here to come to any conclusions about whether the *definition* of humanity is rational animality, nor is there space to weigh in on questions such as whether rational animality is exhaustive of humanity's essence, or whether terms like person, human, *Homo sapiens* and rational animal are interchangeable terms. It may be that the terms human being, person, and rational animal are interchangeable, and that the definition of humanity is rational animality which is exhaustive of our essence.[42] It may be that *Homo sapiens*, or human beings, are merely a type of rational animal.[43] For our purposes it does not matter; what is important is that a crucial part of what makes you, me and every other human being on this planet what and who we are is that we are rational and that we are animals in the senses explained earlier. This unites us and is something important that we all share. Further, if there are any other rational creatures out there, whether they be terrestrial or extra-terrestrial, whether they have fur, feathers or scales, two legs, four legs, eight legs, or no legs, and so on, they will be united to us and the same as us in an important and crucial sense.[44] They will be 'one of us'.

Second, this account in no way, *a priori*, rules out the possibility of other terrestrial rational animals. Some scholars might claim that certain species, such as cetaceans and higher apes, fulfil these criteria. I will not weigh in on this question here since this is a question for the biologist and ethologist to answer. However, it does follow from this account that if there are other rational animals then there is a fundamental break in kind between them and the non-rational animals, whichever those turn out to be. Either way, we have escaped the uncomfortable conclusion that the difference between human beings and uncontroversial non-rational animals is merely one of degree rather than one of kind. If we have to expand the rational animal club to include other species in the future, then so be it.

Two things follow from this in the here and now. First, it may well mean that some of our taxonomic practices need to be re-evaluated. Second, it means that when we are trying to determine whether or not a particular individual is a rational animal, we can no longer appeal to one simple test, property or capacity. Instead, we will need to examine the individual as a whole. We will need to examine not only this being's properties, capacities and abilities, but how it engages in and actualizes those properties, capacities and abilities. From an epistemic perspective in the real world, there may well be individuals whose rationality cannot be unambiguously and definitively ascertained. In terms of the measurements that we can practically make, the difference between a highly sophisticated non-rational animal and a dull-witted rational animal may be slight. However, from a metaphysical perspective every individual will either be rational or non-rational in the senses explained earlier. This makes all the difference 'from the inside'. Their way of being in the world and their very essence will be very different, and this has important ethical implications.

In order to pre-empt a potential objection, it is worth briefly highlighting that, according to this analysis, learning disabled humans (or, indeed, learning disabled transhumans and posthumans) would also count as rational animals. According to this assessment, as human beings they are intrinsically disposed towards rationality. However, their disability, whatever that may be, prevents this disposition from being fully or, in extreme cases, even partially fulfilled. As a result, there is a sense in which they are 'rational' even if they cannot exercise this rationality due to their disability. This insight is crucially important. If we hold that human beings are rational animals, while denying that those with severe learning disabilities are rational, then we risk denying their humanity. I take it as self-evident that this is absurd. As a result, I suggest we interpret the rational component of human nature as an inbuilt tendency to engage in one's multifarious activities in a rational way (as described previously), while observing that this is merely a tendency which can be blocked (by disability), destroyed (by damage), or simply stunted and starved (by neglect, both educational and emotional). The plausibility of this account is evidenced by the fact that a healthy, 'educated' (whatever that means in this context) dog is unable to speak (for example) and is in no way disadvantaged by this. However, a human being who is unable to speak is quite clearly disadvantaged, and, unless they are very young, we can assume that something, sadly, has gone, or is, 'wrong', due to things such as disability or neglect. There is insufficient space here to fully defend or explicate this claim, and some may not be fully convinced, but hopefully my point is clear enough and plausible enough for the purposes of this chapter. The important thing to observe is that it is possible to be fully human (or, indeed, transhuman or posthuman) while being unable to *exercise* one's rational capacities. What is needed, however, is a rational nature as described in the course of this chapter.[45]

At the end of the previous section, I concluded that one of the desiderata when identifying what distinguishes humans from non-rational animals was that it should be intimately linked, but not identical, to language. Does rationality as understood here fulfil this condition?

I believe it does. Rational thought, and thus rationality itself, seems to be intimately tied to language. I struggle to imagine what it would be like to 'think' without language. This might lead us to agree with the English philosopher Michael Dummett's (1925–2011) view that 'language is the vehicle of thought'.[46] Further, as the Australian philosopher David Oderberg has argued, abstract thought seems to require a representational system with a meaningful structure; and what is this if not language?[47] The precise relationship between rationality, rational thought and language goes beyond the limits of this chapter, but it seems highly plausible to believe that they are intimately linked in some manner.

Transhumans and posthumans

We are now in a position to examine transhumans and posthumans. The important question to answer is whether or not they will be rational animals in the sense explained earlier. It seems to me that they will be. They will still have bodies, be they of flesh and blood, metal and silicon or even electrons in a computer system, and they will need to sustain those bodies through the intake of energy (or sources of energy), the expelling of waste and through repair when they sustain damage. As a result, they will be animals even if they are highly unusual animals.[48] They will also be rational. Even if they develop cognitive (or physical) abilities which vastly outstrip normal human cognitive (or physical) abilities. They will still act towards specific goals while knowing, understanding and choosing them as goals. Even if they can do more things than us, and even if they possess properties and abilities which we lack, they will do those things, have those properties and exercise those abilities in a human way. As a result, they will be rational and they will be animals, and thus, they will be united to us and the same as us in an important and significant sense.[49]

It follows from this that if we generate transhumans then we will have the same obligations to them as we do for any other human whom we have brought into existence. Currently, the quintessential relationship and collection of obligations takes the form of parenthood, although other forms may exist. It does not follow from this that we will necessarily have parental obligations towards transhumans. After all, they may be generated fully mature and able to look after themselves. If this were the case, then they would not need parents. However, it does mean that if we generate transhumans who need parents, then their genitors will either need to fill that role themselves or find someone who will in the form of adoptive parents or carers.[50]

While these conclusions close down certain questions, others remain unanswered. It seems to me that the most pressing question is what impact might these transhumans have on our society and what ethical implications this will have for their development and flourishing. Here I can only briefly speculate, but it seems to me that the most worrying plausible impact such individuals might have on our society is to exacerbate existing inequalities and to create entirely new ones.

New issues of inequalities

Currently, just as the English philosopher Thomas Hobbes (1588–1679) pointed out,

> Nature hath made men so equall, in the faculties of body, and mind; as that though there bee found one man sometimes manifestly stronger in body, or of quicker mind then another; yet when all is reckoned together, the difference between man, and man, is not so considerable, as that one man can thereupon claim to himselfe any benefit, to which another may not pretend, as well as he. For as to the strength of body, the weakest has strength enough to kill the strongest, either by secret machination, or by confederacy with others, that are in the same danger with himselfe.[51]

This strikes me as an important observation. Even the world's strongest man can be overpowered by a handful of adults working together or by even the weakest individual through the use of a weapon or trickery. The world's fastest man can still be outrun by a man on horseback. The world's most intelligent person will still make errors in judgement. Further, they can only become an expert on so many topics which means they can be outwitted or fooled when engaging with an expert on something with which they have no experience or education. On top of this, all of us will one day die. This limits the amount of damage that any human being can do to others.

Transhumanism, if completely unchecked, threatens to undermine this delicate balance. If a person supplemented their physical capabilities to such an extent that they could not be overpowered by conventional civil authorities, then the maintenance of genuine law and order would become unfeasible and vastly expensive. You might have to deploy the military every time a cyborg tried to rob a bank! In addition, someone could potentially augment their intellectual powers to such a degree that they were able to manipulate political and economic systems to their massive advantage at a devastating cost to society at large.[52] To some extent these last two concerns are simply the dangers of increasingly advanced technology generally, but the possibility of vastly extending human life expectancy also brings particular risks. Very few people live to be more than 100 years old. This limits the benefits they can bring to society. Imagine if the German-born theoretical physicist Albert Einstein (1879-1955) was still alive today! I have no doubt that he would have made many more worthwhile contributions to science. However, it also limits the amount of damage people can do to society. Imagine if the great dictators of the twentieth century were still politically active today! Our limited lifespan also limits the amount of suffering that we must endure. Death ends suffering, at least for the dead.

These concerns about increased inequalities in power and life experience also go the other way. While some transhumans may have significant advantages over unmodified humans, others may have significant disadvantages. Two possibilities occur to me. First, one can imagine researchers genetically modifying embryos in order to remove 'undesirable' qualities (such as aggression) or to exaggerate 'desirable' qualities (such as cuteness). One need only compare a chihuahua to a wolf to see why this might put certain transhumans at a disadvantage compared to unmodified humans. Second, with the rise of computers and artificial reality technologies, certain kinds of transhumans and posthumans could end up in a very vulnerable position. If the conscious experiences of a group of posthumans were entirely computer-based, unmodified humans might be able to reprogram or manipulate the computers in which the posthumans 'live'. It would be an understatement to say that this could put them at significant disadvantage.[53]

How we should respond to these possibilities goes beyond the scope of this chapter. However, I will raise some questions for future conversation based on these possibilities. If modifying humans through technology puts them at an advantage compared to their unmodified peers, then one way to avoid the resultant inequalities would be to modify everyone. However, it seems obvious that some will not wish to be modified. How do we protect them? Another way to avoid the resultant inequalities would be to prevent anyone and everyone from modifying themselves. However, there are genuine and legitimate reasons why people might wish to be modified. For example, a blind person may want artificial eyes to restore their sight. This option also risks losing the potential advantages that these technologies might make to the human condition. How do we weigh up the risks and benefits of these technologies? What are the legitimate, and illegitimate, reasons for modifying ourselves or others?

There are also questions about who controls these technologies. Do we leave it to private corporations? If so, how do we prevent an elite few modifying themselves in a way that is unaffordable to the rest of the population which would then exacerbate the already existent inequalities between them and the population at large? Further, how do we prevent a modification 'arms race' between corporations and wealthy individuals? Alternatively, we could hand over control of these technologies to the state. However, this opens up the possibility of totalitarian and dystopian states that are currently, and thankfully, purely in the realm of science fiction. I doubt there are any easy answers to these questions, but these are the questions we should be asking.

Notes

1   Nick Bostrom, 'Transhumanist Values', *Journal of Philosophical Research* 30, Issue Supplement, Ethical Issues for the Twenty-First Century (2005), 3.

2 My thanks go to Matthew James for making this distinction.
3 From now on, I will simply talk about transhumans unless the distinction becomes relevant.
4 Ps 8.4 KJV.
5 Aristotle, Pol. 1. 1253a.
6 For a discussion of some of these issues from a philosophical perspective, see Michael Dummett, *The Seas of Language* (Oxford: Oxford University Press, 1996). For a discussion of some of these issues from something of a psychological perspective see Anne C. Reboul, 'Why Language Really Is Not a Communication System: A Cognitive View of Language Evolution', *Frontiers in Psychology* 6 (2015), 1434.
7 Andrew F. Russell and Simon W. Townsend, 'Communication: Animal Steps on the Road to Syntax?' *Current Biology* 27 (2017), R746–R769.
8 Francine G. P. Patterson and Ronald H. Cohn, 'Language Acquisition by a Lowland Gorilla: Koko's First Ten Years of Vocabulary Development', *Word* 41, no. 2 (1990), 97–143.
9 Pietro Perconti, 'Context-Dependence in Human and Animal Communication', *Foundations of Science* 7 (2002), 341–61.
10 I will return to this topic later.
11 Charles Darwin, *The Descent of Man, and Selection in Relation to Sex*, 2nd edn (London: John Murray, 1874), 85.
12 Perconti, 'Context-Dependence in Human and Animal Communication', 341–61.
13 J. Perry, 'Indexicals, Contexts and Unarticulated Constituents', in *Proceedings of the 1995 CSLI-Amsterdam Logic, Language and Computation Conference* (Stanford: CSLI Publications, 1998).
14 Perry, 'Indexicals, Contexts and Unarticulated Constituents', 2.
15 Perconti, 'Context-Dependence in Human and Animal Communication', 343.
16 Perconti, 'Context-Dependence in Human and Animal Communication', 344.
17 Perconti then highlights that we might object to this label because this act (of using the context to determine the meaning of a word) is itself a semantic move. As a result, perhaps it is misleading to label it pre-semantic given it is a semantic move itself. However, for the purposes of Perconti's paper this distinction is unimportant and so he continues to use Perry's terminology. I will follow him in this for the same reason.
18 Perconti, 'Context-Dependence in Human and Animal Communication', 345.
19 Perconti, 'Context-Dependence in Human and Animal Communication', 345.
20 Presumably the distinction between pure indexicals and true demonstratives allows for the possibility of 'impure' or 'mixed' indexicals. Potential examples that occur to me are 'faraway' and 'nearby'. A television remote can be 'faraway', but in a very different way to a distant country. At the same time, if the remote is in my lap, it is definitely 'nearby'. As a result, the context and the meaning are both relevant to fixing the content or referent of the words.
21 See David Kaplan, 'Demonstratives', in *Themes from Kaplan*, eds. Joseph Almog, John Perry and Howard Wettstein (New York: Oxford University Press, 1989), 481–563 for an example and more details.
22 Perconti, 'Context-Dependence in Human and Animal Communication', 346.
23 Perconti, 'Context-Dependence in Human and Animal Communication', 346–7.
24 Presumably, this is why he labels human language context-dependence 'indexicality'.
25 Perconti, 'Context-Dependence in Human and Animal Communication', 353.
26 Perconti, 'Context-Dependence in Human and Animal Communication', 356.

27 Matthew Boyle, 'Essentially Rational Animals', in *Rethinking Epistemology*, Volume 2 of Berlin Studies in Knowledge Research, eds. Günter Abel and James Conant (Berlin/Boston: De Gruyter, 2012), 1.
28 Bertrand Russell, *The Basic Writings of Bertrand Russell* (Routledge: London, 2009), 45.
29 J. St. B. T. Evans, Julie. L. Barston and Paul Pollard, 'On the Conflict Between Logic and Belief in Syllogistic Reasoning', *Memory and Cognition* 11, no. 3 (1983), 295–306.
30 P. N. Johnson-Laird and Fabien Savary, 'Illusory Inferences about Probabilities', *Acta Psychologica* 93 (1996), 69–90.
31 Boyle, 'Essentially Rational Animals', 1.
32 Excuse the pun.
33 Winslow R. Briggs, 'How Do Sunflowers Follow The Sun – And To What End?' *Science* 353, no. 6299 (2016), 541–2.
34 Boyle, 'Essentially Rational Animals', 18.
35 Boyle, 'Essentially Rational Animals', 18–19.
36 Boyle, 'Essentially Rational Animals', 19.
37 Boyle, 'Essentially Rational Animals', 19.
38 Boyle, 'Essentially Rational Animals', 20.
39 Boyle, 'Essentially Rational Animals', 21–2.
40 Boyle, 'Essentially Rational Animals', 22.
41 See *Summa Theologica*, IaIIae, Q. 6, A. 2 and FQ. 12, A. S.
42 See: D. S. Oderberg, 'Could There Be a Superhuman Species?', *The Southern Journal of Philosophy* 52, no. 2 (2014), 206–26 for an example of this view.
43 This is the option Matthew Boyle takes in 'Essentially Rational Animals'.
44 Thus, Locke's rational parrot and Swift's Houyhnhnms are rational animals, united to us and the same as us in an important and crucial sense. See J. Locke, *An Essay Concerning Human Understanding*. First published in 1689. Reprinted and edited by P. H. Nidditch (Oxford: Clarendon Press, 1975): Vol. I, Bk. II.xxvii. 8 and Jonathan Swift, *Gulliver's Travels*. Originally published 1726. Reprinted with notes and introduction by Robert DeMaria Jr. (Harmondsworth: Penguin, 2008) for more details.
45 For a more detailed discussion of this topic, please see Justin Matchulat, 'Rationality and Human Value', *Faith and Philosophy* 32, no. 4 (2015), 404–22, and also my co-authored paper Richard C. Playford and E. Diane Playford, 'What Am I? A Philosophical Account of Personhood and Its Application to People with Brain Injury', *Neuropsychological Rehabilitation* 28, no. 8 (2018), 1408–14.
46 Dummett, Michael, *The Seas of Language* (Oxford: Oxford University Press, 1996), ch. 6. In this chapter, 'Truth and Meaning', Dummett also explains why it is so difficult to really understand what it is like to be a non-rational animal. The moment we try to express what it is like to be a non-rational animal in words we are already ascribing properties to them and their experience which they lack.
47 Oderberg, 'Could There Be a Superhuman Species?'.
48 I have not explored animality in a huge amount of depth due to limits on space, but I assume that the precise elements and molecules out of which their bodies are made is unimportant.
49 One could even argue that we have already entered the dawn of the transhuman age and that many of us are already transhumans, if a bit primitive compared to what might be possible in the future. After all, reading glasses, lazer eye surgery, hip replacements, prosthetics, plastic surgery as well as our increasing interaction with, and dependence upon, electronics and computers could all be seen as first steps into

the transhuman age. If we are *already* transhumans, then it seems less strange to hold that future transhumans will be 'one of us'.
50 The most famous story of someone generating a transhuman and failing to care for him appropriately is of course Mary Shelley's *Frankenstein*: Mary Shelly, *Frankenstein*. Originally published 1818. Reprinted with notes and introduction by Maurice Hindle (London: Penguin, 2003).
51 Thomas Hobbes, *Leviathan*. First published in 1651. Reprinted and edited by Christopher Brooke, (London: Penguin, 2017), 100.
52 I do not think it is uncontentious to say that we are probably already seeing this, to some extent, in certain political and economic domains due to the rise of computers.
53 For a disturbing fictional account of what this might look like, see Black Mirror Series 4 Episode 1: USS Callister: C. Brooker and W. Bridges, (Writers), and T. Haynes (Director). USS Callister (television series episode). In C. Brooker (Producer), Black Mirror (London, Britain: House of Tomorrow, 2017).

3

Remaining human

The philosophy of Charles Taylor aimed at the ethics of generating trans- and posthuman persons

Gregory Parker Jr.

Introduction

In 2016, Charles Taylor was awarded the Berggruen Prize for Philosophy and Culture from the Berggruen Institute. This $1 million prize is awarded annually to scholars who are profoundly shaping human self-understanding amidst a rapidly changing world. Taylor's literary output beckons readers to see humans not only as biologically constituted but also as linguistically, and physically immersed in a network of relationships, which provide a multifaceted description of what it means to be human. Therefore, Taylor's philosophy offers an appealing opportunity to reflect on what it means to be human[1] and the ethical implications this has on the generation of transhumans and posthumans.

A conception of 'fullness' is necessary to draw upon and help frame our entry into Taylor's description of humans. In his tour de force, *A Secular Age*, which was published in 2007 and probably the work leading him to receive the award, Taylor examines what it means to believe. More specifically the conditions of belief within a society in which it was 'virtually impossible not to believe' at one point, to one in which faith is just another option on the pluralist *à la carte* menu.[2] He does so by focusing attention on the condition of the lived experience and the construals of this experience. He describes this shift historically because who we are and our understanding of ourselves is shaped by our interpretation of the past and our expectation of the future. This axiomatic shift, in which there is a movement from the norm of belief to the norm of unbelief, Taylor connects with a shift from the pre-modern 'porous-self' to the modern 'buffered-self'.

In the social imaginary of the porous-self, the individual is open and susceptible to the 'enchanted' world, to the transcendence of God, etc. By contrast, the social imaginary of the buffered-self is isolated from, and in some ways closed to, the 'enchanted' world. For the buffered individual this world is all that there is. Nonetheless, the buffered-self experiences what Taylor calls a loss, in moving from the 'enchanted' to the 'disenchanted world'. Popular Australian songwriter Kevin Parker captures this loss well:

> I don't have the verve to belong to the dead side
> Oh, why have I ever tried, I don't know
> Oh, dare I face the real world?
>
> Everyday
> Back and forth what's it for?
> What's it for?
> Back and forth, everyday
> Everyday[3]

What are we here for? What is so special about being human? If this is all there is, why do we try? These questions typify what Taylor calls the modern malaise, which is a discontentedness with the loss of the transcendent. This conception of malaise coincides with a conception of fullness. In former times, the porous individual found fullness outside of humanity, namely in God. Today this fullness is conceived by the hand of human beings themselves.

Taylor perceives two competing visions of fullness. The first one is embraced by models of transhumanism through technology.[4] This technological vision of fullness has been called by some, borrowing from Taylor's 'social imaginary', the 'socio-technical imaginary'.[5] This makes it clear that the philosophy of transhumanism[6] through biotechnology is putting forth a particular vision of 'fullness' to confront a particular 'malaise'. This socio-technical imaginary is not ethically neutral. The governors of 'fullness' today are those at the front of the socio-technical imaginary. The American science and technology scholar J. Benjamin Hurlbut states:

> The 'scientific community' thus acquires a gatekeeping role, based ... on an imagination that science is *the* institution most capable of governing technological emergence. Normative questions of what is at stake, what is the public good, and who had the authority to define benefits and harms are thereby rendered subsidiary to expert assessments of novelty.... This division of labour is institutionalized in the role of contemporary bioethics, with its focus on downstream consequences and its preoccupation with the question of whether a given technological domain is sufficiently novel to engender new problems.[7]

Hurlbut's assessment is important to grasp. What is good, what is normative and what is healthy for humanity is absent from naturalist technological assessments.[8] Biotechnology, thus governs our current conceptions of the ideal future, regardless of what the highest good is for humans, such that contemporary novelty becomes the highest good. The question thus shifts from one of 'should it be done?' to 'can it be done?'[9] This socio-technical imaginary has explicit implications on what it means to be human.[10] For it places this meaning and human agency *under* technology and puts forth a particular posthuman horizon of fullness.

Taylor's second vision of 'fullness' does not abandon technology. Rather, it seeks to engage technology *through* human agency. This opens humans up to technology in a different manner and forces technology to be *under* what it means to be human.[11] In other words, instead of humans creating and being recreated in the image of technology, technology might be utilized to make us more human. Taking Taylor's *A Secular Age* into consideration, we may note that our shifting understanding and conception of the cosmos has placed stress on our understanding of what it means to be human. An understanding of our purpose and place within this universe has moral significance. In the next section, we will take a closer look at what it means to be human. This concept has been placed in the backdrop of competing visions over the highest good and an acknowledgement that transhumanism and posthumanism have their own conception of the highest good and fullness for humans.

What does it mean to be a human?

For Taylor, humans are introspectively self-aware finite creatures[12], capable of responses, emotions, desires, aversions, making and discovering meaning, relational,[13] religious, lingual,[14] organisms[15] endowed with a mind,[16] embodied,[17] able to die[18] and create,[19] active agents, moral subjects[20], who are embedded in the world, created in the image of God, but have indeed fallen.[21] These themes all orbit Taylor's central claim, that humans are self-interpreting animals.[22] This theme is unfurled in the *Sources of the Self*, which presents something of a meta-ethics, a way of considering what it means to be human and to live as humans.[23] He tells this story through a philosophical and historical genealogy of how we have come to the modern identity which 'involves tracing various strands of our modern notion of what it is to be a human agent, person, or a self'.[24] One may see his historical account as presenting two dimensions of being human, one static and the other dynamic. For Taylor, there is an essential link between who we are as humans and our ethics and this will be drawn out here.

The dynamic component of being human is that which changes alongside the passing of time, or from culture to culture. This dimension develops out of earlier conceptions of the self. They are dynamic because they are subject to change and are moulded by the contours of history. Our role within the narrative, our narrative identity, is how we come to understand ourselves. Of course, this narrative itself is not static but is always evolving.[25] How individuals views themselves as a child is different from their conception of themselves as an adult. Our identity as humans is shaped by our visions of the highest good.[26] Taylor identifies three features of the modern identity that are dynamic: (1) modern inwardness, (2) the affirmation of the ordinary and (3) the notion of nature as a moral source. We are always in a state of becoming or change, with these three shifting alongside the sands of time.[27]

The first to consider is the dynamic of modern inwardness. This is the modern conception of a self, who is distinct from other selves and is somewhat timeless but has been amplified in modernity by the further inner dimension of the subject. Taylor identifies the universal by stating, 'we can probably be confident that on one level human beings of all times and places have shared a very similar sense of "me" and "mine'".[28] Of the further internal dimension of modern humans, he writes: 'There is a sense of 'inside' which designates the thought or desires or intentions which we hold back for ourselves, as against those we express in speech and action.'[29] This is traced historically from the Greek philosopher Plato to the Roman Augustine and then upward through the Frenchman Descartes and the Englishman Locke. This shift for Taylor coincides with a shift of the good or fullness as external to humanity to one in which the source is internal.

An additional dynamic of the modern identity develops in the enlightenment, with the affirmation of ordinary life. Taylor ties a thread here between the rise of Protestantism and the idea of universal benevolence.[30] There are three aspects to the affirmation of ordinary life, namely the value of the family, of ordinary work,[31] and benevolence towards others.[32] One might notice that the affirmation of ordinary life is inherently communal, while it develops in an individualistic direction. That is because a self requires a community and humans are 'language animals'. As Taylor writes, 'One cannot be a self on one's own. I am a self only in relation to certain interlocuters. A self consists only within ... webs of interlocution.'[33] Moreover it ties in with the shift from an external to an internal picture of fullness; that which could only be attained in the afterlife shifts to being searched for in the present day.[34]

The last dynamic dimension of the human is the notion of nature as a moral source. Where does morality come from for this modern human? Taylor explores what he calls the expressivist turn, which is a turn away from Lockean deism. For the heirs of Locke the world could only be grasped through a detached reason. The Romantic expressivist turn alternatively perceives human expression/language as providing an alternative path. These moral sources have been partly internalized because they are our own articulations of the beautiful and the good. This is where the static and dynamic dimension come together. The static dimension of being human is namely that of human ontology or essence, it is that which does not change.[35] The *Sources of the Self* does not focus directly on this static component, but rather it becomes clear as one recognizes our moral reactions through language.[36]

The static component is our physical ontology, which gives us, according to the Romantics, access to morality. Taylor writes, 'we should treat our deepest moral instincts, our ineradicable sense that human life is to be respected, as our mode of access to the world in which ontological claims are discernible and can be rationally argued and sifted'.[37] Our physical ontology is distinct from how we perceive ourselves, that is, 'we are living beings with these organs quite independent of our self-understandings or -interpretations, or the meanings things have for us'.[38] Taylor resources the Romantics to argue that nonetheless, as a linguistic creature, it is through language that the moral sources external to us become within us as part and parcel of who we are. This ultimately leads to threefold split in where we might receive our ethics in the West today: (1) the theism of Augustine, (2) the naturalism of science or (3) the expressivism of the Genevan philosopher Jean-Jacques Rousseau. Taylor perceives a potential reconciliation in the original Christian notion of love. Therein there is a divine affirmation for humans as they participate through God in his love.[39] Therein is a moral source that is both infinite and embodied, static and dynamic.

For Taylor, there is an essential link between who we are as humans and ethics. This essential link is tied to his understanding of humans as self-interpreting creatures. We come to know and understand the world through language which provides both a dynamic and static dimension to being human. The dynamic component takes a narrative form as we come to understand ourselves through history and with other humans. The static is introduced through language as moral sources external and universal to us become a part of us. For Taylor, this is supremely expressed in the Christian notion of love. In the next section, we consider Taylor's articulation of being a person. This concept will build upon but differentiate itself from Taylor's understanding of what it means to be human.

What does it mean to be a person according to Charles Taylor?

It is important to note three features of Taylor's conception of a being a person: (1) a person is an agent with significance, (2) this agent possesses original purpose and (3) is capable of evaluations. These three main features have significant overlap with one another as they are each bound together through language. Taylor's articulation of what it means to be a person would facilitate space for the personhood of transhumans and posthumans, but their generation would be problematic to the second feature of being a person.

In 1985 Taylor writes two separate accounts about his understanding of the concept of a 'person'.[40] In his work *Philosophical Papers*, Taylor has a chapter titled 'On the Concept of a Person'. In the second paragraph of the chapter he gives a distillation of his view of a 'person'. He writes:

> Where it is more than simply a synonym for 'human being', 'person' figures primarily in moral and legal discourse. A person is a being with a certain moral status, or a bearer of rights. But underlying the moral status, as its condition, are certain capacities. A person is a being who has a sense of self, has a notion of the future and the past, can hold values, make choices; in short, can adopt life-plans. At least, a person must be the kind of being who is in principle capable of all this, however damaged these capacities may be in practice.[41]

In this paragraph, Taylor notes that 'person' is often equivalent or synonymous with 'human being'. Beyond this, the word person is often used in legal or moral discourse. In this discourse, a 'person' is attributed a particular moral status and given certain rights. This status and rights rest on an account of a particular picture of the concept of a person. All three features of Taylor's conception of a person are in germ in his definition above, and they will be explored in turn later.

One must first begin with Taylor's concept of agency. This is perhaps clearest in Taylor's other 1985 essay 'The Person'. Here, an agent is 'a being who encompasses purposes, who can be said to go after, and sometimes attain goals'.[42] An agent is thus reflective and forward looking, although they may not always attain that for which they strive. Persons are not simply agents, however, but agents with significance according to Taylor.[43] By this, he means a being 'who can make life plans, hold values, choose'.[44] In other words, 'things matter to them'.[45] For what is special about agents with significance is 'that we can attribute purposes, desires, aversion to them in a strong original sense'.[46]

This is intimately connected to the second feature, that persons possess original purpose, which begins to differentiate his account of agency from more reductionist accounts that limit agency to consciousness. The distinction between agents and persons is made clearer when one considers other kinds of agents (i.e. nonhuman animals, machines, angels). Nonhuman animals are agents, but not agents with significance.[47] They lack the ability to grasp and evaluate significance. Machines can be agents, but they are agents with a derivative rather than an original purpose. Likewise, machines are agents that lack significance.[48] So, what makes the agency of persons different from a nonhuman animal or mechanical agency? To reply to this question, it may be relevant that persons are 'agents plus' or 'agents with significance'; persons are agents with original purpose, desires, aversions and so on.

The third feature of what it means to be a person for Taylor is the ability of evaluations, which is deeply connected to the previous two features. For all three are intimately bound up with language. For language is the instrument by which we grasp significances, such as emotions, good and evil, morality, art, religion and so on. But it is also through participation in the language community that we understand these significances and make evaluations.[49] Language expresses a particular way of being. Thus, a human is always a person on account of the latent capacity to become such a language animal. One really 'becomes a person and remains one' through conversation.[50] In other words, language opens the door for significance and evaluations of significance which are external to the human.[51] Thus, according to Taylor, we must not think of the person as a set of capacities, nor as strictly an agent, but one who is capable of evaluations through language.

For there to be a person, it is necessary for Taylor that this being has its own viewpoint, by which he or she responds to things. But to draw out the significant features of Taylor's understanding of what it means to be a person, we will need to look at Taylor's understanding of humans as language animals. Taylor develops a fuller account of humans as *The Language Animal* in his 2016 book of that name. The significance of language for agents with significance however is already present in his 1985 reflections on personhood. The ability to evaluate or possess human significances is intimately tied to language. As Taylor writes, 'only a language animal could have them'.[52] But what enables language to play such an important role in human significances? Taylor breaks this into two propositions: (1) language enables us to be aware of what we are focusing on and (2) language creates a communal space for discourse. As Taylor points out, there is no analogue for these two dimensions of language for non-linguistic animals.[53] Thus, 'Language makes things clear in two ways: it brings them into articulate focus, and it brings them out into public space.'[54] One further dimension that Taylor draws out in *The Language Animal* is the development or formation of language for humans,[55] which develops organically as they are embedded within a particular community.[56]

This organic development of language brings us to the question of transhumanism and posthumanism. How might Taylor handle the question of a transhuman or posthuman agent? Would there be a distinction between human, transhuman and posthuman agents? Taylor does not address this question head on, but perhaps by briefly reflecting on how Taylor might handle angelic agents, we may reach some distinction. Humans and angels seem to both be agents with significance possessing purposes, desires, aversions in a strong original sense. Likewise, angels seem to be language animals.[57] One might suggest, however, via Italian theologian Thomas Aquinas, that they are language animals in a different way.[58]

This has two threads: (1) the nature of angelic creation and (2) the nature of angelic language.[59] Only the second concerns us here. Aquinas explores this second point in his *Summa Theologia* Q.107.[60] He argues that 'speech manifests to another what lies hidden in the mind'. However, angels' minds are not hidden from one another and thus 'it is not necessary that one angel should speak to another' at least not in the same exterior fashion that humans do with voice, embodied movement and so on. Rather, angelic speech is interior, which includes 'not only the interior speech by mental concept, but also its being ordered to another's knowledge by the will'. This interior speech is not fragmented, but rather the entire mental concept is made known. The English writer, Matthew Sperling, commenting on Q. 107 in Aquinas stated, 'The minds of angels for Aquinas, move immediately to concepts, and the angels swap concepts with each other frictionlessly, by the perfect action of the angelic will, like a sort of divine file-sharing.'[61]

Under this trajectory, we might then say that the difference between human and angelic agents is split along the nature of language. Humans learn language within an embedded community and our significances are shaped by our participation in such a community. As Taylor writes, 'Thus our grasp on our emotions, on what is deep and what is superficial, what is fundamental commitment, and what is passing fancy, what is profound love and what is mere dalliance, can depend crucially on our conversations with others.'[62] Alternatively, angels are created and possess this language already. They do not learn languages through participation in the pre-existing language community, but rather possess it already. Humans and angels are thus playing entirely different language games and participate in different language communities. Therefore, while angels might possess 'significances' they are ultimately unshared with human 'significances'.[63] They would still be 'persons' according to Taylor, and 'agents with significance', but it would be a different kind of 'agent' with a different kind of 'significance'. This we will return to when we consider the generation of transhumans and posthumans. For Taylor, then, we might identify a person as 'a being who has a sense of self, has a notion of the future and the past, can hold values, make choices; in short, can adopt life-plans'. This could be succinctly summarized by indicating that a person is an agent with significance, who possesses a sense of self.[64]

Taylor's philosophy applied to the generation of transhuman and posthuman persons

In the final portion of this discussion, we turn to consider how Taylor's conceptions of what it means to be a human and his conception of personhood might be turned towards the question of the generation of transhuman and posthuman persons.

Taylor might also have addressed the question through the lens of political theory, in which issues of equality, justice and class conflict may have all been raised. Here the question is approached strictly through the lens of what it means to be a human and a person. So what might Charles Taylor say about the generation of transhuman and posthuman persons? (1) Across the corpus of Taylor's writings, he has often exhibited a concern for the preservation of what it means to be human in relation to technology, (2) transhuman and posthuman persons are robbed of their original 'human' purpose and (3) there is a loss of shared significances that may further buffer transhuman and posthuman persons. The latter two concerns hinge on Taylor's conception of what it means to be a person. Although of course, Taylor draws a clear line between being a person and a human through language. Each of these three will be approached in turn.

Retaining our humanness

First, Taylor has often exhibited a concern for the preservation of what it means to be human in relation to technology. Across his works, he has often lamented the role of instrumental reason in the use of technology.[65] He writes of this most clearly in *Ethics of Authenticity*, where he advocates for an 'ethic of caring' in relation to technology and not an ethic of 'domination'.[66] He pushes for us to place technology *under* what it means to be human, rather than what it means to be human *under* technology. Taylor's articulation for this is that the abuse of instrumental reason coincides with a certain flattening of human life. This coincides with Taylor's conception of the 'malaise' in the buffered-self. Taylor does not believe that this malaise can be simply overcome through technology and the 'socio-technical imaginaries' vision of fullness.

Taylor's vision of retaining what it means to be human offers very little room for the generation of transhuman and posthuman persons. What is fundamentally human about humans should be retained in any movement towards transhumanism and posthumanism. This requires a recognition that a certain moral ontology is implicit in visions of the future. The ethics of generating transhuman and posthuman persons, in other words, turns on our understanding of what it means to be human in the first place. And the generation of transhuman and posthuman persons places humans *under* technology rather than over.

The loss of original purpose

The second concern deals largely with the second feature of being a person. That humans are agents with original purpose (p.51). If you recall, nonhuman animals, angels and humans were all creatures that were afforded original purpose in Taylor's schematic. Although, by virtue of second-order evaluations humans and angels have a stronger kind of original purpose than nonhuman animals. The generation of transhuman and posthuman persons raises an interesting question along these lines, as does the artificial generation of any kind of creature. To draw out the point, I will make an appeal to pop-culture. In the 2019 TV series *The Boys*, mega corporation Vought has medically modified children across the nation. These children then grow up to become superheroes. When one superhero 'Starlight' (Annie January) discovers that she was not originally intended to be born with these powers, but was medically modified, she confronts her mother (Donna January), and they have this exchange:

> *Donna*: I did it because they promised that you'd have a chance at an extraordinary life, that you'd be strong and successful and special. Who wouldn't want that for their children?
> Annie: You made me think that I was chosen by God
> *Donna*: You were. God brought Vought into our lives. He made this possible.
> Annie: Bullshit. You did! And then you controlled every single minute of it. You woke me up 5am to train for those stupid pageants and the tap dancing and tae kwon do.
> *Donna*: I gave up every moment of my life and I was happy to do it. This was our dream.
> Annie: This was your dream. I never got a chance to choose my own dream. No wonder I don't know who the f*** i'm supposed to be.[67]

Annie's plight captures in a moment a potential argument against generating transhuman and posthuman persons from Taylor's perspectives in that it robs them of their original human purpose. Biotechnologically generated transhuman and posthuman persons have been robbed of their agency. While of course an individual's life trajectory is susceptible to countless variables, to mechanically disrupt this organic process causes a loss of agency. One can also see how the corporation Vought, which is representative in this illustration of the socio-technical imaginary of the biotech field, has offered a novel conception of fullness. Life will be 'extraordinary' for those who traverse this transhuman path. However, what is the transhuman experience of Annie January? She experiences a loss of agency, having been subjugated to the intentions of entities beyond the norms of human development.[68] This coincides with the first point. In Annie's human life being submitted *under* technology, she is robbed of original agency and loses something of her humanness.

Loss of shared significances

The third issue that Taylor's framework brings to bear on the question of the generation of transhuman and posthuman persons is the loss of shared significances. Taylor provides a thought experiment in this direction in his essay 'The Person' in which a gaseous, sapient race comes to humans from a faraway galaxy. He describes the creature in the following way:

> They are not living organisms in our sense but they understand, and care about things in their own (to us incomprehensible) way. They might come to understand that some process, for example, electric shock, had some significance for us, they would perhaps understand that this significance was negative, provided they saw

us as sapient, and thus took our avoidance of it as purposeful. They might be able to understand the physiological conditions of this being unpleasant, that is to say, something we want to avoid, so they could identify thresholds. But just what the experience of pain was would forever be beyond them.[69]

While potentially beyond even a transhuman, the illustration draws out the point that there is a loss of shared significances. The engendered transhuman would potentially no longer share the same experiences as those shared by present humanity. An illustration may be drawn again from *The Boys*. It is revealed that Vought had medically engendered one 'supe' in particular, Homelander (John). In a scene reminiscent of Victor Frankenstein in Mary Shelley's 1818 novel, the 'supe' Homelander's loss of shared significances is demonstrated.

> *Jonah*: The thing about crossbreeding dogs, if ya get the right genes you can get the perfect creation. But it doesn't matter how perfect they are. It is not enough. When I raise subjects without their mothers they become violent, aggressive, downright hateful. You should have been raised in a home with a family who loved you. Not in a cold lab with doctors.
> John: And yet I turned out great.
> *Jonah*: When I think what it has done to you and what you can now do to everyone else. I'm sorry.
> John: I don't want your f***ing apology.
> *Jonah*: All this is my fault.
> John: What do you want? What? What do you want forgiveness? Now? After you raised me like a f***ing lab rat. No. Too little too late.
> *Jonah*: I'm just an old man thinking about his mistakes
> John: I'm the world's greatest superhero.
> *Jonah*: You're my greatest failure. [70]

Throughout the show, the transhuman Homelander is repeatedly isolated from human beings and demonstrates difficulty fraternizing with them. When considering the socio-technical imaginary, we must not only consider what is gained, but also what is lost. The transhuman no longer has a set of true interlocuters, there is a loss of true community, and therefore a loss of self. One might recall Taylor's language of self considered above: 'One cannot be a self on one's own.' Humans learn language within an embedded community and our significances are shaped by our participation in such a community. Moreover, there is the loss of family. In the generating of trans- and posthumans, the person does not overcome the malaise of modernity, nor does the fullness of the 'socio-technical imaginary' offer them a balm. Just as the modern self is 'buffered' and is still vulnerable and longs for connection, the 'Supe' John still experiences this 'malaise'. Social connections and love are central to Taylor's understanding of being human, and the trans- and posthuman is vulnerable to great social suffering.

Conclusion

Through the lens of the work of Taylor, a synthetic description of what it means to be a human being and a person was offered. It was noted that the socio-technical imaginary was not neutral and that there were competing visions of fullness. Furthermore, this chapter unfurled a static and dynamic dimension of being human. This centred on human beings as self-interpreting creatures. Our attention was then turned to what it means to be a person. This focused on persons as agents with significance. What it means to be a human and a person was then turned on the ethics of generating transhuman and posthuman persons. The competing visions of fullness make it difficult to perceive how Taylor would positively approach the ethics of generating transhuman and posthuman persons. Personhood and human ontology both have implicit moral implications. An apprehension of Taylor's perception of what it means to be human and personhood raises three issues to the surface. That technology must not rule over humanity, the issue of the loss of original purpose, and the loss of shared significances. These three are connected to the nature of humans as self-interpreting creatures. Other possible lines of inquiry to be explored in the future might include the nature of the relationships between, on the one hand, human beings and on the other transhuman and posthuman persons in the generation of yet more transhuman and posthuman persons. What community would exist for transhuman and posthuman persons? Altogether, the chapter asserts that Taylor would have difficulty affirming the ethical viability of the generation of transhuman and posthuman persons and any path forward would need to keep 'being human' above 'technology'.

Notes

1. Charles Taylor, *Sources of the Self: The Making of Modern Identity* (Cambridge, MA: Harvard University Press, 1989), 79 (Hereafter, *SOS*). SOS, 49. 'Personal identity is then a matter of self-consciousness. But it is not at all what I have been calling the self, something which can exist only in a space of moral issues.'
2. Charles Taylor, *A Secular Age* (Cambridge, MA: The Belknap Press of Harvard University Press, 2007), 3 (Hereafter, *ASA*).
3. Kevin Parker 'Desire Be Desire Go.' Track#2 on *Innerspeaker*. Modular, 2010, mp3. Tame Impala.
4. Charles Taylor, *Ethics of Authenticity* (Cambridge, MA: Harvard University Press, 1991), 6, 98–101, 105 (Hereafter, *EOA*).
5. *ASA*, 172. A social imaginary is 'the way ordinary people, "imagine" their social surroundings, and this is often not expressed in theoretical terms, it is carried in images, stories, legends, etc.'; *Dreamscapes of Modernity: Sociotechnical Imaginaries and the Fabrication of Power*, eds. Sheila Jasanoff and Sang-Hyun Kim (Chicago: University of Chicago Press, 2015), 4. Jasanoff and Kim define socio-technical imaginaries as 'collectively held, institutionally stabilized, and publicly performed visions of desirable futures, animated by shared understandings of forms of social life and social order attainable through, and supportive of, advances in science and technology'.

6   Popular definitions of what it means to be transhuman have suggested that it is an intermediary state of humanity between what we were and what we could become as posthumans. In the literature, neither posthuman nor transhuman are well defined, because the teleology is transitory in nature; the end goal is undefined. Thus, we might conceive transhumanism as a process to a posthuman vision, a sort of guided evolution through bio-technological advancement to transcend the limitations we possess organically as humans. The 'sociotechnical imaginary' continues to change and with it what it means to be trans/posthuman (See for example, https://whatistranshumanism.org/#what-is-a-transhuman (Accessed on 8 January 2021)).

7   J. Benjamin Hurlburt, 'Remembering the Future: Science, Law, and the Legacy of Asilomar', in *Dreamscapes of Modernity: Sociotechnical Imaginaries and the Fabrication of Power*, eds. Sheila Jasanoff, and Sang-Hyun Kim (Chicago: University of Chicago Press, 2015), 126–51, 129.

Asilomar is shorthand for a 1975 conference, which took place in Pacific Grove, California at the Asilomar conference centre. The conference met to assess the risks associated with recombinant DNA technology. Hurlburt examines the role of memory in the perpetuation and preservation of Asilomar as a sociotechnical imaginary. He does so in three ways: (1) looking at technoscience as a source of novelty and origin of change in society, (2) ascribing agency, competency, and responsibility to the 'scientific community' to introduce and regulate change and (3) offering a programmatic vision for the future through 'Asilomar-in-memory'.

8   SOS, 79. We have noted at least initially that this shifting understanding of our conception of the cosmos has led to deprivation of the consideration of the highest good in the 'socio-technical imaginary' which values novelty over the good. For Taylor, our understanding of the good has large import on how we understand ourselves.

9   This could also be seen as being birthed out of the larger movement towards pragmatism at the turn of the twentieth century.

10 SOS, 78.

11 EOA, 105–7.

12 ASA, 30, 583–4.

13 ASA, 137–8.

14 ASA, 147–8, 343–4, 353–4, 357, 755–5.

15 ASA, 182.

16 ASA, 31–2. The enchanted world has meaning independent of discovery while the disenchanted world has meaning only 'in the mind'.

17 ASA, 33.

18 ASA, 67.

19 ASA, 114.

20 ASA, 605.

21 ASA, 668, 678, 701; SOS, 5; Charles Taylor, 'A Catholic Modernity?', in *A Catholic Modernity? Charles Taylor's Marianist Award Lecture*, ed. James L. Heeft (Oxford: Oxford University Press, 1999), 13–37, 15–16, 35. In this lecture, he briefly delves into a discussion of humanity as the Image of God: 'Human diversity is part of the way in which we are made in the image of God.' He also suggests in this article that we are '*homo religiosus*' (28); that is, humans are religious by nature.

22 Charles Taylor, *The Language Animal: The Full Shape of the Human Linguistic Capacity* (Cambridge, MA: The Belknap Press of Harvard University Press, 2016) (Hereafter, TLA); Charles Taylor, 'Language and Human Nature', in *Philosophical Papers*

(Cambridge: Cambridge University Press, 1985), 215–47, 246–7. 'The issues concern the nature of man, or what it is to be human. And since so much of this turns on what it is to think, to reason, to create; and since all of these points towards language, we can expect that the study of language will become even more a central concern of our intellectual life.'
23   Michael Zuckert, 'Charles Taylor, *Sources of the Self*', in *The Oxford Handbook of Classics in Contemporary Political Theory*, ed. Jacob T. Levy (Online. February 2016).
24   *SOS*, 3.
25   *SOS*, 57.
26   *SOS*, 63.
27   *SOS*, 47.
28   *SOS*, 112.
29   *SOS*, 113.
30   *SOS*, 23, 215, 218.
31   *SOS*, 44, 211.
32   *SOS*, 258.
33   *SOS*, 36.
34   *SOS*, 214.
35   It should be noted that there is some recognition that Taylor has a 'weak' ontology. He says as much (see Charles Taylor, 'The "Weak Ontology" Thesis', *The Hedgehog Review* 7, no. 2 (Summer 2005), 35–42.). This is not to say that humans are immutable, but rather that there is something irreducibly human to humans. The static remains ontologically stable. In this chapter, ontology is understood to be the set of concepts that together compose what it means to be human. Thus, the dynamic and static components interplay with one another and together make up human 'ontology'.
36   *SOS*, 5. 'a moral reaction is an assent to, an affirmation of, a given ontology of the human.'
37   *SOS*, 8.
38   *SOS*, 34.
39   *SOS*, 510.
40   Charles Taylor, 'The Concept of a Person', in *Philosophical Papers Vol.2: Philosophy and the Human Sciences* (Cambridge: Cambridge University Press, 1985), 97–114; Charles Taylor, 'The Person', in *The Category of the Person*, eds. Carrithers Michael, et al. (Cambridge: Cambridge University Press, 1985), 257–82.
41   Taylor, 'The Concept of a Person', 97.
42   Taylor, 'The Person', 258.
43   This too is linguistic. This takes place through the form of first and second-order evaluations. In his essay *What is Human Agency*, Taylor introduces his notion of human agency, which is tied to notions of first and second-order desires. All creatures have desires (first-order), but only humans evaluate those desires (second-order). This first and second order of desires corresponds with weak and strong evaluations. True agency requires the existence of strong evaluations. These strong evaluations make implicit ontological claims on humans by compelling them towards a vision of a higher good. (See: Charles Taylor, 'What Is Human Agency', in *Philosophical Papers Vol 1: Human Agency and Language* (Cambridge: Cambridge University Press, 1985), 15–44; *SOS*, 33. Taylor identifies that human agency is crucially connected to an orientation of the highest good.)
44   Taylor, 'The Person', 261.
45   Taylor, 'The Concept of a Person', 98–9.

46 Taylor, 'The Concept of a Person', 97.
47 Taylor, 'The Concept of a Person', 99–103.
48 Taylor, 'The Person', 260.
49 Taylor, 'What is Human Agency', 36–7.
50 Taylor, 'The Person', 260.
51 Taylor, 'The Person', 277–78. Thus, being a person for Taylor opens us up to something that is beyond us. We might see here then the door to religion, morality, culture, ethics and so on.
52 Taylor, 'The Person', 271–2. This is intimately connected with issues of morality, meaning, dignity etc. 'It is only in language, or some other symbolic activity, that we can be aware of standards qua standards. It is in language, at least in a broad sense … that standards can be disclosed.'
53 Taylor, 'The Person', 272–75.
54 *TLA*, 42, 51–64, 344.
55 Taylor, 'The Person', 268–9.
56 *TLA*, 52, 55.
57 Taylor does discuss angels in relation to humans in *Ethics of Authenticity*. Here, he links the changing vision of our relation to the cosmos as lending itself to a vision of angels as having more in common with humans than a previous era and this change is 'language related' (see *EOA*, 84–87).
58 David Keck, *Angels and Angelology in the Middle Ages* (Oxford: Oxford University Press, 1998), 99–105. Keck draws out two paths: (1) Bonaventure who perceived angels as sharing a species but possessing individual personhood. (2) Aquinas who believed each angel is their own distinct species along with possessing individual personhood.
59 If one follows a more traditional path of reflection on the creation of angels, they are created fully developed. They are not subject to development within time as are humans. This connects intimately with the nature of angelic intellect. The intellect of an angel acquires knowledge in a different fashion than humans according to Bonaventure and Aquinas. As Etienne Gilson masterfully puts it, the intellect of an angel 'would be comparable to a canvas covered with its painting, or better still, a canvas reflecting the luminous essence of things'. This is not to say that Angels are omnipresent, or that they do not grow in knowledge. Rather angels do not develop in the same way as humans do (See Etienne Gilson, *The Philosophy of St. Thomas Aquinas*, trans. Edward Bullough, ed. G. A. Elrington (Cambridge: W. Heffer & Sons, Ltd., 1929), 178. Gilson is reflecting on Aquinas' angelology but his statement is relevant nonetheless; Keck, *Angels and Angelology in the Middle Ages*, 101–2; Augustine, *City of God*, 439–40, 659–60.
60 Thomas Aquinas, *Summa Theologia*, trans. English Dominican Provinces (Notre Dame, IN: Christian Classics, 1948), Q. 107 (see also I, Q.50.4).
61 Matthew Sperling, *Visionary Philology: Geoffrey Hill and the Study of Words* (Oxford: Oxford University Press, 2014), 166.
62 Taylor, 'The Person', 275.
63 See 1 Pet. 1.12.
64 Taylor, 'The Concept of a Person', 97. Taylor identifies in his account these capacities as *necessary* but not *sufficient* conditions. By this, he means that these capacities must be present, but do not inevitably have to be active. For example, for a child to eat ice cream, ice cream must necessarily be present. Nonetheless, the presence of ice cream does not inevitably lead to the consumption of ice cream. Likewise, the presence

of these capacities provides for the attribution of being a person, not their current employment. This makes room in Taylor's articulation of personhood to be used ethically to protect the unborn, the physically or mentally disadvantaged, and so on. Taylor summarizes these capacities under the term 'respondent', which makes way for his concept of self-interpreting beings.

65 *ASA*, 294; *SOS*, 456.
66 *EOA*, 105–7.
67 *The Boys*. 'You Found Me.' Episode 8. Directed by Erik Kripke. Written by Anne Cofell Saunders and Rebecca Sonnenshine.
68 Nonetheless, it is important to assert that a transhuman would indeed be a 'person' according to Taylor's threefold scheme.
69 Taylor, 'The Person', 268–9.
70 *The Boys*. 'The Self-Preservation Society.' Episode 7. Directed by Dan Attias. Written by Craig Rosenberg and Ellie Monahan. Thank you to Camille Simpson for bringing this to my attention.

4

Being somebody

Towards a categorical imperative for the age of transhumanism

Christian Hölzchen

Can generating posthuman persons be ethical?

The following chapter looks for an answer to this question by building upon the philosophical framework of humanism as it was most prominently developed by the German philosopher Immanuel Kant. This is not arbitrary: Kant quite literally lays a broad groundwork for modern ethical thought in the humanist tradition, with consequences for our understanding of human (or personal) rights up to this day. This concept of ethical personalism, of a grounding in humanism, has become a persistent strand in our ethical tapestries. It is clearly more visible in Continental patterns, but when issues of human or personal rights are concerned, this classical philosophy of the enlightenment is still a principal frame of reference for ethical thought.

Yet, this chapter is not meant to discuss Kantianism in depth. Rather, Kant and the tradition building upon him (and departing from him) serves as an example for an ethics that informed human rights, and thus as a lens through which we can examine the relation of ethics and personhood in a certain way.

Kant's most famous 'formula' for morality is the 'categorical imperative'.[1] The idea of a categorical imperative is to find a general principle for acting morally, which does not depend upon circumstances but allows us to judge different circumstances and interests from a shared moral vantage point. This perspective itself is derived from how we can act morally as persons.

Since this question is more concerned with a specific strand of ethical thought and its implications for our moment in time, the possible scenarios of trans- or posthuman persons can be drawn with a broader brush. This reflects the current state of the debate: we are in the fortunate position of thinking about the issues (mostly) *before the fact*. Even though some areas of uncertainty have to be discussed, there are currently no uploaded consciousnesses, strong artificial intelligences (AIs) or heavily genetically edited transhuman beings protesting their moral (and legal) rights. In this situation, it is justified to focus more on how our ethical personhood can be understood in the light of some proposed scenarios of posthuman persons and extrapolate from there.[2]

Moral imperatives and the ethical implications of being a 'person'

When we are discussing the ethics of generating 'persons' from a normative perspective – as one does when discussing categorical imperatives – there is more than one dimension to consider.

To begin with, there is the basic question of the morality of doing something: is this action morally acceptable? We can consider motives, means and immediate results of an action, and judge accordingly. The act of generating trans- or posthuman persons could, for example, be compared to giving money to charity, stealing a bicycle, yelling at a cat, lying on an insurance form, and so on. Depending on the action, and on its moral value, we might come to the conclusion that this action is right, or wrong, maybe even categorically so (one should never yell at a cat – it's pointless).

There is also a broader question of what an action might mean for the shape of our world in a wider sense, of responsibility for the present, and the future of our shared world: How will a proposed technological or social development change the world and the future? Is it an acceptable change? In this sense, the issue of generating transhuman persons can be compared to, for example, the discussion about fossil fuels, nuclear weapons or about the scale of industrial automation.[3] In this setting of responsibility, we can ask about the mediate effects of actions on other persons as well as on the world as a whole, and derive right or wrong from there.

But there is yet another dimension which comes into play when persons directly interact with other persons. Here, we are not just moral agents acting in a way that influences ourselves or the world we inhabit but are interacting with other moral agents. If we do not just act as persons but *upon* persons, we are faced with the ethical dimension of personhood itself. The point behind the concept of rational ethics, especially in the logic that led to the notion of a 'categorical imperative', rests upon the understanding that persons are fundamentally different from mere things. In the German philosopher Robert Spaemann's (1927–2018) terms, we need to recognize the difference between 'someone' and 'something'.[4] Persons are not just objects for ethical discourse, but subjects of ethical discourse. Or in Kantian terms: they are never just means to an end, but always also ends in themselves.[5]

For an ethical discourse in this Kantian tradition, much of the discussion of trans- and posthumanism would already end here: The amount of design involved in creating these entities appears to treat them as objects in such a way that it must be unethical; this is not something one does to a person. But stopping here would be risky, as some now-plausible technological developments would threaten to undermine the logic of human dignity and human rights that is a pivotal ethical achievement of the enlightenment. We have already seen (in the argument on 'speciesism') how conceptual failures to deal with nonhuman beings (which might be persons) call the concept of human dignity into question. And the failure of rationalist ethics to adequately address the ethical personhood of humans with impaired cognitive capabilities has been justly criticized in other contexts.

In this sense, the challenge of trans- and posthumanism may serve as a wake-up call to ethical theories that believe in the categorical importance of human rights and dignity to search for stronger foundations for their ethical approach, so that it can apply not only to ungenerated entities as yet, but to all humans and (depending on a discussion that is beyond the scope of this chapter) maybe certain other animals as well.

The challenge of defining persons

If we are indeed generating persons, the ethical discussion must take this into account. But how do we assess the personhood of an entity? If ethicists are pressed for an answer, there are two well-travelled roads. One is the empirical definition, often favoured by utilitarians, and another is a more metaphysical strategy.

The first strategy has, in recent years, been most prominently proposed by Australian ethicist Peter Singer. Without going into the heated debates around his more controversial proposals, the challenges of an empirical definition can be observed clearly here. Singer is rooted in the discussion on animal rights,[6] and from this vantage point he proposes to look at certain capabilities of an entity – a baby, an adult, a chimp, a person suffering from dementia – and to judge their personhood accordingly.

Whether or not the said being is a person can then be determined with clear criteria. Singer's argument works well if it is meant to *include* potentially personal beings; maybe some apes show enough features of personhood to warrant special protections. The problem lies in an equally strong potential to exclude many beings we might morally want to regard as persons. In the framework of Singer, there are no intrinsic reasons against euthanizing severely handicapped human beings. They may only live because of extrinsic reasons (our not wanting to kill them), not because it would be intrinsically wrong to kill them (as with fully functioning human adults).[7]

More conceptual problems with the argument exist, such as in the developmental and gradual nature of 'realized' human personhood – we do not just turn from 'mere mammals' into rational humans overnight on our first, tenth or eighteenth birthday.[8]

But there is still a deeper problem when we discuss personhood, in that the act of questioning the personhood of a person is in itself problematic. If I am a person, then my ethical claims and rights may not be infringed upon. Whatever claims I issue as a person are always accompanied (and superseded) by a 'higher order claim' of personhood itself: I demand to be respected as a person, and because of that I raise my (more concrete) claim. If personhood is to have direct ethical implications, then the first and unspoken implication must be for my personhood to be recognized.[9] But evaluating my personhood means to suspend my immediate claim towards recognition as a person. The moral point of this presumption becomes immediately apparent when we consider issues of race or gender; most of us would concede that we cannot morally doubt that a Bavarian, or a man, is a person. If we start there, we can only end up going wrong – because their personhood supersedes any of their personal attributes.

Because of this logic, many discussions in ethics and ethical discourse in matters of medicine and biology still resort to humanist foundations. But here, we are faced with a different quagmire. If we want to understand personhood as something before or beyond measurable individual capacities, then we are left with a foundation that appears, for better or worse, metaphysical. We might, for example, assume that a certain 'nature' (in an Aristotelian[10] sense) is the nature of persons – if they are actively rational or not. All beings of a certain kind are instances of one nature, and if this nature is personal, then all of these beings are persons.[11] This notion harks back to a biological framework for understanding the development of organisms and living beings in a more general sense, a framework that was finally made obsolete by an understanding of genetics and heritability that can explain speciation and development without any principles beyond the organism.

From a biological perspective, there is no singular human nature, only a multitude of individual human natures capable of interbreeding, with genetic variations and combinations waxing and waning in the mix. The metaphysics of a shared nature no longer provides an explanation for the theory of biology, but it lives on in some metaphysical understandings of morality.

We might agree that a non-falsifiable claim about human nature is a justified price to pay for an ethics that is immune to the temptations of involuntary euthanasia or eugenics. The current bioethical challenges, however, undermine this strategy: What about possible persons that have a distinctly different nature, be it by extensive genetic or technological modifications, or by exchanging the biological substrate for the digital? What about a being that shares some human and some nonhuman biology? If they are persons, we may not exclude them, and our anthropocentric definition of all humans as persons would then be undermined. But to settle this question, we would again have to resort to an empirical analysis and leave the moral safety of a metaphysical claim behind. In other words, our ethically cautious choice of a metaphysical foundation for morality might fail in the face of the new challenge.

With the enlightenment arose an attempt at a 'third way', between empiricism and metaphysics. Such 'transcendental'[12] strategies of considering personhood can be understood as an attempt to evade this quagmire, as they seek to avoid mere empiricism as well as classical metaphysics. A transcendental stance seeks to begin at the point where we start asking where our understanding begins, and to develop the consequences of how we understand this beginning of understanding itself. The first modern example of this strategy, Kant's *Critique of Pure Reason*,[13] is based upon affirming and containing empiricism, and moving towards a metaphysics grounded in personhood itself, as it leads to scientific endeavours as well as morality and art. With this strategy, a concept of how reason must operate for science to be possible leads to his centrepiece: an understanding of practical reason as a feature related to material nature,[14] but not directly tied to it. And from this stance we can say: a person needs the kind of biology a person might have (as humans do), but there could be more than one such biology. (This is why Kant could conceive of extra-terrestrial beings to be considered 'humans' in moral terms.[15])

Indeed, if we seek to walk this tightrope of a transcendental understanding of personhood, the next step must lead us deeper into the concept of personhood and practical reason.

The synthetic nature of personhood

So far, we have addressed personhood almost as a thing, as a singular concept, even though it contains a notion of biology and a portion of rationality. If we reject an understanding of personhood as a property that some humans might possess and that others might not, we must now examine these parts of a personal whole and their relation to each other.

As aficionados of educated banter know, 'person' can be traced back to the masks of ancient theatre. On these ancient boards, we already encounter two parts coming together to form a whole, a duality that is synthesized during a dramatic impersonation. The character in a play is a combination of a hidden element, the individual behind the mask, and the mask the individual wears, which defines his or her role and outward appearance.

The modern understanding of personhood as an ethical concept still contains such a duality, notably in the ethical notion of autonomy. Autonomy contains the notion of a self, an 'autos', and a law, the 'nomos'. The ethical focus tends to be upon the latter component: individuals are able to give moral laws, and because of that they have to be regarded as a source of moral obligations. These laws, usually tied to the faculty of reason, allow individuals to govern themselves and others in the same moment. If I raise a rational claim, it is binding for all rational beings and has to be respected: It is the form that matters. So far, so categorical.

The 'self', the 'autos', usually receives far less attention. Yet if rationality can be decoupled from human biology (as can be done with an AI capable of learning), we notice its importance. We could feed moral philosophers like Cicero, David Hume, Kant and John Rawls into a clever neural network, and (after some learning) it might start producing perfectly fine normative statements. If we look at the form only, they might appear to be practical laws. But we would be right to regard them differently than if they came from a person. They are not the 'nomos' of an 'autos' but just sentences devoid of life, the epitome of the abstract formalism of which Kant is often accused.

If we take both components of autonomy seriously, we can see that it implies not a simple, but a twofold relationship. The nomos relates an individual, seen as a whole, to other individuals, insofar as the rational self-determination claims validity for all rational beings. Thus, personhood means a relationship that is directed outwards, from one person to another, with a special obligation. But the precondition of this outward relation is a relation within the individual himself or herself, insofar as the autonomous individual is determining a self, an 'autos', that is not just a generic instance of reason. This practical synthesis of a self and an ethical claim is what we mean by autonomy. In other words, autonomy is not merely 'getting one's way' in everything, it refers to the mode of, and the respect for, our moral agency as finite, individual beings.[16] The ethical status of persons entails this duality of being a unique individual and a generic individual, a self that is not merely reason, yet able to give practical laws for everybody by reason.

This means that the outward relation of persons, their ethical claim to recognition, is intricately linked to a relationship within a person, between two facets that lead to the ethical expression of a personal self. The interplay between these two 'internal' facets directs the person outward and posits the necessarily ethical claim of personhood: autonomy is what we present as we relate ourselves ethically to others, as persons among persons.

This is still a rather traditional understanding of enlightenment ethics: practical reason, in an interplay with personal individuality. And we still cannot account for human beings who cannot self-determine rationally, like a person suffering from a severe mental disorder: they might have the self, but does it matter without reason? Does their incapacity of giving a rational 'nomos' deny not only their effective autonomy but also their ethical claim to personhood and its respect?

Again, in this case, trans- and posthumanism can focus our attention: for if we consider the kinds of changes and replacements being proposed by such ideologies, these do not initially occur in the mind but at the level of the body. We often tend to discuss the different rationalities of beings with the same types of bodies. But trans- and posthumanism rely more on an identical, generic rationality with different or radically altered bodies. So, how do our bodies figure into the moral issues of personhood?

The body as a self

That our material bodies might matter is not a new notion. One early philosophical decision of Christianity was to reject purely spiritual understandings of the universe in favour of a rich theology of creation and incarnation.[17] Of course, human beings appear different from other living beings we know; we go above and beyond our biological existence, so we are tempted to focus upon our more transcendent properties, our 'spirit' and 'soul'. But we were living as bodies before we spoke, developed a character, a personality or a sense of self. When we are asleep, we still breathe, and we wake up not as minds in a tired or refreshed body but simply tired, or refreshed.

The fact that we are embodied informs more general and more individual aspects of our personhood. In general, being embodied creatures means that we are finite and mortal entities, dependent upon others at least in the beginning of our lives, and in almost all cases beyond this stage as well. We cannot survive for long without fulfilling our basic needs, our mood (and our rationality) may quickly suffer for lack of sugar or coffee. And we cannot wait forever to fulfil our ambitions, before our bodies start declining and giving up on us.

But our individual bodies are uniquely different as well. Some of us have brilliant genes, are smart, beautiful and healthy. Others are plagued by illness or other limitations. Most of us comprise a mixture of the two. We develop ourselves and our personalities in the bodies with which we are born. In this sense, our bodies are almost our fate. However, that does not need to be fatalistic: we can rebel against our bodies' limits, work upon them and go beyond or against them. But all the while, our bodies remain the stage and backdrop of our lives and personal existence. And while we can generalize aspects like mortality or 'natality'.[18] our concrete individuality as persons cannot be neatly separated from our bodies.

The concreteness of our individual bodies plays a key role in our continued development of self, or as selves. Our individuality, our personhood, in the more concrete sense of the term, is what we make of ourselves, in or as the bodies that we are. If our selves are negotiated between more general, social and cultural concepts and something individual and different, then the body is part of the concrete and unique.

This understanding of our embodiment ties into the composite nature of personal autonomy. If we understand autonomy as a synthesis of some kind of self and practical reason, not just as something rational, and if we accept that this self is inseparable from our concrete embodiment, the ethical significance of the body even for seemingly rationalist ethics becomes inevitable.

Personhood, as an ethical concept, cannot be separated from the fact that we have to negotiate our limited and individual lives in coexistence. And if the body plays a crucial role in our individuality, it plays a comparable role for ethics. The German philosopher Jürgen Habermas, usually a theorist of discursive reason, puts it thus:

> I conceive of moral behaviour as a constructive response to the dependencies rooted in the incompleteness of our organic makeup and in the persistent frailty (most felt in the phases of childhood, illness, and old age) of our bodily existence. Normative regulation of interpersonal relations may be seen as a porous shell protecting a vulnerable body, and the person incorporated in this body, from the contingencies they are exposed to. Moral rules are fragile constructions protecting *both* the physis from bodily injuries and the person from inner symbolic injuries.[19]

The twofold nature of embodiment

If we follow this last argument, we can now assume that ethical personhood entails the elements of a bodily nature and of communicative reason – one related to the 'autos' and the other to the 'nomos' in autonomy. But the shift in perspective does not have to end here, as we can also develop the foundations of the element of rationality much closer to embodiment – if we understand embodiment itself as a dual concept.

Any dual understanding of embodiment is usually explored in languages that (conveniently) provide more than one word for 'body'. In theology, we can come across the distinction of 'sarx' and 'soma' (often translated as 'flesh' and 'body') in the Greek writings of Apostle Paul.[20] In German, the (semantically identical) words *Leib* and *Körper* gave rise to a philosophical distinction, mostly employed in the discourses of Phenomenology as well as Philosophical Anthropology.[21] In this regard, the different schools of thought have a different focus: Phenomenology is more interested in personal experience, while Philosophical Anthropology seeks to understand human existence from a biological as well as philosophical perspective. But these differences need not concern us now.

The claim, in short, is that embodiment itself is a twofold reality for persons. On the one hand, persons experience themselves as bodies in an immediate way. If somebody hits my body, they hit me. The world can impress itself upon us – literally, and in a more sensual or emotional fashion. In this sense, we *are* a body. On the other hand, we are beings that can have very real influence upon ourselves by acting and interacting with our own bodies in a material sense, as an object or a tool. We undertake sporting activities, we kick a printer to make it work, and we also drink coffee, take medicines and drugs or maybe start to enhance our bodies by means of genetics or technological augmentations. In this sense, we *have* a body.

These aspects of being-a-body and having-a-body intersect, as in the famous example of one hand touching the other, where one hand touches actively and one is being touched, both within our own body. And these negotiations are open to creativity and to cultural expressions, as means of translating our immediate bodily presence into the mediated shapes and expressions. We can jump a fence, but also dance – or act rationally.

In a more general sense, our embodiment contains the distinction between immediate and concrete embodiment in situations, and between the mediated parts of our lives that are open to cultural norms. For example, we dress, behave and perform according to our plans and ambitions. Thus, our embodied existence can be described as a negotiation between those two aspects of embodiment as a whole. Therefore, human embodiment actually means the challenge of negotiating these two facets consistently.

The crucial point in this argument is that we can see the complexities of autonomy on a more fundamental level, within the embodied nature we share and which differentiates us as human persons. Autonomy, in the Kantian sense, now appears as an extreme, almost as an abstraction of a fundamental feature of human existence. But the personal self-relationship appears to be much broader. Now, an incapacity for rational law-giving would not take away from an underlying of personal self-relationship that is, to a degree, visible. The self-relation and expressiveness of personhood can already be seen in a certain relationship to one's body, indicated for example in dressing a certain way, in doing one's makeup and so on. If we are rational and educated accordingly, we might be capable of proper 'nomos', with rational arguments and words. But the more immediate bodily self-determination would be of the same ilk and would have to be respected accordingly and immediately: as an expression of bodily autonomy.

Ethical autonomy, then, is not just reason communing with reason (by the mere means of matter), but building upon our embodied self-relationship. That we *are* bodies is intricately linked to what we have to say in ethical terms: If we were not these discrete bodily entities, these ineffable sources of immediate personal experience, there would be no need to translate our lives into (even normative) shapes and forms – and no need for others to heed our claims. And this immediate embodiment, our existence as the bodies we are, as we try to transcend and re-shape them, is of crucial importance when we consider trans- and posthumanism.

In short, seeking to understand posthuman personhood has led us to the question about how the body in general might be important to our understanding of personhood. This has then led us to the possibility of deriving our conception of personhood and its ethical dimension from a phenomenological and anthropological understanding of embodiment as a practical composite: Being a person means being somebody, in a quite literal sense.

Thus, a more intricate understanding of embodied nature provided a way forward, towards describing personhood on a transcendental level, in other words, between a metaphysical claim and the sceptical glance of empiricism. Persons are bodies and make use of them, in ways that can be moral and demand our recognition.

Posthumanism, the body and a categorical imperative

So what does trans- and posthumanism mean for this tradition of ethical personhood, and what are the ethical consequences? The general implications of trans- and posthumanism, the permanent modification or abolition of our embodied nature, are consistent with a broader trend within Modernity. They can be regarded as an expression of its ambivalent relationship to the body. On the one hand, Modernity can appear almost disembodied (or 'excarnated', as the Canadian philosopher Charles Taylor would say[22]). But on the other hand, bodies are everywhere; we are bombarded with fit and naked bodies, and we are all supposed to work on our own bodies constantly. But if we look at the dual embodiment sketched out above, this apparent paradox is dissolved. We can understand it as a devaluation of the immediate and concrete – 'porous'[23] – dimension of being-a-body, in exchange for more and more control over our bodies as objects we have, use and shape.

The proposals of trans- and posthumanism appear like a logical next step on this path of Modernity, be it by exerting an increasing control over our chemical or genetic make-up and eliminating their contingencies or by completely exchanging our unique but frail biology in favour of a designed machine.

Controlling or discarding our body reduces or eliminates the pressure of having to negotiate the immediate and sometimes ineffable parts of ourselves – that which we did not choose to be – with what we want to do and who we want to be (or are expected to be by our societies, cultures and economies). Trans- and posthumanism provide a solution for the challenge of leading a personal life – by eliminating a constitutive factor of personhood. If we assume personhood to be valuable, and if we accept our embodiment as a crucial factor in this personhood, then this solution resembles curing a headache by removing our head. It is to change ourselves, so that we fit into a world that challenges or even clashes with personal existence, instead of making the world and life more habitable for persons.

Usually, this might be the point where normative ethics passes the baton to endeavours such as virtue ethics, which do not just list prohibitions but develop an understanding of a good (personal) life. Here, we must content ourselves with the promised 'imperatives', with some normative parameters for a world within which personal existence retains its ethical value.

Kant states that there can only be one categorical imperative – but he provides different formulations of the idea. In the light of our discussion, we might add another version: *Act so that your actions are in accordance with your personhood and the personhood of whomever you act upon.* On this basis, we can add more concrete imperatives.

In the first section of this chapter, three levels of ethical challenges were distinguished. They were (in reversed order): our special obligation to persons, our responsibility for our shared world and future and the immediate morality of an action. Each of these dimensions can be addressed in an imperative informed by the reflections on personhood and on the generation of trans- and posthuman persons.

The imperative of certainty

The reflections on what an ethical understanding of personhood presupposes and how posthumanism relates to these underpinnings have already led to a looming question: Can these new entities even be regarded as persons? Or are their bodies so far changed, or even abolished, that we must reasonably doubt their personhood?

However, this cannot be the question if we accept that doubting the personhood of a person contradicts the moral implications of the said personhood. The transcendental logic of personhood, of its required recognition, hinges upon the fact that it cannot reasonably be doubted. The only ethical way forward to avoid this ethical dilemma is to not create such uncertainties. Only by abstaining from the generation of entities whose personhood could reasonably be doubted can we avoid situations that resemble racist or sexist judgements of the past.

This is not meant to justify rejecting the claim to personhood of entities that have already been brought into existence. The high esteem placed upon personhood indicates that we should always err on the side of protecting potential persons, and this might (for example) reasonably be extended to any being that carries human genes, even if it outwardly resembles a pig: Part of the biology that makes up the bodies of persons is present, so we cannot be certain that we are not faced with the body of a person. The possibility that pigs bred for humanized organs might be persons, yet groomed and slaughtered for parts, is too gruesome to be ignored out of hand.

If we hold that it is unethical to call the personhood of persons into question, then one imperative must be: *Do not generate beings whose ethical personhood can be doubted.*

This need not, for example, preclude any and all therapeutic interventions in the genome, but it speaks against the overarching goals of trans- or posthumanism; the more they are realized, the more dubitable the personhood of the generated beings becomes. This is a pointlessly cruel endeavour when regarded from the ethical perspective of the resulting beings.

The imperative of difference

The generation of beings whose personhood appears possible, but dubitable, is not only problematic regarding our possible obligations to these entities. It is also relevant to the ethical discourse for our moral world which is (not entirely, but in significant parts) based upon our obligations towards persons.

Building on the second section of this chapter, one such challenge is obvious: if our shared world is slowly filled with beings whose personhood is in doubt, then the presumption of personhood of all its members becomes increasingly difficult or implausible. A reasonable doubt that some participants in our discourse are actually persons, a kind of 'moral dissonance', threatens the entire presumption of personal value for this discourse. Uncertainty regarding entities with a plausible but not irrefutable claim to personhood presents a credible (and unnecessary) threat to these very foundations of a personal framework of ethics. In other words, it would be foolish to risk our understanding of personal value in such a manner without dire necessity.

In addition, the direction of posthumanism erodes a fundamental source of meaning for our personal existence. The deeper interplay of persons relies upon them having something to tell each other, something that needs to be expressed and can only be expressed. The fundamental difference we all come from (and fall back upon) plays the necessary counterpart to the shared world of culture, and even to the most abstract claims of ethical rationality. The less there is to say, the less ethical claims might matter.

Yet trans- and posthumanism erode this very font of difference, the font of our self-expressions. Each optimized or designed gene that is inserted millions of times in place of the usual differences takes away from a real difference at the deepest levels of personhood. While being-a-body and unique biology are not to be conflated, an attack on one will diminish the other. Each optimizing intervention leads to more of the same, and less to tell.

The safeguard against this development is to preserve the fundamental difference that preserves the necessity and meaning of individual expressions and self-determination. A reliable way to this end lies in 'traditional' procreation, but again, not all interventions in human biology need to lead towards a generic human nature.

With a slight adjustment, we can apply the already cited imperative of Hans Jonas (see note 3): *Act so that the effects of your action are compatible with the permanent occurrence of different personal life.* This ensures a world where persons always have something to tell – and are obliged to listen.

The imperative of humanity

The final imperative (focused on the action as such) is well explored in literature and philosophy, so that it does not need to be redeveloped. The ethical way of relating to persons is to interact, maybe to raise and nurture, but not to design or to shape them to our personal desires. Relating to potential persons as if they are not persons, but treating them as objects, also erodes our own personhood.

To conclude, this means: *Do not treat potential persons as objects that you can generate at will (not even yourself).* Such humanity, with a certain humility, preserves our place as persons among persons. Whether we want to understand this theologically, or just as a phrase from literature, we can shorten this last imperative: *Do not play God.*

Notes

1 A 'categorical imperative' in Kant's concept is meant to be a single principle that must always apply and ground or supersede all concrete ethical norms we encounter. In this sense, the idea that any motivations for our actions should be generalizable to a law for everybody is 'the' categorical imperative, as developed in Immanuel Kant, *Groundwork of the Metaphysics of Morals [1785]*, trans. Mary Gregor (Cambridge: Cambridge University Press, 1998), 31 (= AA 4, p. 421). But Kant also relates this formula for morality to principles that are not 'the' singular categorical imperative, but still apply broadly in certain areas (such as telling the truth). This idea of ethical principles that relate back to the fabric of moral reasoning is the strand that is taken up in this chapter. The relationship between the idea of the categorical imperative as such and its application in principle is discussed critically and lucidly in chapters VIII and IX in George Marcus Singer, *Generalization in Ethics: An Essay in the Logic of Ethics, with the Rudiments of a System of Moral Philosophy* (New York: Atheneum, 1961).
2 This also means that the discussion is focused more upon practical and less upon (for lack of a better word) ideological notions of posthumanism. If posthumanism is intended as an alternate philosophy to humanism with some technical additives, or if the proposed new entities are not even meant to be persons or individuals, this discussion does not apply directly.
3 The idea of such an 'imperative of responsibility' has its inspirations in Kantian thought, but is explicitly developed by German-born American philosopher Hans Jonas (1903–1993) in *The Imperative of Responsibility: In Search of an Ethics for the Technological Age* (Chicago: University of Chicago Press, 1984). Here, Jonas proposes different variations of a 'new' imperative, e.g.: 'Act so that the effects of your action are compatible with the permanence of genuine human life' (Jonas, *Imperative of Responsibility*, 11).
4 Robert Spaemann, *Persons: The Difference between "Someone" and "Something,"* trans. Oliver O'Donovan (Oxford: Oxford University Press, 2006).
5 Cf. Kant, *Groundwork*, 38.
6 Peter Singer, *Animal Liberation: A New Ethics for Our Treatment of Animals* (New York: Harper Collins, 1975).
7 This distinction is clearest in Peter Singer, *Practical Ethics*, 3rd edn (Cambridge: Cambridge University Press, 2011), 160–1.
8 In fact, the Swabians of Southern Germany profess to only turn rational at the age of forty.
9 Spaemann, *Persons*, 180–96.
10 Ancient Greek philosopher, Aristotle develops a theory of the things in existence where every individual of a species shares in a specific nature (the nature of petunias or sperm whales, for example).
    This definition was taken up most influentially by Christianity as a template for understanding a fixed order of creation.
11 This argument is presented in Spaemann, *Persons*, 236–48.
12 A lucid case for the workings and limitations of transcendental arguments can be found in Charles Taylor, 'The Validity of Transcendental Arguments', in *Philosophical Arguments* (Cambridge, MA: Harvard University Press, 1995), 20–33.
13 Immanuel Kant, *Critique of Pure Reason [1781/87]*, trans. Paul Guyer and Allen W. Wood (Cambridge: Cambridge University Press, 1998).
14 For only a finite being needs moral law – a divine will would have no need for it; see Kant, *Groundwork*, 25 (= AA 4,419).

15 For Kant, 'humanity' in its moral sense is not a biological factor. It is our rational nature, our moral agency as finite beings, that makes us 'human' in a full sense. Kant's notions of extra-terrestrial beings are documented before, during and after he wrote his seminal 'critiques'. For excerpts of a (speculative but entertaining) early text and a few essential later references, see Michael J. Crowe, *The Extraterrestrial Life Debate: Antiquity to 1915* (Notre Dame: University of Notre Dame Press, 2008), 138–51. In this light, some central passages gain clarity as to how Kant relates human moral nature to human biology: 'A *human being* is indeed unholy enough but the *humanity in his person* must be holy to him. In the whole of creation everything one wants and over which one has any power can also be used merely as a means; a *human being* alone, and *with him every rational creature*, is an end in itself' – Immanuel Kant, *Critique of Practical Reason [1788]*, ed. and trans. Mary Gregor, revised edn (Cambridge: Cambridge University Press, 2015), 72 (= AA 5,87; emphases added).

16 Of course, many actions we encounter might not be the result of moral reflection. But since we are dealing with persons, which are able to self-govern in a moral way, we are justified (and probably obliged) to assume that others do not just act out of base desires. In that sense, we are likely to over-ascribe autonomy when looking at the actual behaviour of people – as a consequence of our respect for the moral nature of others and ourselves.

17 Cf. James F. Keenan, 'Embodiment and Relationality: Roman Catholic Concerns', in *Transhumanism and the Body: The World Religions Speak*, eds. Calvin Mercer and Derek F. Maher (London: Palgrave Macmillan, 2014).

18 German-born American philosopher Hannah Arendt (1906–1975) coined the term 'natality' for the new that comes into the world with each new person; see Hannah Arendt, *The Human Condition*, 2nd edn (Chicago: University of Chicago Press, 1998), 8–9.

19 Jürgen Habermas, *The Future of Human Nature*, trans. William Rehg, Max Pensky and Hella Beister (Cambridge: Polity, 2003), 33–4. The terminology is employed in the sense that sticks and stones might hurt my 'physis', while words might injure my 'person' (without breaking physical bones).

20 See James D. G. Dunn, *The Theology of Paul the Apostle* (Grand Rapids, MI: William B. Eerdmans P. Co., 1998), 55–73.

21 The distinction of two aspects of embodiment in German philosophy is first employed by Max Scheler (1874–1928), who is influential for phenomenology as well as philosophical anthropology, in his ethical classic, Max Scheler, *Formalism in Ethics and Non-Formal Ethics of Value: A New Attempt toward the Foundation of an Ethical Personalism [1918]*, trans. Manfred S. Frings and Roger L. Funk (Evanston: Northwestern University Press, 1973), 399 ff. In phenomenology, it is taken up in the later writings of the German Edmund Husserl (1859–1938), as well as by the Frenchman Maurice Merleau-Ponty (1908–1961). In philosophical anthropology, the German Helmuth Plessner (1892–1985) provides a deeper interpretation, in his *Laughing and Crying: A Study of the Limits of Human Behavior*, trans. James Spencer Churchill and Marjorie Grene (Evanston: Northwestern University Press, 1970), 32–8.

22 Charles Taylor, *A Secular Age* (Cambridge, MA: Belknap Press, 2007), 554–5. Taylor's principal intention appears to be a rejection of Protestantism and its cultural impacts in favour of the more incarnate theology of Catholicism. Yet the bigger picture stretches beyond a confessional squabble.

23 The distinction of a 'porous' and a 'buffered' self is employed by Charles Taylor to explain the changes in the self brought about by modernity.

Part II

How can transhuman and posthuman persons be generated?

5

On the scientific plausibility of transhumanism

Chris Willmott

Introduction

Until recently I was, like many,[1] somewhat dismissive regarding the real-world significance of the transhuman or posthuman. Transhumanism seemed to be a thought-experiment conducted by enthusiasts, many of whom exhibited a distinctly religious fervour for their cause. For me, this was an interesting, but wildly speculative, debate since science was never going to achieve the kinds of alterations to the human form being advocated.

In hindsight, this was a ridiculously naïve position. Given the pace at which scientific advances have delivered other developments once considered unlikely, if not impossible, I ought to have heeded the advice to 'never say never'. As we shall see, some recent innovations really do open up the feasibility of creating various transhuman and posthuman beings in the relatively near future.

In a short introduction on any topic, decisions need to be made about the scope of coverage. These considerations are particularly problematic on a subject such as transhumanism where there are already so many variations in the application of core terminology. I am fully aware that some readers will be exasperated by the inclusion or exclusion of certain aspects here. So, already conscious that 'you cannot please all people all of the time', let me begin by outlining the underlying principles being applied.

First, this chapter focuses specifically on the *science* of bringing new transhuman and posthuman persons into existence. Other chapters will examine the *ethical implications*.

Second, in keeping with other authors of this book, I will be informed, but not constrained, by the notion that transhumans must, of necessity, be an *improved* version of the existing species *Homo sapiens*.[2] As others have noted, the definition of 'improvement' is itself problematic.[3] More importantly, our aim here is to prompt reflection on the moral, ethical and religious status of beings that go beyond the natural boundaries of the human. It is far from certain that any part-human creature will de facto be an improved person, regardless of the definition of 'improvement' applied.

Third, I will not limit the notion of the posthuman to an uploaded virtual existence. While an entirely digital version of personhood may be one ultimate endpoint, constraining the posthuman to a being entirely detached from any physical form renders redundant the much important discussion about transhumanism which focuses on alterations to our bodies.

Finally, I will give consideration to developments whose applications are initially therapeutic, if they involve mechanisms by which subsequent modifications of the human form may be achieved. Here we touch upon another classic conundrum regarding transhumanism. How much alteration does someone need to have before they cease to be human and require re-classification as a *trans*human? How many additional abilities are required before I exceed being a highly developed human? Nevertheless, on the basis that we must inevitably start the process of any transition from human to transhuman from our current state, it seems appropriate to include some reflection on approaches which primarily compensate for genetic or physical impairment.

Overall, I consider interventions having the potential to intentionally drive human development in directions that 'blind' evolution would be extremely unlikely to deliver. I also touch upon various 'biotransformative technologies'[4] that may lead to alterations along two independent trajectories – the human-animal (biological dimension) and the human-machine (mechanical or technological dimension). In both directions, there is scope for the percentage of retained 'humanness' to vary considerably.

I do not discuss uses of nootropic drugs, claimed to improve cognitive function. Although convinced that these will play a growing role in the enhancement of cognitive abilities, my view is that they will not be a method for transitioning to *new sorts of persons* that is the focus here.

Altering biology

I begin with reflections on the biological alteration of humans, for which two different approaches exist. One is the creation of human-animal hybrids and chimeras. The second, already realized, involves attempts at genetic manipulation of humans. Recent dramatic developments in the capacity to intentionally modify the human genome demand our attention first, and are considered in greater depth than other approaches.

The most popular tool for genome editing is currently the Crispr system (pronounced 'crisper') or more formally Crispr-Cas9.[5] It is no exaggeration to call this a game changer, which has revived the notion of 'designer babies'. Hitherto, that term has most frequently been employed to describe the use of preimplantation genetic diagnosis (PGD), an adaptation of IVF technology, that facilitates checking particular genes in an embryo before deciding whether or not to implant it into the gestational mother. In truth, 'designer baby' was always slightly misleading in that original context, since PGD only allows selection between embryos on the basis of their naturally occurring gene combinations (to ensure they were free from an inheritable disease and/or to be a stem-cell donor for a sick sibling) – the intentional modification or introduction of a different gene via PGD is impossible. As we shall see, this is no longer a constraint for Crispr and related techniques.

The first attempts to target alteration of an individual's genes came with the advent of gene therapy.[6] There was no expectation this method would achieve changes beyond the correction of genetic disease. If someone had an illness caused by inheriting faulty copies of a particular gene from both parents, the aim was to overcome this by adding in a functional copy of that gene. Even this, more limited, goal proved far trickier to achieve than anticipated. To be a stable, permanent, treatment, that third copy of the gene needed to be integrated into the individual's DNA. This, however, was hard to regulate – you could not be certain where the gene would end up within the patient's genome. Arrival of the additional gene could itself cause damage at the site of integration, as well as triggering the unwanted expression of other nearby genes. In a famous early case, the plan to overcome a life-threatening immune deficiency in children by adding a functional copy of the faulty gene was scuppered because the strong promoter (the control box, if you like) for the integrated gene also activated another nearby gene, leading to leukaemia.[7]

Recognizing these difficulties, attention switched to methods to *correct* the faulty gene in its original location rather than adding an extra copy. In addition to avoiding problems with integration events, this has the significant advantage since it leaves the gene in the correct context for natural factors to regulate its expression. Real excitement in this regard is being driven by the Crispr–Cas9 genome editing system, which is relatively simple and inexpensive to use. Unlike previous tools which floundered due to the complexity of re-engineering the proteins involved, Crispr only needs the manufacture of a short piece of sequence-specific RNA, a molecule related to DNA, which acts as a kind of homing mechanism, and a standard Cas protein, that works as molecular scissors. Such is the contrast with earlier editing schemes, that employing Crispr is like changing music by switching CDs rather than having to rebuild the HiFi sound system each time.

In the Crispr system, the guide RNA directs the Cas enzyme (typically one of the family called Cas9) to cut at a specific location within the genome you want to alter. To complete the process, a piece of DNA containing the desired changes has to be included in the cocktail, in order that the cell's natural repair mechanisms can be tricked into introducing the altered sequence in place of the original gene.

Biological generation of transhumans

Globally, researchers are employing Crispr and related methods to modify organisms as diverse as mice and mosquitoes, wheat and pigs, even mammoths (in an attempt to achieve de-extinction)[8] and, of course, humans.

Despite prevailing weaknesses in the technique, Crispr has been widely used with human cells. Usually, this work is conducted first in cultured cell lines, both for basic research and, where there is an expectation of treating patients, to allow for appropriate checks to be made.[9] However, on at least one occasion, germline (that is heritable) genetic modification of humans has already been conducted. In this infamous case, Dr He Jiankui announced at the Human Genome Editing Conference in November 2018 that he had genetically modify twin girls, by altering a protein called CCR5 which is exploited by HIV to enter cells.[10] He used Crispr-Cas9 to alter the gene for CCR5 in the girls, introducing a mutation that made a non-functional version of that protein and ought therefore to protect them against HIV.

Had He been premature in crossing this particular Rubicon? The international science community and bioethicists certainly thought so. Even the usually libertarian philosopher Julian Savulescu was quoted describing the work as 'monstrous'.[11] The Chinese authorities ultimately agreed, sentencing He to three years in prison.[12] The twins He used are the first known examples in whom someone has intentionally modified the hereditable human genome. However, since Crispr use does not require specialist training and equipment, it is highly plausible that attempts to perform other germline alterations are already underway somewhere in the world.

Is gene editing a mechanism for creating *trans*humans? Perhaps not initially, but the Crispr-Cas9 system and related technologies have the potential to not only tinker with existing human genes but to deliver into our genomes the genes derived from other organisms, or even codes that are entirely synthetic. Apart from adherence to certain size restrictions, any DNA sequence could, in theory, be integrated into the recipient's genome once the double-strand breakage has been orchestrated. Novel attributes could be introduced, including '*radical* augmentations', a term used to define changes (e.g. the capacity to fly) beyond the '*extraordinary* augmentations', which would be abilities to perform some natural human task unnaturally well (e.g. being able to run at 50 mph).[13]

If something was not achievable in one round of changes, it might be possible to carry out sequential modifications. One arena in which this is already being done is in the 'humanization' of pig organs to render them less susceptible to rejection when transplanted into a human patient. Scientists at a company, eGenesis, have been able to remove several immunological triggers (plus some unwelcome virus sequences) that had previously curtailed endeavours to get over the shortfall in human organs for transplantation by using xenografts, organs taken from other mammals, especially pigs.[14] Lessons learned during this process will inform attempts to directly alter the human genome.

This example leads us into the second pathway to biological generation of transhumans, namely production of chimeras and hybrids. Of all the possibilities being discussed in this chapter, this is the route most likely to leave some readers questioning whether these are *transhuman* beings. I would, however, refer back to the aim of this book regarding the ethical, philosophical and religious status of transhumans. Chimeras and hybrids may not represent *improvements* to the human form, but as creatures derived from humans they fit very neatly into the definition of the transhuman being employed here.

Although the terms are sometimes used as though they are synonyms, the meanings of chimera and hybrid are actually quite distinct. A chimera consists of *cells* from more than one organism (possibly, but not necessarily, a human and a nonhuman animal). Importantly, individual cells within the chimera contain genetic material from only one source. In contrast, a hybrid is an organism in which all (or most) of the cells contain a combination of genetic material deriving from more than one distinct species or breed. These can occur naturally if the egg of one organism is fertilized following sexual reproduction with the male of a related species. Examples include a zonkey (zebra crossed with a donkey), a liger (male lion with a female tiger) and a tigon (male tiger with female lion).

Creation of both part-human hybrids and chimeras is likely to necessitate molecular biological interventions. Interest in chimeras is principally fuelled by the possibility to manufacture human organs, either for transplantation or for research purposes. Whereas the eGenesis strategy for making xenografts is about alteration of the original animal genome to render an organ less likely to evoke an immune response when transplanted into a human, the chimera-based approach looks to achieve bona fide human organs grown within a source animal.

Attempts to form interspecies chimeras have generally involved manipulation at the stage of the development of the blastocyst (a hollow structure early in embryogenesis, containing the inner cell mass (ICM), which will form the embryo proper, and a layer of trophectoderm cells, which will become the placenta). There has been some, but limited, success producing chimeras via the fusion of blastocysts from two different species; it only works with very closely related species (e.g. rats and mice, sheep and goats[15]), and even then the rate of chimera formation is very low.

Over the past decade, the ability to make sustainable chimeras has been bolstered by blastocyst complementation.[16] In this strategy, the host cell is genetically modified to have a deficiency in one or more cell lineage(s), leaving it with a tissue-specific niche that can be compensated only by cells from the other organism. So, for example, a pig embryo engineered to be incapable of making its own kidney cells, would only survive if it developed an organ made of tissue grown from human cells injected into the blastocyst.

There remain technical difficulties with the use of such animal-grown human organs for transplantation. For example, the presence of any remaining host cells within the organ could trigger an immune response.

Although blastocyst complementation (or some future variation) seems essential to achieve the intentional growth of a transplantable organ, this does not rule out the potential for simultaneous occurrence of chimera formation at lower rates in other tissues. There is particular concern regarding risks of chimeric brains or sperm and egg cells developing since they might, respectively, influence the consciousness of the recipient animal or allow acquired characteristics to be passed on to the next generation.

Research is also being conducted using brain organoids, brain-like materials grown from human stem cells. Currently, these are only small, less than 5mm in size, and lack both blood supply and appropriate brain organization. Nevertheless, their development are relevant to the notion of transhumans in two ways. Firstly, there is active research underway to transplant human brain organoids into animal models.[17] Initially, such experimentation is likely to worsen not improve the mental capacity of the recipient animal. However, in the fullness of time, this work might lead to modification of behaviour and the acquisition of more human-like capabilities, such as self-awareness. Secondly, improvements to our understanding of the factors controlling brain architecture might reach a point where it is feasible to grow an entire functional brain from stem cells – a brain that has never existed in the context of a human body. This has a bearing on consideration of the mechanically augmented posthuman.

It is worth noting, in passing, that the UK *Human Fertilisation and Embryology Act 2008* actually employs the term 'human admixed embryo', which includes not only cybrids but also 'any embryo . . . in which the animal DNA is not predominant'.[18] This would encompass a variety of beings up to and including a 50 per cent human 50 per cent nonhuman combination, sometimes termed a 'true hybrid' or amphimictic embryo. This type of pairing is most commonly associated with an assessment of male fertility, in which the ability of human sperm to penetrate hamster eggs (that have had their jelly coating removed) and trigger one round of cell division is examined. Once again, however, there is no serious intention to allow such constructs to develop further.

Machine-based generation of transhumans

Let us turn our attention to the second dimension of development, the human-machine. If we were to consider this as a spectrum from fully human at one extreme to fully machine at the other, many might be surprised by how far we have already traversed towards the machine end of that scale. It can be argued that people's ever-burgeoning reliance on their smartphones for a variety of tasks over and above the making of telephone calls represents the shallow end of our move towards technology-enhanced life. We could add to this the use of wearable technology such as Fitbit to record biometric data that influence our subsequent lifestyle choices, and the use of voice-command tools such as Alexa and Siri to schedule reminders about tasks we need to perform.

Perhaps, these examples seem too trivial to represent a real shift towards a transhuman, let alone posthuman existence. However, at a minimum, they reveal how much technology is already interwoven into our lives. A step on from these applications might be the use of electrical brain stimulations such as transcranial magnetic stimulation (TMS) and transcranial direct current stimulation (tDCS) to influence mood. The latter has become a recognized medical treatment for depression, but there is also a growing community of enthusiasts advocating self-administration of tDCS for a range of brain-related applications, including bolstering memory and language acquisition.[19]

All of these interventions are non-invasive; that is, they occur outside the body. There are unquestionably some additional factors for consideration as soon as you place a device *within* the body, not least the potential for infection. But for many observers, penetrating the skin to implant a device represents an ideological as well as a physical barrier; a threshold is quite literally being crossed.

Back in 1998, UK academic Kevin Warwick garnered considerable publicity when he became reportedly the first person in the world to have a radio-frequency identification chip (RFID) inserted into his hand.[20] The device triggered an automated greeting when he arrived at work, and doors were programmed to open as he came towards them. Warwick's device was a proof-of-principle experiment. Since then, similar appendages have become commonplace among body modification enthusiasts, known as grinder biohackers, to the extent that one commentator observed, 'Magnets and RFID implants are rites of passage.'[21] Although such biohackers like to be portrayed as transhumanist pioneers, I would contend that there is a crucial distinction between these alterations and interventions that involve direct interaction with the recipient's central nervous system.

Once again, humankind already has more experience of direct neural interfaces than many would appreciate. Cochlear implants overcome deficiencies in the normal acoustic hearing process by passing electrical signals directly to the auditory nerve. Deep brain stimulation involves electrical impulses being sent to electrodes implanted in the brain, for example, for treatment of movement disorders.

Most pertinent to transhumanism are dramatic developments in the control of neural prosthetic limbs. Brain-machine interface (BMI) work of this kind is often funded by the US Defence Advancement Research Project Agency (DARPA). In one groundbreaking study, two ninety-six-electrode grids were implanted into the primary motor cortex (M1) of a tetraplegic woman.[22] Via cables connected to her skull, she was able to operate a prosthetic limb by thinking about the intended movement. This achievement is far from trivial; after implanting the electrodes, the researchers spent several weeks getting the patient to think through the manoeuvres while they identified the specific neurons principally involved in controlling movement in different directions.

In parallel developments, other researchers have been working on passing sensory (proprioceptive) information regarding touch, pressure, limb position and velocity directly to the brain via intracortical microstimulation (ICMS). One research team made important observations about the detection of sensory information by implanting minute electrodes into the primary somatosensory cortex (S1) of a man with a spinal injury and asking him to describe the senses he experienced (albeit phantom) with a combination of stimuli.[23] A second team achieved limited sensation of touch and pressure in the brain of a paralysed man, when they interacted with a robotic hand wired to his S1 region.[24]

The holy grail of this work is to achieve a closed loop, combining both the sensory input information and the motor response within one bidirectional system in a manner that allows for improvement to fine control of the process. A recent paper reports the successful addition of tactile information via ICMS to a patient who was already familiar with controlling a robotic arm via wires connected to their M1 region.[25] The proprioceptive information coming from the prosthetic limb enabled them to accomplish some standard movement tests with greater proficiency than when guided by visual stimuli alone.

It is worth reiterating that, hitherto, these uses have been in the realm of rehabilitation. However, once refined these technologies could be used to facilitate the control of larger super-human limbs (the generous funding of this kind of research by DARPA might be considered a tacit acknowledgement of the potential military capabilities of machine-enhanced humans).

Away from the control of movement, what other brain-machine interface advances are there? One involves so-called 'augmented cognition', which is the extension of cognitive capacities via the ability to access remote computing facilities directly from one's own mind.[26] Uses might include expansion of someone's working memory such that they could, for example, conduct complex mathematical calculations 'in their head' without needing to resort to pen and paper or a hand-held device. Similarly, they might be provided with greater perception of events so that they 'take-in' more detail as something is occurring (they would never be caught out by the popular perception test where instruction to count the number of times a ball is passed between participants leaves the observers oblivious to the fact someone dressed in a monkey-suit walked slowly through the scene). Additionally, the accuracy of long-term memory might be bolstered by routine storage of audio or visual records that are accessible at will. It might even prove feasible to instantly download expertise to perform some task, for example, becoming fluent in a language in moments.

It should be self-evident that the development of all of these brain-machine interfaces is utterly reliant not only on our growing understanding of the operation of the mind but also upon cybernetic innovations. These includes computational developments, such as improved algorithm decoders and other means to speed up the information transfer rate.[27] Crucially, they will also require advances in material science to deliver stable and effective connectivity between the organic 'wetware' of the brain and the technological hardware.

Experience with existing brain implants has highlighted a number of key obstacles that need to be overcome. These include damage of tissues around electrodes, degradation of the electrodes themselves, or progressive loss of signal due to small-scale shifting of the connections (micromotion) at the interface, the build-up of scar tissue and/or the triggering of immune responses.[28] Bolstering the biocompatibility and longevity of electrodes is therefore a top priority. Carbon nanotubes, cylinders of one or more layers of graphene, have emerged as a material of particular interest for a range of biomedical applications, including for BMIs.[29] They are relatively stable structures of appropriate dimensions for such roles. The shared carbon-based nature of nanotubes and organic life also contributes to their biocompatibility.

Other frontiers for improvement include miniaturization of components, wireless transmission of signals and means to recharge any implanted devices.[30] To huge fanfare, Tesla and SpaceX owner Elon Musk held a press conference in 2019 to describe innovations being made as part of the Neuralink project he began in 2016. In the near future, the company expects to start human trials of their first brain-machine interfaces which will have thousands of electrodes emerging from a coordination chip that will communicate wirelessly with an external device, such as a telephone. The threads into which the electrodes will be organized are so small a specialist robot has been designed to insert them into precise locations within both the M1 and S1 cortexes, while avoiding blood vessels.

Musk's vision is genuine; we are now on the cusp of such feasible developments, not science fiction. This is not to say his plans are beyond scepticism. It has been suggested, for example, that he demonstrates a naïve understanding of the biology of neurons, and has overlooked the individualized architecture of each person's brain. These may delay the successful implementation of the approach, but Neuralink and other companies[31] are at the point of trials in human volunteers.

Success in this arena will herald the capacity to jump along our human-machine axis from a patient operating a 'smart' prosthetic limb, to individuals with increasing percentages of their body replaced by cybernetic components. Although the initial applications are for rehabilitation, Musk is overt that the ultimate ambition is to achieve 'symbiosis with Artificial Intelligence (AI)'.[32] Once perfected, this could deliver scenarios in which technology interfaces with a brain as the only remaining organic remnant of a once-human individual.[33] This would place us emphatically in the category of cyborg, the fusion of cybernetic technology with a biological organism (indeed, many would argue that we reach that point as soon as a controllable prosthetic is achieved).

Musk envisages this research as the gateway to such outcomes as non-verbal communication and the capacity to archive versions of your memory in the same way you might save versions of a document.[34] The capacity to fully detach our memories from an organic body and to generate an entirely electronic version of ourselves is also fundamental to the concept of the *post*human. Enthusiasts such as Nick Bostrom describe uploading of the human mind onto computers as 'whole brain emulation'.[35]

Such a posthuman must at some point in proceedings, however, actually have been an organic being. This stands in contrast to our final category, the android. Here we are effectively traversing the human-machine dimension from the other end, since the android remains entirely machine, but manifesting human characteristics. Since an android has never existed in an embodied biological form, it is inevitably, to some measure, a *fake* human. If we adopt a liberal definition of personhood, however, can such a creation qualify?

The principal technologies to consider here are artificial intelligence and robotics. Machine learning plays an increasingly common role in our lives, from the algorithms that recommend websites on an internet search, through to the programmes that assist in analysis of X-rays or other medical data. In the jargon, these are 'weak AI', tools capable of performing a narrow range of pattern recognition or other defined tasks. Though they perform an invaluable service, no one is under any illusion that these are achieving anything worthy of the status of persons. What, however, of deep learning systems that attempt to replicate human characteristics such as reasoning or intentionality? These would be 'strong AI', otherwise known as 'artificial general intelligence' or 'full AI'; could they be *persons*?

Although we are considering the implications of developments in computer engineering, the discussion of strong AI gets rapidly intertwined with philosophy, requiring a brief detour. Pivotal to these reflections is the notion of *consciousness*, since this is perceived to be the gateway for personhood and thereafter for grounding ethical and moral rights. Some observers argue that consciousness involves a level of self-awareness that can never be achieved by a machine[36] (indeed a few suggest that consciousness is even illusory for humans[37]). Others note that despite significant recent advances in weak AI and popular representations of humanoids such as in the film *Ex Machina* and the TV series *Humans*, strong AI remains a distant objective.[38]

Since we are indulging in a degree of 'horizon spotting', let us elaborate upon some of the extensive fulminations surrounding machine consciousness. Active debate includes not only ways that consciousness might be demonstrated, but even the definition of consciousness itself. Undoubtedly, the most famous test for machine intelligence (which is not quite the same thing as consciousness, as we shall see in a moment) is Alan Turing's Imitation Game, often called the 'Turing Test'. Could a computer answer questions posed by an unsighted interrogator in such a way as to be indistinguishable from a human respondent? There are plenty of objections that the Turing Test does not demonstrate genuine intelligence. A well-known example is the Chinese Room, in which philosopher John Searle posited that he could operate a symbol-processing program, written in English, that could respond to questions posed in Chinese characters sufficiently well that the recipient was fooled into thinking the person operating the machine understood Chinese.[39] The clear implication is that a computer with sufficient symbol-processing capability could pass itself off as human without really understanding.

In recent years, a burgeoning collection of other tests for intelligence and consciousness have been envisaged.[40] Some are variations on the original Turing Test, substituting different methods, even wine appreciation or jazz improvisation rather than speech, for demonstrating interaction. In seeking to distinguish consciousness from intelligence, there is a growing recognition of the importance of subjective experience, that is, what it means to *feel* something, as distinct from the process of parsing information. The self-awareness of subjective sensory experiences, for example, the emotional response to a smell or emotions triggered by a view, are sometimes termed qualia. In this regard, Finnish philosopher Pentti Haikonen argues that if qualia equate to self-explanatory information, then a machine manifesting self-explanation would have qualia and thus be 'conscious', without any requirement for human qualia and machine qualia to be phenomenologically identical.[41] Therefore, if an artificial neural network can be constructed which demonstrates qualia, then an essential threshold for personhood has been crossed.

Hitherto, our discussion of androids has focused on AI, consciousness and personhood, without reflection on the physical shape of the machine. If a whole brain emulation can qualify as a posthuman, then, presumably, it follows that manifestation of these capabilities in the absence of humanoid form would also be sufficient to count as a person. Nevertheless, significant effort has been directed towards development of anthropomorphic robots and investigating the influence this may have on human–robot interactions. This may influence a willingness of humans to consider an android to be a person.

Evidence suggests that a complex blend of characteristics contributes to our perception of humanized robots, such as physical appearance, linguistic, behavioural and other psychological aspects.[42] Physical dimensions include bipedal stance, the manner by which movement is achieved upon those two legs, gender and racial features. In this regard, the emerging potential to produce soft, skin-like materials with embedded electro-mechanical components is of particular interest[43], especially for social robots where physical contact with a human may be significant, such as in education, healthcare and sexual services (which are a major market in this field).[44]

Linguistic, behavioural and psychological components are more the realm of AI and software design, although facial expressions and body language clearly involve physical movement as well.[45] Capacity to mimic human traits such as empathy can be programmed with increasing plausibility. This process of humanization has led several authors to consider classifying some robots as persons, and to reflect on the associated rights and responsibilities following from such a status. These include a degree of genuine autonomy and the right not to be 'murdered' but also a description of the duties and accountabilities that come with personhood.

Whatever their motivation, Saudi Arabia has already crossed this threshold when, in 2017, they awarded citizenship to a robot called Sophia.[46] It seems unlikely that this will be a 'one off'; the European Parliament has, for example, already considered a motion regarding the allocation of liability should a company's robot be found responsible for any damage to the property of others.[47]

Conclusion

In this chapter, we have summarized the science that could contribute to the generation of various beings who may possibly fall into the definitions of the transhuman or the posthuman. We have considered current and future advancements along both biological and technological/mechanical axes. We need to be particularly mindful of Amara's Law: 'We tend to overestimate the effect of a technology in the short run and underestimate the effect in the long run.'[48]

Some of the innovations discussed, especially with genome editing, have moved unexpectedly fast and offer perhaps the strongest indications yet that evolution of humans beyond the natural constraints of *Homo sapiens* are plausible. However, I still believe it is premature to say that a transhuman, let alone a posthuman, is imminent. Transhumanism will probably remain more science fiction than science fact for a while longer, but the reality of recent progress obliges us to examine closely the moral, ethical and religious status of such beings. which is the focus of the other chapters in this collection.

Notes

1 E.g. Mark Gubrud, 'Why Transhumanism won't work', *The New Atlantis*, 10 June 2010; John Gray, 'Humanity Mk II: why the future of humanity will be just as purposeless as the past', *New Statesman*, 13 October 2016; Rose Eveleth, 'Transhumanism is tempting – until you remember inspector gadget', *Wired*, 27 May 2019.

2 In an oft-quoted definition, Bostrom sees 'fundamentally improving the human condition' as the goal of the transhumanist movement. See The Transhumanist FAQ, https://nickbostrom.com/views/transhumanist.pdf (Accessed on 9 January 2021).

3 For example, Hava Tirosh-Samuelson, 'In pursuit of perfection: the misguided Transhumanist vision', *Theology and Science* 16, no. 2 (2018), 200–22.

4 Allen Porter, 'Bioethics and Transhumanism', *The Journal of Medicine and Philosophy: A Forum for Bioethics and Philosophy of Medicine* 42, no. 3 (2017), 237–60.

5 Clustered regularly interspaced short palindromic repeats with the Cas 9 protein. The acronym is sometimes rendered in capitals as CRISPR. However, in this chapter we have followed the more general convention on lower case letters when the acronym is said as a word (e.g. Nato) rather than as letters (e.g. BBC).

6 R. Michael Blaese et al., 'T Lymphocyte-directed Gene Therapy for ADA – SCID: Initial Trial Results after 4 years', *Science* 270, no. 5235 (1995), 475–80.

7. Emma Young, 'Miracle' Gene Therapy Trial Halted', *New Scientist*, 3 October 2002.
8. Britt Wray, 'CRISPR May Prove Useful in De-extinction Efforts', *The Scientist*, 1 September 2017; Beth Shapiro, 'Mammoth 2.0: Will Gnome Engineering Resurrect Extinct Species?' *Genome Biol* 16, no. 228 (2015).
9. Tim Wang et al., 'Genetic Screens in Human Cells using the CRISPR-Cas9 System', *Science* 343, no. 6166 (2014), 80–4; Ophir Shalem et al., 'Genome-scale CRISPR-Cas9 Knockout Screening in Human Cells', *Science* 343, no. 6166 (2014), 84–7.
10. BBC News, 'He Jiankui Defends "world's First Gene-Edited Babies"', 28 November 2018, https://www.bbc.co.uk/news/world-asia-china-46368731 (Accessed on 8 January 2021).
11. BBC News, 'He Jiankui Defends "world's First Gene-Edited Bbies"', 28 November 2018, https://www.bbc.co.uk/news/world-asia-china-46368731 (Accessed on 8 January 2021).
12. Antonio Regalado, 'He Jiankui Faces Three Years in Prison for CRISPR Babies', *MIT Technology Review*, 30 December 2019; BBC News, 'China Jails 'gene-edited babies' Scientist for Three Years', 30 December 2019, https://www.bbc.co.uk/news/world-asia-china-50944461 (Accessed on 8 January 2021).
13. John Shook and James Giordano, 'Neuroethics Beyond Normal: Performance Enablement and Self-transformative Technologies', *Cambridge Quarterly of Healthcare Ethics* 25, no. 1 (2016), 121–40.
14. Begley Sharon, 'Birth of CRISPR'd Pigs Advances Hopes for Turning Swine into Organ Donors', *StatNews*, 10 August 2017.
15. Benjamin S. Freedman, 'Hopes and Difficulties for Blastocyst Complementation', *Nephron* 138, no. 1 (2018), 42–7.
16. Toshihiro Kobayashi et al., 'Generation of Rat Pancreas in Mouse by Interspecific Blastocyst Injection of Pluripotent Stem Cells', *Cell* 142, no. 5 (2010), 787–99. NOTE ADDED IN PROOF: Blastocyst complementation was the method used by Juan Carlos Belmonte and colleagues to produce human-animal chimeric embryos which were grown for up to 20 days as reported in April 2021, see Tao Tan et al., 'Chimeric Contribution of Human Extended Pluripotent Stem Cells to Monkey Embryos *ex vivo*', *Cell* 184, no. 1 (2021), 2020–32.
17. Chen Hi et al., 'Transplantation of Human Brain Organoids: Revisiting the Science and Ethics of Brain Chimeras', *Cell Stem Cell* 25, no. 4 (2019), 462–72.
18. Gill Haddow et al., 'Not "human" Enough to be Human but not "animal" Enough to be Animal – the Case of the HFEA, Cybrids and Xenotransplantation in the UK', *New Genetics and Society* 29, no. 1 (2010), 3–17.
19. Puya Yazdi, 'Effects of Transcranial Direct Current Stimulation (tDCS)', *SelfHacked*, 22 September 2020.
20. Steve Connor, 'Professor Has World's First Silicon Chip Implant', *The Independent*, 23 October 2011.
21. Alice Hines, 'Magnet Implants? Welcome to the World of Medical Punk', *The New York Times*, 12 May 2018.
22. Jennifer Collinger et al., 'High-Performance Neuroprosthetic Control by an Individual with Tetraplegia', *The Lancet* 381, no. 9866 (2013), 557–64.
23. Michelle Salas et al., 'Proprioceptive and Cutaneous Sensations in Humans Elicited by Intracortical Microstimulation', *eLife* 7 (2018), e36137.
24. Sharlene Flesher et al. 'Intracortical Microstimulation of Human Somatosensory Cortex', *Science Translational Medicine* 8, no. 361 (2016), 361ra141.
25. Sharlene Flesher et al., 'A Brain-Computer Interface that Evokes Tactile Sensations Improves Robotic Arm Control', *Science* 372, no. 6544 (2021), 831–6.

26　Pieter Roelfsema et al., 'Mind Reading and Writing: The Future of Neurotechnology', *Trends in Cognitive Sciences* 22, no. 7 (2018), 598–610.
27　Mikhail Lebedev et al., 'Editorial: Augmentation of Brain Functions: Facts, Fiction and Controversy', *Frontiers in Systems Neuroscience* 12, no. 45 (2018).
28　Vadim S. Polikov 1, Patrick A. Tresco and William M. Reichert, 'Response of Brain Tissue to Chronically Implanted Neural Electrodes', *Journal of Neuroscience Methods* 148, no. 1 (2005), 1–18.
29　Rossana Rauti et al., 'Properties and Behavior of Carbon Nanomaterials when Interfacing Neuronal Cells: How Far have We Come?' *Carbon* 143 (2019), 430–46.
30　Stephan Waldert, 'Invasive vs. Non-invasive Neuronal Signals for Brain-Machine Interfaces: Will One Prevail?' *Frontiers in Neuroscience* 10, no. 295 (2016).
31　Zoë Corbyn, 'Are Brain Implants the Future of Thinking?' *The Guardian*, 22 September 2019.
32　Olivia Solon, 'Elon Musk Says Humans must Become Cyborgs to Stay Relevant: Is He Right?' *The Guardian*, 15 February 2017.
33　This is precisely the development envisaged many times over in science fiction, for example, *Doctor Who*'s nemesis the Cybermen (see Green and Willmott (2013)) The Cybermen and Human.2 in *New Dimensions of Doctor Who: Exploring Space, Time and Television* (Reading Contemporary Television), edited by Matt Hills. I B Tauris and Major in *Ghost in the Shell*.
34　Elon Musk Reveals New Details About Neuralink, His Brain Implant Technology, https://youtu.be/Gqdo57uky4o
35　Cited by Tirosh-Samuelson, 'In pursuit of perfection: the misguided Transhumanist vision'.
36　Robert K. Logan, 'Can Computers Become Conscious, an Essential Condition for the Singularity?' *Information* 8, no. 4 (2017), 161.
37　Anna Buckley Is consciousness just an illusion?, 4 April 2017, https://www.bbc.co.uk/news/science-environment-39482345 (Accessed on 11 January 2021).
38　Pentti O. A. Haikonen, 'On Artificial Intelligence and Consciousness', *Journal of Artificial Intelligence and Consciousness* 7, no. 1 (2020), 73–82.
39　David Cole, 'The Chinese Room Argument', *Stanford Encyclopedia of Philosophy* (2002), https://plato.stanford.edu/entries/chinese-room/
40　David Cole, 'The Chinese Room Argument', *The Stanford Encyclopedia of Philosophy* (Winter 2020 Edition), ed. Edward N. Zalta, https://plato.stanford.edu/archives/win2020/entries/chinese-room/ (Accessed on 11 January 2021).
41　Haikonen, 'On Artificial Intelligence and Consciousness'.
42　Jean-Christophe Giger et al., 'Humanization of Robots: Is It Really such a Good Idea?', *Human Behaviour and Emerging Technology* 1, no. 1 (2019), 111–23.
43　Daniela Rus and Michael T. Tolley, 'Design, Fabrication and Control of Soft Robots', *Nature* 521 (2015), 467–75.
44　Brian D. Earp and Katarzyna Grunt-Mejer, 'Robots and Sexual Ethics', *Journal of Medical Ethics* 47, no. 1 (2021), 1–2.
45　Ruud Hortensius, Felix Hekele and Emily S. Cross, 'The Perception of Emotion in Artificial Agents', *IEEE Transactions on Cognitive and Developmental Systems* 10, no. 4 (2018), 852–64.
46　Andrew Griffin, 'Saudi Arabia Grants Citizenship to a Robot for the First Ever Time Independent', *The Independent*, 26 October 2017.
47　Giger et al. 'Humanization of Robots: Is It Really Such a Good Idea?'.
48　Cited by Rodney Brooks, 'The Seven Deadly Sins of AI Predictions', *MIT Technology Review* 120, no. 6 (2017), 79–86.

Part III

Philosophical aspects in generating transhuman and posthuman persons

6

Domination and vulnerability

Herman Bavinck and posthumanism in the shadow of Friedrich Nietzsche

James Eglinton

This chapter is on the emergence of bioethics in the writings of the Dutch Christian ethicist Herman Bavinck (1854–1921), a figure best known for his work in dogmatic theology, the four-volume *Reformed Dogmatics*,[1] but who was also one of the most interesting and significant Dutch Christian ethicists of his day. Although bioethics would only become the object of direct and clear focus relatively late in Bavinck's life, this chapter will chart the roots of his views on bioethical issues through his criticisms of the German atheist philosopher Friedrich Nietzsche (1844–1900) during the first two decades of the twentieth century.

Born in 1854, Bavinck studied in the Netherlands at the Theological School in Kampen (the seminary of the theologically conservative Christian Reformed Church), and at the University of Leiden, completing a doctorate on theological ethics there in 1880.[2] Following a short period in the pastorate, Bavinck spent his academic career teaching in Kampen (1883–1902), and then at the Free University of Amsterdam (1902–21), a Christian university established by the Reformed theologian and statesman Abraham Kuyper (1837–1920).[3] In the course of those decades, he became the most important intellectual in the neo-Calvinist movement – a branch of the Reformed theological tradition that aimed to articulate a species of Calvinism that was both recognizably orthodox *and* modern.[4]

In those two phases in his career, Bavinck wrote prolifically within the field of Christian ethics. During the Kampen decades, he wrote a long but never finished manuscript on Reformed Ethics – a work that has now been transcribed and published in Dutch and English.[5] While working in Amsterdam, he published books and articles on the ethics of war, the family, and of politics, on medical ethics, on the ethical implications of individualism, among other topics.

With regard to the theme of this book – on the ethics of generating transhuman and posthuman persons – unsurprisingly Bavinck has nothing to say directly. Historically, Bavinck came some time before either trans- or posthumanism. It is certainly the case, however, that one could build a constructive theological engagement from Bavinck's dogmatics and ethics that would offer interaction with posthumanism. This chapter, though, is primarily historical in focus. It will give an account of Bavinck's belief that a profound ethical shift became clear in Western culture at the beginning of the twentieth century following the death of Nietzsche who argued that as God is dead 'because we have killed him', all values should be revalued.

Bavinck understood (and agreed with the logic of) Nietzsche's core and novel assertion: namely, that if atheism is true, we are under no obligation to retain any of the moral trappings of theism. For Bavinck, the Western ethical imagination pre-1900 was the Western ethical imagination *pre-Nietzsche*. It was an ethical imagination in the shadow of Christ. After 1900, due to the impact of Nietzsche, he thought, the ethical imagination should be considered under the long shadow of the Nietzschean *Übermensch* – a new kind of idealized post-Christian human who was mighty, dominant, strong and this-worldly. From the early 1900s onwards, Bavinck perceived that Nietzschean ethics had changed the lay of the land in the Western ethical imagination, and would continue to do so long into the future. During the last two decades of his life, Bavinck's ethical writings became, in effect, an unfolding commentary on the contrast between Nietzschean and Christian ethics as applied to issues like war, the family, industrialized labour and towards the end of Bavinck's life, also in the realm of bioethics (with a focus on questions about reproduction and eugenics). In tracing out that development, this chapter will provide a historical sketch of Bavinck's Christian ethics pre- and post-Nietzsche, leading to Bavinck's critiques of bioethics in what he viewed as 'the age of Nietzsche'. Following that, it will conclude with reflections bringing this historical chapter to focus more closely on the theme of this book, on questions around the ethics of creating trans- and posthuman persons.

Bavinck and Nietzsche

While a professor at the Theological School in Kampen in the 1880s–1890s, Bavinck was busy writing a substantial but never finished tome, *Reformed Ethics*. That work was intended to be a companion volume to his *Reformed Dogmatics*, and was envisioned as such through Bavinck's view that dogmatics (which concerns God's deeds for us) belongs alongside ethics (what we do in response to God) as organically connected, twin disciplines. The production of the *Reformed Ethics* manuscript was also informed by the belief that the ethical challenges of the day required fresh reflection: for Bavinck, the late nineteenth century was not well served by the ethics texts of previous decades or centuries. Rather, each age stood in need of its own articulations of dogmatics *and* ethics. In the 1880s–1890s, Nietzsche was alive, but was an almost unknown figure in the Netherlands, for which reason *Reformed Ethics* pays almost no attention to him. (Indeed, Nietzschean thought only began to gain mass traction posthumously.)

Historians of neo-Calvinism have sometimes made much of the claim that Nietzsche was first introduced to the Dutch public by the neo-Calvinist theologian, Abraham Kuyper, who served as Prime Minister of the Netherlands from 1901 to 1905, and whose 1892 speech 'The Blurring of the Boundaries' referenced him as an obscure German atheistic philosopher,[6] and incidentally brought him to the attention of the Dutch public. Although this claim is not quite true – the German philosopher Michael Georg Conrad (1846–1927) had published on Nietzsche in Dutch a decade before Kuyper[7] – it was certainly the case that Nietzsche was not a figure of any outstanding influence in the Netherlands during his own lifetime. In the 1890s, he became something of a curiosity to Dutch theologians. In 1894, for example, the arch-conservative (and anti-neo-Calvinist) Reformed theologian Lucas Lindeboom (1845–1933) traced a direct line between Nietzsche's impiety and blasphemy, and the collapse of Nietzsche's mental health in the 1890s.[8] While other theologians attempted to make sense of Nietzsche among the post- and anti-Christian thinkers active in that decade, none of them seems to have foreseen the extent to which his influence would grow posthumously.[9]

In this long and unfinished ethics manuscript, Bavinck only mentions Nietzsche once: in a section of the appendices, Nietzsche is referenced in passing as an example of hedonistic ethics. At the time of writing (at some point in the 1880s–1890s), Bavinck saw Nietzsche as one of a line of thinkers and philosophers who taught an ethic of individual happiness and egotistical utilitarianism.[10] In this appendix, Nietzsche does not appear to pose any great threat to the basic structure of Christian ethics. Rather, he was described as a figure whose attempt to define 'the good' by the goal of creating 'individual happiness' was a disordered form of the Christian ethical imagination, rather than an outright rejection of it. Although there is no evidence as to which of Nietzsche's published works Bavinck might have read in the 1880s, it may be the case that his impression of Nietzsche as an unintimidating hedonistic philosopher was rooted in the title of Nietzsche's 1882 book *The Gay Science* [*Die fröhliche Wissenschaft*], while suggesting a degree of unfamiliarity with that book's content. (Nietzsche's argument that 'God is dead' was aired in *The Gay Science*.)[11] This lack of careful attention to Nietzsche was perhaps typical of the intellectual trends of the Netherlands in the 1880s and early 1890s.

In the 1880s–1890s, the kind of Dutch atheism that Bavinck knew entailed a denial of God's existence, but also made no effort to overthrow the ethical norms generated by the Christian faith: there may be no God, this logic argued, but it is still wrong to murder, steal or exploit the poor. This kind of atheism, which had been present in Dutch culture since the 1860s, was both powerfully moralistic (under the influence of the moralistic Dutch atheist and novelist Multatuli (1820–87)), and materialistic in spirit.[12] In Bavinck's own view, the 1880s and 1890s were the 'age of Renan' (named after the French philosopher Ernest Renan (1823–92)). In the 1890s, just as Bavinck was writing his own fledgling account of Christian ethics, this moralistic and materialistic atheism began to run out of steam. Materialist atheists began to move back to some kind of theism, although to Bavinck's disappointment, few of these atheists moved towards orthodox Christian faith.[13] During these decades, while Nietzsche was still alive, it seems that Bavinck was only exposed to a variety of atheism that carried over a Christian ethical imagination that Bavinck himself recognized, and that he could address directly. In those decades, the denial of God's existence nonetheless left the world's moral order more or less untouched.

In comparison to the moralistic atheism of the 1880s–1890s, Nietzschean atheism – which grew rapidly in popularity and influence after his death in 1900 – was thoroughly novel in that it denied both the *roots* and *fruits* of Christianity. If we kill God, its logic went, we must also revalue all values, as nothing in the moral framework produced by Christian theism automatically deserves an ongoing right of existence. If there is no God, it is not a given that murder, theft or the exploitation of the poor is wrong. Rather, those values must be revalued. For that reason, Nietzsche's atheism was intended as a wholesale and radical departure from the theism it had rejected, and as such, it was unlike anything that had come before. After 1900, a new kind of atheist had emerged – one who felt under no obligation to carry over any of the moral remnants of a former theistic age. As such, Nietzsche's atheism was not intended to supersede a previous stage of Christianity's long history. Rather, it would shun Christianity entirely, and create something utterly new in its place.

Crucially to its appeal, Nietzschean thought made atheism purposeful by its focus on another of his novelties, the *Übermensch* – a mighty, this-worldly way of being human, a kind of human who prefers the concreteness of domination to the flighty pursuit of happiness. (Although Bavinck's earlier ethics manuscripts saw Nietzsche as an example of the ethics of hedonism, Nietzsche's long-term contribution to ethics would actually be the ethics of domination). For the *Übermensch*, domination was the goal (rather than survival, à la Darwin, or self-sacrifice, à la Jesus). Nietzsche's own New Testament hero was the Roman Governor Pontius Pilate, rather than Jesus Christ.[14] Jesus laid down his life meekly, and put the needs of others before his own, associated with the poor and took their sicknesses upon himself, and bore their griefs and sorrows. Pilate, however, acted in self-interest and the pursuit of power, and (in Nietzsche's estimations) did the right thing in scorning both the hopelessly voluntarily weak Jesus at his trial, and looking down on the notion of 'truth'.

After Nietzsche's death in 1900, a cult of Nietzsche began to develop in the Netherlands. The poet and novelist Frederik van Eeden (1860–1932), for example, popularized the *Übermensch* in his character Vico Muralto.[15] In some Dutch circles, it became popular to disdain Jesus' model of grace and servanthood, and also to criticize Darwin's model of the survival of the fittest (on the grounds that survival is far inferior to domination). Rather, the idea of the domination of the strongest began to gain ground. It was a new species of atheism that had no interest in the Netherlands' Christian past, and it pointed to an unimaginable future wholly untethered from it.

For that reason, although Bavinck's interactions with Nietzsche pre-1900 were very limited, Nietzsche would become Bavinck's regular opponent in his writings on ethics from 1900 onwards, until Bavinck's own death in 1921. After 1900, Bavinck knew he had moved from the 'age of Renan' into the 'age of Nietzsche'.[16]

Ethics in the age of Nietzsche

During Nietzsche's own lifetime, while Bavinck was writing his ethics manuscripts, Dutch society had gone through a process of deconfessionalization and secularization. The state church had been disestablished, and rates of church attendance had begun to drop. Nonetheless, in the 1880s–1890s, Bavinck believed that the Dutch nation was on the verge of a return to its (Calvinistic) Christian roots. While some Dutch people were flirting with moralistic atheism, he thought that atheism would never satisfy them like their first love (Calvinism) had. At that time, he was convinced that the roots of Christianity, and particularly Calvinism, were spread deep and wide through the soil of Dutch culture. Any attempt to pull those roots out was doomed to fail: the roots held the soil together, to the extent that without them, the remaining soil would fall apart. In those decades, Bavinck believed that the Dutch people knew this, deep down, and that they would soon return, en masse, to Christianity.[17] After Nietzsche's death, however, the fact that some Dutch people were willing to venture into Nietzsche's unknown de-Christianized future made Bavinck reconsider his earlier view of the Dutch as indelibly Calvinistic. He now saw that they were much less rooted in Calvinism than he had previously thought. In *Present Day Morality* (1902), he now recognized that 'in his moral philosophy, Nietzsche has only given voice to what lived unconsciously in many hearts'.[18] At this point, Bavinck saw Nietzsche as a poster-boy for a broader cultural change: he put into words what many Dutch people were already thinking and feeling.

A common feature in Bavinck's interactions with Nietzschean ethics after 1900 is the importance of Christology: for Bavinck, Christian ethics ultimately hinged on Christ. And for that reason, the core of Nietzsche's consequences for ethics, he believed, was Christological. In Bavinck's 1912 book *Christianity*, he argued that the Christian religion has both *phenomena* (manifestations in the real world, including Christian ethics) and an *essence* (Christ himself).[19] The *phenomena* of Christianity, as diverse as they may be, are produced by reflection on its shared *essence* – by reflection on Christ. Applied specifically to ethics, this view means that Christian ethics (as one of Christianity's phenomena) emerges as a result of contemplation on Christ himself.

Building on this, he argued that those who reject Christianity's *phenomena* (in this case, Christian *ethics*) must ultimately reject Christianity's *essence* (Christ himself). This particular book is a warning that the Nietzschean *Übermensch* was fast approaching. Indeed, Bavinck's argument for the Christians of the later decades of twentieth century was that they would face as yet imaginable ethical novelties, the core of which will always be a rejection of God having disclosed himself in Jesus Christ. This particular connection is important in interpreting Bavinck's responses to Nietzsche in the ethics of war, pedagogy and bioethics.

Ethics and war

Three months after the outbreak of First World War, Bavinck published a short article that was soon reissued as a booklet entitled *The Problem of War*.[20] In this, he argued that as the religion of the Prince of Peace, Christianity naturally leaned towards mercy, rather than violence. For that reason, declarations of war are the calling of the state, rather than of the church. However, as a religion called to promote righteousness and defend the oppressed (as Christ himself had done), he claimed, 'Christian ethics indeed allows no other conclusion that this, that good and justified wars *are possible*.'[21] In claiming this, however, he expressed scepticism of whether any of the wars of history had truly been just. After all, every previous war contained elements that were deplorable to both 'Christianity and humanity'. Bavinck argued that war could not be justified on account of,

> the rights of the strongest, the virtues of patriotism, bravery, courage, patience, steadfastness, the consensus of the majority, sacrifice, etc, that it can cultivate . . . and less still for the beneficial [financial] consequences, the extension of territory, the expansion of culture, or even of the [spread of] Christianity that might accompany it.[22]

However, having supported 'just war' theory, he found himself unable to imagine how in the age of Nietzsche, conflict between any of the countries in Europe could be entirely just. Europe had now become a continent in which Christianity's influence had been replaced by the pursuit of economic and nationalistic dominance. Bavinck feared that in a godless world (godless because 'we have killed God'), all wars would be unjust.

> Who can tell us what the reason is for this war, why it is being waged, and what purpose it serves? From whatever angle one looks at it, no light shines on it. It is surrounded by darkness.[23]

In his judgement, the growing Nietzschean rejection of the way of the Prince of Peace, which was deemed 'no longer to apply to our age', played a central role in Europe's descent into violence. The nihilistic First World War was inextricably linked to the new atheism of the age, the blame for which he laid squarely at Nietzsche's feet.

At the end of the War, Bavinck offered a second assessment of it, again arguing that it was occasioned by the development of Nietzschean atheism. The War had left Bavinck deeply troubled by the state of a Christendom that had grown utterly estranged from Christianity, and prompted him to ask why Europe's long Christian history had not prevented historically Christian nations from marching into (what he still believed to have been) a needless and meaningless war – dragging the rest of the world with them. The answer, he argued in 'Christianity, War, and the Bond of Nations',[24] was that towards the end of the nineteenth century, Darwin's notion of the 'survival of the fittest' and Nietzsche's anti-Jesus 'philosophy of domination' had migrated from the realms of biology and philosophy into the world of nationalist politics. As a result, international politics had been transformed into a race for domination at all costs, with no regard for Christianity as a restraining factor – a development that occurred just as the dominant liberal theology of the day realized it was no match for an *Übermensch* intoxicated with its sense of evolutionary superiority.

(Bio)ethics and pedagogy

In the 1917 book *The New Education*,[25] Bavinck offered a lengthy exploration of the future of education against the backdrop of First World War, engaging with new developments in child psychology, new pedagogical theories, emerging views of politics and statehood, and new ideas on the role of the individual and the community.

In attempting to plot a path forward for Christian thought on education in that setting. Interestingly, Bavinck's argument moved readily from pedagogy to bioethics, on account of his belief that the spirit of the age's influence on pedagogy – in its blend of Darwin and Nietzsche – was intimately linked to changes and trends in bioethics. Modern pedagogy, he thought, had come under the influence of Darwin and Nietzsche's *Übermensch* idea, which Bavinck understood as merging to form a dangerous cocktail that taught children two particularly damaging ideas: first, that they are *only* their bodies, and secondly, that powerful bodies are *better* than weak bodies. Bavinck was troubled by the increasingly common view that those whose bodies were deemed 'less worthy' should be sterilized. In this book, Bavinck charted the development of eugenics in England (through the eugenicist Francis Galton (1822–1911), and his protegee, the atheist eugenicist Karl Pearson (1857–1936)), and also in the United States. In context, for example, moves were made to pass compulsory sterilization for those deemed unworthy of reproductive rights in the states of Indiana (1907), Washington, California, Connecticut (1909), Nevada, Iowa and New Jersey (all 1911), New York (1912) and Minnesota (1913): this movement attempted to remove the deaf, the blind, serial offenders, alcoholics, psychopaths, those with a particularly low IQ and the 'general degenerate' from the gene pool. In his account, Bavinck listed the statistics of hundreds of people in different states who were sterilized, often without individual consent.

Interestingly, Bavinck's analysis of this movement highlighted a cultural shift regarding the perceived rights of every child. He argued that Western culture had shifted to affirm what seemed superficially to be noble aspirations for children: every child has the right to be born into a healthy body, to be of sound mind and to live in a stable home environment. (Stated more cynically, these rights could mean: every child has the right to be strong, and well equipped to dominate, and that children who do not enjoy physical or mental health, or a stable home, do not have the right to exist). As a consequence, he noted that the general public sentiment was clear: it was now widely held that children who do not have one or more of those things – a healthy body, good mental health or a stable home environment – will inevitably become the drunks, prostitutes, criminals and chronically mentally or physically ill of society. And for that reason, he observed, the public sentiment in some states was that the 'less than worthy should be excluded' from reproduction.

Bavinck believed he had exposed a fault line in the bioethics of his day: in New York in 1912, for example, a law was proposed that would also extend sterilization to epileptics and people with other chronic physical illnesses. That law had supporters, but was defeated because it clashed with other modern liberal values around individual freedom. In the next year, the United Kingdom Parliament passed the *Mental Deficiency Act*, which legalized the compulsory segregation of those deemed 'feeble minded' in colonies where they were kept separate from the general population. (This practice carried on until 1959, with at one point 65,000 United Kingdom citizens being legally detained on account of low intelligence).[26]

By raising these examples in a book on education, Bavinck's point was to highlight that what children were now learning in schools was part and parcel of that Nietzschean culture – where the *Übermensch* was the new norm, where physical and psychological dominance was man's chief end, and where the physically and mentally 'weak' were now a problem to be removed from the gene pool or the general population in one way or another. Bavinck argued that this new bioethics began in the classroom as children were taught anti-Christian lessons about their own bodies and the bodies of others.

In 1920, Bavinck published a collection of essays on *Biblical and Religious Psychology*,[27] in which he argued – perhaps presciently, with regard to the history of the mid-twentieth century – that a terrible change had been introduced to popular Western psychology through 'the emergence of Friedrich Nietzsche', who, 'with deep disdain for the masses glorified only a few great men who came forth from humanity, and vindicated for them that "might is right"'.[28] In response to the *Übermenschen* who would enter history in the remainder of the twentieth century, Bavinck posed Christ's own question: 'What does it profit a man if he gains the whole world, but loses his soul?'

In this example, it is again clear that Bavinck believed the problem with Nietzschean ethics is Christological in nature: rejection of the essence of Christianity (Christ himself) necessarily generates an ethic (as a phenomenon of Christianity) that is not shaped by reflection on Christ.

While there are numerous other interactions with Nietzsche in Bavinck's ethical writings throughout the last two decades of Bavinck's life, this chapter has dealt with the aforementioned examples for two reasons. First, they cover the years between 1902 and 1919, from shortly after Nietzsche's death, to just before Bavinck's own health went into terminal decline, and his work ground to a halt. As such, these writings enable the reader to see a coherent account of the changed Western ethical imagination that emerged in the 'age of Nietzsche'. Secondly, they show us a consistent Christian response to the ethics of a newly de-Christianized age. To return momentarily to the *Reformed Ethics* text written before Nietzsche's rise to prominence, it is true that Bavinck's ethical writings from that earlier period offered no meaningful interaction with Nietzsche. This lack of engagement, though, could hardly be less representative of his pattern of writing from 1902 onwards. In fact, in dealing with the most important questions on ethics and society during the final two decades of Bavinck's life, Nietzsche was certainly his most important and regular interlocutor.

Conclusion: Bioethics, dominance and vulnerability

Thus far, this chapter has been historical in focus, and has not addressed the theme to which this volume is dedicated: namely, is it possible to generate transhuman and posthuman persons ethically? As was stated in the introduction, it would certainly be possible to develop a constructive answer to that question from Bavinck's writings (particularly drawing on his theological account of 'being human'). That approach, however, would necessitate an altogether different kind of investigation (i.e., close exegesis of Bavinck's theological anthropology, account of culture, human vocation, and technology, in order to create a framework that would address more recent ethical questions) to that taken thus far in this paper. Nonetheless, on the basis of this chapter's account of Bavinck on Nietzsche leading into bioethics, it is possible to make some preliminary comments that address this book's theme directly.

One of the most striking divergences between Bavinck's account of 'human nature' and the new thoughts on 'being human' that emerged in the age of Nietzsche (as understood by Bavinck) are the issues of vulnerability and power. The Nietzschean ethic of domination aimed at the elimination of one's own vulnerability and the simultaneous acquisition of power over those who are weaker than you are. Its goal is that the invulnerable *Übermensch* comes to exercise domination over those whose mode of existence he finds intolerable, for which reason he factors them out of the equation by forced sterilization or compulsory segregation. As the sad history of the twentieth century indicates, every *Übermensch* needs to determine his *Üntermensch*. Nietzsche had nothing good to say about weakness. For him, there was no virtue to be found in it, and those foolish enough to do so – Christians – deserved scorn. Conversely, the Christian notion of humanity advanced by Bavinck portrayed an invulnerable God as embracing vulnerability, finitude and weakness in the incarnation of Christ. The self-existent second person of the Trinity assumed a real human nature, including a frail human body that was capable of injury and death, and a human psychology that could be deeply distressed. The Son of God became *Mensch*, a human, *homo vulnerabilis*. Nietzsche's revised human aimed to become something different, not a *Mensch*, but an *Übermensch* – a profound revision of what it means to be human. Rather than the *homo vulnerabilis*, this new anti-Christian kind of human was a *homo dominus*.

Does this divergence have anything to contribute to this volume's discussions of trans- and posthumanism? Perhaps it does. To return to this chapter's introduction: in the two phases of his working life (the 1880s–1890s, in Kampen; and then 1902–21, in Amsterdam), Bavinck interacted with two different species of atheism. In the 1880s–1890s, his atheist interlocutors were committed to a more or less untouched Christian moral imagination: inspired by the novelist Multatuli, the average Dutch atheist at that time was ashamed, for example, of his country's exploitation of the poor and powerless Indonesian population, and was firmly convinced that the core assertions of Christian morality were correct. Thou shalt not murder, God or no God. As a Christian ethicist, Bavinck's interaction with them was quite straightforward. He disagreed with them on the existence of God, but there was no great disagreement on what it meant to be human – at least as far as questions of ethics and society were concerned. And when he appealed to Jesus as the ideal human, these atheists were fairly receptive to definitions of the human that centred on vulnerability.

In the second phase of his working life, in Amsterdam and in the 'age of Nietzsche', all this had changed. Suddenly he found himself trying to speak with a new breed of atheists with whom he had no shared prior ethical commitments regarding God or humanity. And the central feature of Bavinck's account of the ethics of human nature – the God-Man Jesus Christ – had suddenly come to function as the antithesis of the Nietzschean ideal humanity. In context, Bavinck found that there was insufficient common ground for dialogue on the ethics of being human. Rather, interestingly in the context of his biography, Bavinck's engagement with Nietzscheans prompted him to begin investing himself heavily – both in theological reflection and in practice – in evangelism: Nietzscheans would only think differently about ethics if they thought differently about Christ, who Bavinck thought must now be communicated to them as to pagans.[29]

What does this have to say to the issues of trans- and posthumanism, and particularly the ethics of generating transhuman and posthuman persons, in the early twenty-first century?[30] Taken in the as yet fantastical *Humanity+* sense – in which ordinary human organic components might one day be 'upgraded' and 'outmoded' by functionally 'superior' replacements – transhumanism is an effort to flee vulnerability, leaving open as a consequence that the modified (trans)human would then occupy a position of dominance over the unmodified (ordinary) human. The point of transhumanism is certainly not to *acquire* extra weaknesses or vulnerabilities. It is, rather, to exceed what even the most optimally functioning unmodified human can do. Posthumanism, in the sense given by the American inventor and futurist, Ray Kurzweil,[31] exists as an admission that transhumanism's effort to flee vulnerability is in vain as long as we remain tethered to these mortal bodies, which are susceptible to death for as long as they retain and depend on organic components. In that sense, the posthuman attempt to defeat vulnerability is a process of *excarnation* – an exodus from the body – rather than of *incarnation*. (Accordingly, it is through this process that posthumanism would make us something other than 'human'.)

Faced with Kurzweilian posthumanism, a theologian working within Bavinckian categories today might well be struck by the degree to which their views on 'human nature' are poles apart – perhaps to the same degree that Bavinck saw himself as having no meaningful shared language or imagination when trying to discuss ethics with the Nietzscheans of his day. A Christian theological account of 'being human' is shaped by the perfect human, Jesus Christ, perfect in love *and* willingly vulnerable. Significantly, that view ties together the embrace of vulnerability with the capacity to love. To be vulnerable is to admit my capacity to be affected by others – either to aid my flourishing, or to crush my heart. To affirm my vulnerability is to ask others to see me as I am, to love me, to protect me – as I do the same to them.

The British Christian writer C. S. Lewis (1898–1963) gave voice to this anthropology by writing that:

> To love at all is to be vulnerable. Love anything and your heart will be wrung and possibly broken. If you want to make sure of keeping it intact you must give it to no-one, not even an animal. Wrap it carefully round with hobbies and little luxuries; avoid all entanglements. Lock it up safe in the casket or coffin of your selfishness. But in that casket, safe, dark, motionless, airless, it will change. It will not be broken; it will become unbreakable, impenetrable, irredeemable. To love is to be vulnerable.[32]

Lewis' words could be modified slightly to address the posthuman aversion to vulnerability:

> To love is to be vulnerable. Love anything and your heart will be wrung and possibly broken. If you want to make sure of keeping it intact you must give it to no-one, not even a person whose flesh is mortal, whose IQ is low, of chronic ill health, an

alcoholic, or the long term unemployed. Store it carefully in an algorithm, avoid all entanglements. Encrypt it safely, upload it into a singularity where there is only your self. But in that mainframe, safe, dark, motionless, airless, excarnate, it will change. It will not be broken; it will become unbreakable, impenetrable, irredeemable. To love is to be vulnerable.

As a historical theologian, I am not qualified to speculate on the future of technology, or whether the Kurzweilian posthuman 'upload' [of a human consciousness being replicated in a computer environment] scenario is likely to become a reality any time soon – although I retain a deep sense of scepticism towards that prospect – or whether it is likely that Artificial Intelligence might soon be capable of creating a 'person' in the classical sense defined by the Roman politician and philosopher Boethius as 'an individual substance of rational nature'. Such questions fall far beyond the limits of my discipline. However, my avenue of inquiry does create some scope to address the interaction between Christian ethics and posthumanism in the present day. When approached with 'Bavinck on the age of Nietzsche' as a primer used to trace the contours of the Western ethical imagination across the previous century, it becomes clear that the most pressing areas of today's ethical discussion between aspiring posthumans and those with no such aspiration concern the rival desires to be *homo dominus* or *homo vulnerabilis*. Exploration of those clashing desires – particularly in relation to our capacity to love – is increasingly common in science fiction, which functions as a useful vehicle to imagine humans, as beings whose lives are oriented around love, in their interactions with disembodied artificially intelligent beings.[33] For the most part, though, direct theological engagement with these questions is lacking. While some theological engagement with posthumanism has pointed towards love as the fulfilment of a Christian account of human flourishing,[34] more work is certainly required on the part of theologians in questioning whether the rival ideal of posthuman flourishing involves love at all, or whether the quest to become posthuman is also an attempt to become post-love.

Notes

1 Herman Bavinck, *Reformed Dogmatics*, ed. John Bolt, trans. John Vriend, 4 vols (Grand Rapids, MI: Baker Academic, 2003–8).
2 Herman Bavinck, *De ethiek van Ulrich Zwingli* (Kampen: Zalsman, 1880).
3 James Bratt, *Abraham Kuyper: Modern Calvinist, Christian Democrat* (Grand Rapids, MI: Eerdmans, 2013).
4 James Eglinton, *Bavinck: A Critical Biography* (Grand Rapids, MI: Baker Academic, 2020).
5 Herman Bavinck, *Gereformeerde ethiek*, ed. Dirk van Keulen (Utrecht: KokBoekencentrum, 2019); *Reformed Ethics*, ed. John Bolt (Grand Rapids, MI: Baker Academic, 2019).
6 Abraham Kuyper, 'The Blurring of the Boundaries', in *Abraham Kuyper: A Centennial Reader*, ed. James Bratt (Grand Rapids, MI: Eerdmans, 1998), 363–402. Cf. Bratt, *Abraham Kuyper*, 244.

7 Michael Georg Conrad, *Vlammen voor vrije geesten* (Kampen: Laurens van Hulst, 1883), 45.
8 Lucas Lindeboom, *Godgeleerden* (Heusden: Meerburg, 1894), 48.
9 See, for example, J. H. Gunning, *Komt de vroomheid des harten aan?* (Nijmegen: Ten Hoet, 1893), 12; A. F. Savornin de Lohman, *De aanval op Seinpost en mijn antwoord* (Utrecht: Kemink, 1895),118; Anne Anema, *Calvinisme en rechtswetenschap* (Amsterdam: Kirchner, 1897), 93; J. H. Gunning, *Rekenschap* (Nijmegen: Ten Hoet, 1898), 19.
10 Bavinck, *Gereformeerde ethiek*, 941. NB. The English edition *Reformed Ethics* does not include this appendix. The figures listed alongside Nietzsche by Bavinck were the Greek Aristippus (c. 435–c. 356 BCE), the Frenchmen Helvetius (1715–71) and La Mettrie (1709–51), as well as the German Stirner (1806–56).
11 Friedrich Nietzsche, *The Gay Science*, trans. Thomas Common (Mineola: Dover Publications, 2006), 90–1.
12 Multatuli, *Max Havelaar, or The Coffee Auctions of the Dutch Trading Company*, trans. Baron Alphonse Nahuÿs (Edinburgh: Edmonson & Douglas, 1868).
13 For an account of this period, see Eglinton, *Bavinck: A Critical Biography*, 225.
14 Friedrich Nietzsche, *The Antichrist*, trans. H. L. Mencken (New York: Knopf, 1918), 46. 'Must I add that, in the whole New Testament, there appears but a *solitary* figure worthy of honour? Pilate, the Roman viceroy.'
15 Frederik van Eeden, *De kleine Johannes*, 3 vols. (Amsterdam: Elsevier, 1979).
16 Eglinton, *Bavinck: A Critical Biography*, 226.
17 Eglinton, *Bavinck: A Critical Biography*, 206.
18 Herman Bavinck, *Hedendaagsche moraal* (Kampen: Kok, 1902). 'Inderdaad heeft een man als *Nietzsche* in zijne zedelijke wijsbegeerte slechts uiting gegeven aan wat onbewust leefde in veler harten.'
19 Herman Bavinck, *Het christendom* (Baarn: Hollandia, 1912).
20 Herman Bavinck, *Het problem van den oorlog* (Kampen: Kok, 1914).
21 Bavinck, *Het problem van den oorlog*, 16. 'De Christelijke ethiek laat dus inderdaad geene andere conclusie toe dan deze, dat er goede en rechtvaardige oorlogen *kunnen* zijn.'
22 Bavinck, *Het problem van den oorlog*, 16. 'Zijn recht rust dus niet op het recht van den sterkste, op de deugden van patriotisme, heldenmoed, geduld, standvastigheid, eendracht, offervaardigheid enz., die hij kweeken kan; nog minder op de zegenrijke gevolgen, verruiming van den gezichtskring, verbreiding der cultuur, of zelfs van het Christendom.'
23 Bavinck, *Het probleem van den oorlog*, 1. 'Wie kan ook aangeven, wat de oorzaak van dezen oorlog is, waarom hij ondernomen werd en waartoe hij dienen moet? Van welke zijde men hem beziet, nergens valt een lichtpunt op te merken, rondom is hij in duisternis gehuld.'
24 Herman Bavinck, 'Christendom, oorlog, volkenbond', *Stemmen des Tijds* 9 (1919), 1–26, 105–33.
25 Herman Bavinck, *De nieuwe opvoeding* (Kampen: Kok, 1917).
26 Maggie Potts and Rebecca Fido, *"A Fit Person to be Removed": Personal Accounts of Life in a Mental Deficiency Institution* (Tavistock: Northcote House, 1991).
27 Herman Bavinck, *Bijbelsche en religieuze psychologie* (Kampen: Kok, 1920).
28 Bavinck, *Bijbelsche en religieuze psychologie*, 75. 'en met name is toen Friedrich Nietzsche opgetreden, om, met diepe verachting voor de massa, de enkele groote

mannen te verheerlijken, die uit de menschheid voortkomen, en voor hen het recht van den sterkste te vindiceeren.'

29 For an account of the growing importance of evangelism in Bavinck's thought and practice in the 'age of Nietzsche', see Eglinton, *Bavinck: A Critical Biography*, 249–59.
30 This chapter concerns 'posthuman' in the Kurzweilian sense, and does not refer to 'critical posthumanism' as an approach to philosophy. See, for example, Pramod K. Nayar, *Posthumanism* (Cambridge: Polity Press, 2014).
31 Ray Kurzweil, *The Singularity Is Near: When Humans Transcend Biology* (London: Penguin, 2005).
32 Clive Staples Lewis, *The Four Loves* (New York: Harcourt Brace Jovanovich, 1960), 169.
33 See, for example, Anneke Smelik, 'Film', in *The Cambridge Companion to Literature and the Posthuman*, eds. Bruce Clarke and Manuela Rossini (Cambridge: Cambridge University Press, 2017), 109–20.
34 See, for example, Brent Walters, *From Human to Posthuman: Christian Theology and Technology in a Postmodern World* (London: Routledge, 2006), 134.

7

The question of technology and relationships

How might Martin Heidegger's idea of enframing shape how posthuman persons and their generators relate to one another?

Matthew James

Introduction

When asked the secret of his success, the great Canadian ice hockey player Wayne Gretzky famously offered the following advice: 'Skate to where the puck is going, not where it has been.'[1] Dealing with questions concerning the future does require us to look back, reflect and consider where we have come from and where we currently find ourselves. But to better understand the future, we are also required to look ahead in order to anticipate the likely trajectories of science and technology and grasp more fully the implications for the future of humanity and our relationship with technology.

The advent of new emerging technologies is set to challenge and cut straight to the core of our anthropology: our fundamental relationship between technology and human being, between our ability to manipulate, design and control our own selves. Writing in 1943 what now reads as a strikingly prophetic vision of the twenty-first-century Oxford academic C. S. Lewis argued that while technology is said to extend the power of the human race,

> what we call Man's power over Nature turns out to be a power exercised by some men over other men with Nature as its instrument. . . . . There neither is nor can be any simple increase of power on Man's side. Each new power won *by* Man is a power *over* Man as well. Each advance leaves him weaker as well as stronger. In every victory, besides the general who triumphs, he is a prisoner who follows the triumphal car. . . . *Human* nature will be the last part of Nature to surrender to Man. The battle will then be won. We shall have 'taken the thread of life out of the hand of Clotho' and be henceforth free to make our species whatever we wish it to be. The battle will indeed be won. But who, precisely, will have won it?[2]

This idea of taking hold of the power of technology to determine who we shall be and turn ourselves into creatures of our own design is something that those who subscribe to a transhumanist philosophy readily celebrate. Seeking to free themselves from the shackles of human embodiment and limitations of human nature, they actively desire to see the whole human condition evolve and progress. Taking this idea even further, posthumans present a possible future reality of creatures evolved from humanity but with key features and capabilities which distinguish them from present human beings so as to no longer be considered human in any significant degree.[3]

This battle of power won *by* humans and *over* humans is the focus of this chapter, specifically as it relates to its impact on relationships. Even the most cursory of reviews of the transhumanist literature reveals the acutely libertarian perspective of the aspirations underpinning the trans- and posthuman project. The desire for morphological freedom to be whoever you wish to be runs as one of its central tenets but with little real consideration of the implications for collective normative behaviour and wider society. What would it mean for posthumans and humans to live alongside one another? Is such harmony part of the plan or could it be along more dystopian lines involving the fracturing of humanity into disparate groups? What this means for relationships, not least between generators and those they have generated, becomes even more of a pressing question to consider.

This chapter explores the German philosopher Martin Heidegger's (1889–1976) idea of enframing[4] and applies it to how we perceive and relate to the human body. Does Heidegger's notion of standing reserve[5], meaning to see an object or subject as component parts of a technological process to accomplish some other goal, shed any light on how generators of new posthuman persons might relate to the new entities that they create? Heidegger's idea of enframing is considered in light of calls to follow a socialized proactionary approach, as opposed to a more precautionary one, in order to begin to experiment and realize a posthuman future. If technology is going to be used by generators to develop new kind of entities, to what extent does following the proactionary imperative contribute to enframing and considering the human body as standing reserve?

Heidegger and the question of technology

Martin Heidegger was an influential yet divisive twentieth-century philosopher. An original critical thinker, his ideas and unique perspective distinguishes him as a major intellectual of his generation. However, many condemn him as a counter-revolutionary and, along with his affiliation with the Nazi regime, dismiss his contribution to philosophical thought outright.[6] While acknowledging these conflicts, the fact remains that Heidegger's perspective on modern life and the place of technology within it causes him to be a philosopher worthy of consideration concerning technology and the future of humanity. In this chapter, I will draw upon his works *Being and Time* and *The Question Concerning Technology*.

It is necessary to map out some of Heidegger's key ideas and principles relevant to our discussion in order to then apply them to the specific question of relationships between generators and their generated entities. One such idea that underpins Heidegger's philosophy of technology is the essence of technology. He clearly writes that his aim is not to give a definitive account of 'what technology is', rather, his goal is to set out 'a way'.[7] A way that begins with calling into question our *relation* to technology. He wants us to be questioning concerning technology and by doing so, set up the dynamics for us to enter into a free relationship to it. The relationship will be free if it opens our human existence to the essence of technology. When we can respond to this essence, we shall be able to experience the technological within its own bounds.[8]

Typically, technology is considered as something 'other', as some activity that takes place 'out there' external to us, as a collection of *things* that one can choose to use or not or something that we *make* or *do*. It cannot be used to describe a set of instruments, nor is it a particular aspect of human activity. Heidegger considers this instrumentalization of technology as a misunderstanding on our part, arguing that 'technology is by no means anything technological'.[9] We might be experiencing the increased digitalization of society, with the proliferation of technological devices impacting our day-to-day lives and the automation of services, but to Heidegger the *essence* of technology remains the same. His concern is ontological, or as the American philosopher Iain Thomson puts it, 'ontological technologization, that is, with the disturbing and increasingly global phenomenon . . . by which entities are transformed into intrinsically meaningless resources standing by for optimization'.[10]

Technology is not something that we make but rather it is a mode of being or revealing. A key idea first set out in Heidegger's work *Being and Time* and subsequently developed in *The Question Concerning Technology* is how theoretical activities such as science and technology, help to reduce and narrow down our perception and understanding of how we interact and negotiate the ordinary world of action and concern.[11] The objective view that science and technology afford us, while of value, cannot provide us with the richness of understanding that we need. It obscures the essential being of many things including their nearness, or how we relate to them. Distance and nearness concern how close or far we are from the essence of things so as to encounter things in their truth. For example, as I look out my study window, I see a cherry tree. From a scientific perspective, the distance can be measured objectively and given a value of 10 metres. But the real distance between my house and the tree is not just based on physical measurement but relates to how intimately and distantly the tree and house concern me.[12] As I walk towards the tree, its shape becomes larger as my separation from the house increases. This results in what Heidegger refers to as *Gestell* [enframing].[13] While *Gestell* means frame or skeleton in German, to simply understand enframing as providing a framework through which we understand the world would be to miss Heidegger's deeper meaning here. In contrast to the poetic (*poiesis*) which refers to a 'bringing forth', enframing is more fundamentally a 'calling forth' or 'challenging claim' that is prompting a response and gathers together (into a framework or configuration that is constantly adjusting) so as to reveal. Consequently, we end up considering everything as 'standing reserve' – everything is imposed upon or 'challenged' to be an orderly resource for technical application, which in turn we take as a resource for further use.[14] Under technology, *everything* appears as a 'resource' to be exploited.

By merely restricting things to objective physical terms – the more we become indifferent to things that concern us – we in turn lose a true experience of nearness and distance. The danger of enframing is: 'Where this ordering holds sway, *it drives out every other possibility of revealing*.'[15] To illustrate this mode of revealing, Heidegger famously uses the example of the windmill and the river Rhine. While the windmill's sails turn in the wind, seemingly 'just as' the turbines in the plant turn in the flow of the Rhine, Heidegger claims that there is a fundamental difference. The sails turn in the wind but are at the mercy of the wind to make them turn. The wind is allowed to flow on its own. In contrast, the hydroelectric plant changes the flow of the river, unlocking the energy from its current and storing it.[16] The Rhine 'enframed' by the hydroelectric dam means that the water can be trapped by the plant in a way that a windmill could not do with the wind.

Technology as a way of beholding has transformed how we view the world around us. As we acknowledge other kinds of revealing and pay attention to other realms of truth and being, we begin to allow ourselves to experience the technological within its own bounds. For Heidegger the challenge is found not so much in that technology makes it harder for us to access that realm, but that its 'power' is so pervasive that it makes us forget that other realms even exist, obfuscating that free relationship which recognizes and understands that technology is but one kind of revealing.

Enframing and transhumanism

The importance and relevance of this transformation in our understanding of the world is nowhere more pertinent that in discussions surrounding technology and the human body. How we enframe the body cuts straight to some of the core issues concerning the philosophy of transhumanism and aspirations for achieving a posthuman future. From reviewing the literature, we can see the extent to which technological thinking sets us on a dangerous path of revealing of nature, and our own selves, as standing reserve.[17]

Transhumanism helps to promote 'an interdisciplinary approach to understanding and evaluating the opportunities for enhancing the human condition and the human organism opened up by the advancement of technology'.[18] Any form of technology which allows us to live longer and be stronger and smarter is embraced by transhumanism in order to get us out of the confinement of our human skin and arrive at something better – a 'post-human future'. Here, posthumans will possess vastly greater capacities than those we are presently able to experience.

In transhumanist thought, human nature is regarded as a 'work-in-progress, a half-baked beginning that we can learn to remold (*sic*) in desirable ways'.[19] Braden R. Allenby, American environmental scientist and attorney, and Daniel Sarewitz, professor of science and society at Arizona State University, do not share Heidegger's concerns that technology presents a distinctively new challenge that is present only in hydroelectric dams but absent in windmills. Due to us being a 'work-in-progress', we've always been challenged to take unto ourselves new technology in order to enhance ourselves.[20] As

Nick Bostrom, director of the Future of Humanity Institute at University of Oxford, and Toby Ord, moral philosopher, argue, while the human condition appears to have an irrational, built in, preference for the status quo, humanity needs to push for the 'new thing'; it is part of our evolutionary process to fulfil our biology.[21] Implanting a microchip in the brain to access data that we can control consciously and immediately is therefore considered as one way in which humans are to evolve beyond using the more humble notepad and pen to capture and store important details.

While it is fair to say that Heidegger would not consider enframing as 'fulfilling our biology', the challenge posed by making alterations to human thought and action arose long before transhumanism and human enhancement emerged.[22] This idea that we were cyborgs[23] from the moment humans first picked up a hammer and chisel to hone stone, or use some other tool to perform a task that we were unable to do on our own, is an idea advocated by many engaged in the field of human enhancement.[24] The British cognitive philosopher, Andrew Clark, writes:

> We humans have always been adept at dovetailing our minds and skills to the shape of our current tools and aids. But when those tools and aids start dovetailing back – when our technologies actively, automatically, and continually tailor themselves to us just as we do to them – then the line between tool and user becomes flimsy indeed.[25]

The line may be flimsy but to deny that the line exists at all would equally be a mistake. It must be acknowledged that there is a subtle phenomenological difference between my frail and ageing Grandmother using a walking frame to aid her mobility and exchanging it for a pair of robotic legs, designed by others, which may be strapped to her own legs to perform the act of walking for her. A 'flimsy' line may exist between the robotic legs and the frame, but the facility is *developed* by my Grandmother through interaction and practice, becoming extensions of part of her human body. This is something that we all engage in, to some extent, but is perhaps more distinctly witnessed through those living with disabilities.[26]

Enframing and the impact on identity and relationships

Developing this idea of enframing leads to implications for considering the relationship between generators of new persons and those they generate. A common concern voiced about human enhancement and particularly human–machine interfaces is that of ceding control to machines. Clark foresees any merging of human with machine as maintaining that which we have always experienced, as opposed to presenting any erosion of our ability to maintain control *over* machines.[27] Fear of an interconnectedness of devices taking control of us all is simply misplaced. Bailey argues that this is a rather naïve position.[28] The kind of control we have over technology and it has over us, may be no different in kind to the influence of existing technology on our lives; what warrants further reflection is the extension of that control over our *biology*. Advances in technologies which fall into the broad category of enhancing humanity may extend the reach to which they can enhance, improve and extend the lifespan of humanity, but the Heideggerian issue remains: the essence of technology to enframe – to make our primary, exclusive way of relation to the world through technology.[29] As Heidegger notes, 'Where this ordering holds sway, *it drives out every other possibility of revealing.*'[30]

The resonance of Heidegger's concept of enframing and seeing the human body as 'standing reserve' is pertinent. The danger of seeing the human body and the world around us as standing reserve prevents what Heidegger terms *Dasein* from its interconnectedness with the world.

Dasein is Heidegger's term for the specific kind of existence of humans, in that it is possessed by them individually. They make their own Being an issue for themselves; that is, they live philosophically, aware of their temporal finitude, and defined through their embeddedness in the world.[31] It is inseparable from time and space. *Being-in-the-world* is a condition of *Dasein*, a unified phenomenon. Without reference to a preexisting world of people, objects, relationships, language and culture, an individual's existence cannot be understood nor meaningfully detached from that world. In contrast to the German philosopher Edmund Husserl's (1859–1938) transcendental phenomenology, which focused on the scientific study of how things appear,[32] Heidegger posits that an individual's subjective experience cannot be just observed and described, but instead must be *interpreted* through or via the wider world of which they are a part.

Contrasting Heidegger with Cartesian dualism, whereas the French philosopher René Descartes (1596–1650) considered the world a collection of extended material objects for perception by a thinking mind, Heidegger's formulation binds the world to *Dasein* as an intrinsic existential element. Understanding of objects in the world of necessity involves comprehension of them in relational terms:

- *Ready-to-hand* = understood by *Dasein* in terms of use. For instance, a hammer is useful for hitting and pulling nails but can also be understood in the wider context of carpentry according to its own readiness-to-hand to chisels, planes, wood, nails and so forth[33].
- *Present-at-hand* = quality of objects that simply exist within the world.

As a result of *Dasein's* relation to a particular object there can be a shift between Ready-to-hand and Present-at-hand. Cartesian dualism can often be found at the heart of posthuman aspirations of human enhancement technologies such as mind-uploading, replication of life through silicon chips and super-intelligence. Thus, Heidegger's notion of *Dasein* and a unified relationship with the world might appear to run counter to transhumanism, which appears to seek to 'break free' from the body. However, the American scholar N. Katherine Hayles, a prominent thinker in posthuman studies, sets out her dream of posthumanism in which a posthuman is 'an amalgam, a collection of heterogenous components, a material-informational entity, whose boundaries undergo continuous construction and reconstruction'.[34] The human body is just an original form and substance of something that can be upgraded or improved upon, as opposed to something to be discarded or escaped from, tending to regard the body as something ready-to-hand as opposed to present-at-hand. While there is a difference in opinion as to the extent of the change, the fact remains that enframing challenges our ontological perspective.

One way in which we can seek to resist considering everything as merely standing reserve is to maintain an awareness of our own mortality. This of course runs counter to many of the claims and promises, based within transhumanism, that advances in biotechnology, cybernetics and neurotechnologies will enable the possibility for individuals to download (or 'upload') their consciousness into multiple bodies. Following this path, we give way to enframing: ordering ourselves and taking an *inauthentic* relation to our identity. This means that to properly contextualize technology in our lives means coming to grips with our own mortality. That we become who we are as human individuals, aiding the development of a sense of identity and self-possession as distinct from, but in relation to, another.

Positioning ourselves in the world through such a purely technological lens leads us to consider ourselves as technological producers. We become generators and consumers of identity that are subject to our own design and construction. Weakness, fallibility and finality are eradicated in favour of enhancement and improvement. We pursue a better version of ourselves free of the strife and challenges that resist and define us, but rather which we choose to define instead.

Heidegger warns that the Rhine, enframed by the dam and power plant, 'appears as something at our command'.[35] Transhumanism, on the other hand, attempts to turn the organic into the mechanical and, in so doing, we lose our orientation within the world, our individuality and our inter-relationality. Understandably, enframing the flesh causes it to be considered as a component part of a technological process to accomplish some other goal: what Heidegger defines as standing reserve. To resist this requires us to embrace our finitude and embodiment so that we can become authentic individuals.

Posthuman future

Enframing the body and considering it as standing reserve gives the impression that everything is at our command. In this regard, transhumanist philosophy appears to encapsulate everything that Heidegger warns against, possibly causing him to resist a posthuman future if he were alive today. But is this necessarily the case? Could an alternative reading of what transhumanism actually is align more closely with Heidegger's aspiration for the future of humanity? In other words, what about considering technology as only *one* way of being and integrating it into a whole way of life necessitating other ways of being.

For this to be possible, the origin of the term transhumanism would need to be revisited. Bostrom suggests the term was first used by the English evolutionary biologist Julian Huxley (1887–1975) in 1927[36]. Grandson of the biologist Thomas Henry Huxley (1825–95), who was famous as 'Darwin's Bulldog' for his defence of Charles Darwin's theory of evolution, Julian served as the first director-general of the United Nations Education, Scientific and Cultural Organization (UNESCO). However, both the date and attribution to him are contested particularly when one considers that Jean Coutrot (1895–1941), a French polytechnician and champion of the rational organization of work, appears to use it for the first time in 1939.[37] It is perhaps fairer to propose that Huxley was one of the first people to use the term to advance new ideas about the future of humanity in a lecture given in 1951, which was subsequently published in 1957 entitled 'Transhumanism'.[38] Huxley used the term to capture the idea that what distinguished *Homo sapiens* from other animals was that there is a qualitative difference between *knowing* how evolution works and simply *obeying* it. This distinctive position gives us an ability to act on it from the outside, providing us with opportunities and capabilities to take control of the direction of our evolution.[39]

The challenge, therefore, becomes one of re-asserting the case for human exceptionalism in comparison with other species and defending human beings. It is proposed that Heidegger would not take issue with the idea of human exceptionalism, as it appears to resist enframing the body and considering everything as standing reserve. Our distinctiveness as humans to innovate and progress in our understanding of the world around us appears to resonate with Huxley's idea of humanity having the ability to act on evolution from the outside. Challenges to this begin to emerge when we consider the promises of recent advances in the fields of nanotechnology, biotechnology, information technologies and cognitive science (often referred to NBIC), which promise opportunities of enhancing humanity.

The significance of such opportunities grows in importance when those behind the technology seek to extend their reach into the realm of generating entities that could be considered as beyond (or post-) human. Questions exist in terms of the relationship between the generators of such new persons and those so generated. In seeking to continue to defend the uniqueness of human beings, the question could be framed on the basis of attitudes to risk: whether risk is an opportunity or a threat to humanity. American philosopher-sociologist Steve Fuller argues that responses have tended to be over-precautionary in this regard. The precautionary principle, has been described as 'the Hippocractic oath applied to the global ecology: do no harm'.[40] In response, Fuller and legal scholar Lipinska have coined the term 'the proactionary principle', positing that the only barriers to indefinite extension of human progress and power are fear and ignorance, both of which can be overcome through greater knowledge.[41] In short, the precautionary principle views risk as a threat and something from which people need to be protected, whereas on the other hand, the proactionary principle considers risk an opportunity and something that is good for people. From a regulatory perspective, an overtly precautionary perspective results in policy decisions which aim to prevent the worst possible outcomes, while proactionary approaches aim to promote and advance opportunities. Precautionaries make a clear distinction between the actual world and other possible worlds. Any action resulting in an actual loss can never be compensated for in the attempt to try something new. Conversely, proactionaries accept the opportunity to sacrifice part of their present-day conditions in order to give space to pursue the 'new thing' and keep the future open. This means that an unsuccessful experiment or one which produces unexpected results is not considered a loss, but a learning experience.

Reflecting on these two approaches in the light of Heidegger's ideas of enframing and standing reserve, it initially appears that in relation to the question of generator–generated relationships, Heidegger's position better aligns with a precautionary approach. We are to resist viewing human flesh as standing reserve. Taking a risk to pursue such opportunities is not justified. However, could an alternative interpretation of Heidegger's ideas mean that the proactionary imperative should be pursued? A pursuit that would, in some way, form better relationships between generators and new persons?

This kind of alternative perspective understands the drive to progress and evolve as an inherently human imperative without reaching the extent of enframing the human body. Such a view can be seen as libertarian with its emphasis on the ability to do as one pleases, exercising freedom of choice and autonomy in making decisions. Indeed, these sentiments resonate with much of the transhumanism agenda with its focus on the individual and morphological freedom. However, one danger of such a libertarian take is that it can end up being anti-social, resulting in actions that adversely affect the consideration and well-being of others.

While the proactionary principle may well share aspects of a libertarian approach, it does not consider individual freedom as the ultimate end but as a means to an end for the flourishing and cultivation of humanity. Thus, if generators do use technology to develop new kinds of persons, it is surely better that the proactionary imperative is followed. With its proactive approach to managing risk and providing an environment within which wider experimentation can take place, it allows us to enter into a free relationship with technology. Persons who are far more than just standing reserve and an assembly of component parts can be generated. Instead, they would have a reference to nature, experience and the self. This new bio-social environment sees a new 'social contract' established whereby in return for an individual taking calculated life risks, they receive rewards, reparation or compensation. Wider societal benefits are the learning and insights gained from progress in science and technology,[42] thereby providing a better understanding of science as a public good.

This idea can be applied to the current crisis in pension provision. In this regard, a recent UK House of Lords report concluded that we are 'woefully underprepared'[43] for the consequences of people living longer. Many people are also, apparently, retiring too early, leading to cash flow challenges in terms of pensions provision and ensuring older people are able to have a quality of life they expected to enjoy in later life. As people live longer, they are not necessarily living healthier lives, meaning that the UK National Health Service is being faced with rising demands in care for growing numbers of people living with long-term chronic conditions. One part of the solution to solving this crisis may be to enable people to live healthier and longer lives and raise the retirement age. The English gerontologist Aubrey de Grey is developing Strategies for Engineered Negligible Senescence (SENS) which reverse the ageing process, allowing people to live longer and healthier lives. Contrary to popular opinion that de Grey wants us to live forever, his immediate goal is more concerned with anti-ageing therapies to add years to life expectancy in a faster way than age consumes them.[44]

Significantly, this involves more than just changes within the environment or society but also changing how people operate and function in their own bodies. As the level of data and insight increases from SENS changes, so does the ability to make interventions and changes to improve that level of functionality. Understandably this recapitulates the theme of control addressed earlier in this chapter and presents related implications for matters such as privacy and surveillance. In terms of a socialized proactionary 'social contract' the question is not so much related to what people are giving up in terms of their information but what people are getting back in return. This addresses the asymmetrical power relationship which often colours the enhancement debate, that it is all about the many giving up their data so that a powerful minority harnesses the benefits. This cuts straight to the heart of generator–generated relationships and raises valuable questions if posthuman futures are to be pursued. In order to avoid perceiving one another as simply being standing reserves, the approach should not be to protect them from risk at all cost. Rather it may be to ensure posthumans are part of the process and whatever they volunteer for, they are not so harmed that they could never function again. This appears to consider humans as more than a replacement part in a technological process (ready-to-hand), but retains something of what it means to innovate and experiment as humans and reimagines a new positive expectation with regard to science and technology.[45]

Conclusion

As we look ahead to the advances in science and technology enabling the generation of posthuman persons, Heidegger's ideas clearly speak into the conversation concerning any responsibilities that we might have towards them. He postulates that human beings relating to objects in a technological manner, results in them just seeing these objects as component parts of a process to accomplish some other goal. The red warning light on the dashboard of the human journey begins to flash for Heidegger, when enframing leads us to treat our technological relation to the world as our basic, definitive and indeed *only* way of being. It prevents *Dasein*; in other words, it inhibits humanity from understanding the world and its inhabitants as integral parts of its own existence. In the face of exponential change, the challenge is to resist enframing by allowing, instead, *Dasein* to flourish in its interconnectedness in-the-world, brought about by humans returning to being-in-the-world and ensuring a truly human approach to technology. But does this mean adopting an overly precautionary approach to a natural human desire to innovate and progress in our understanding and testing of ideas? Or can risks be mitigated in some way to allow this to occur?

In this chapter, we have explored how adopting a more socialized proactionary imperative may present a way forward that keeps in healthy tension our interconnectedness in-the-world and our attitudes to risks. It may be possible for us to enter into the kind of free relationship espoused by Heidegger, by establishing an environment that allows for the subjective experience of both the generator and the new person to interpret their being through the wider world of which they are a part. This would be a kind of mutually beneficial relationship which does not consider power as something residing with a minority, but dispersed and shared by the majority. Such an approach stands in contrast to the one that interprets and mediates relationships purely on the basis of scientific observation and definition. New applications of technology will always appear to usher in the promise of a better life. What must remain front and centre, however, is the question of what makes us distinctively human and that in part concerns how we relate to one another. It is both profound and prescient that C.S. Lewis's essay 'The Abolition of Man' opens by quoting from the English writer John Bunyan's (1628–1688) *Pilgrim's Progress*: 'It came burning hot into my mind, whatever he said and however he flattered, when he got me home to his house, he would sell me for a slave.'[46]

Notes

1. Jason Kirby, 'Why Business People Won't Stop Using that Gretzky Quote', *Macleans*, 24 September 2014. Available at: https://www.macleans.ca/economy/business/why-business-people-wont-stop-using-that-gretzky-quote/ (Accessed on 5 August 2020).
2. C. S. Lewis, 'The Abolition of Man', in *C.S. Lewis Selected Books* (London: HarperCollins, 2002), 420–1.
3. Calum Mackellar, ed., *Cyborg Mind: What Brain Computer and Mind-Cyberspace Interfaces Mean for Cyberneuroethics* (Oxford and New York: Berghahn Books, 2019), 163.
4. Martin Heidegger, *The Question Concerning Technology and Other Essays* (New York: Harper Perennial, 2013), 19.
5. Heidegger, *The Question Concerning Technology and Other Essays*, 17.
6. Mark Blitz, 'Understanding Heidegger on Technology', *The New Atlantis: A Journal of Technology and Society*, Winter (2014), 63.
7. Heidegger, *The Question Concerning Technology and Other Essays*, 3.
8. Heidegger, *The Question Concerning Technology and Other Essays*, 4.
9. Heidegger, *The Question Concerning Technology and Other Essays*, 4.
10. Iain Thomson, *Heidegger on Ontotheology: Technology and the Politics of Education* (New York: Cambridge University Press, 2005), 45.
11. Blitz, 'Understanding Heidegger on Technology', 67.
12. Graham Harman, *Heidegger Explained: From Phenomenon to Thing* (Peru: Open Court Publishing Company, 2007), 135.
13. Heidegger, *The Question Concerning Technology and Other Essays*, 19.
14. Heidegger, *The Question Concerning Technology and Other Essays*, 24.
15. Heidegger, *The Question Concerning Technology and Other Essays*, 27, emphasis added.
16. Heidegger, *The Question Concerning Technology and Other Essays*, 14, 16.
17. Jesse I. Bailey, 'Enframing the Flesh: Heidegger, Transhumanism and the Body as 'Standing Reserve'', *Journal of Evolution and Technology* 24, no. 2 (2014), 14.
18. Nick Bostrom, 'Transhumanist Values', in *Ethical Issues for the 21st Century*, ed. Frederick Adams (Philosophical Documentation Center Press, 2005), 3.
19. Bostrom, 'Transhumanist Values', 4.
20. Braden R. Allenby and Daniel R. Sarewitz, *The Techno-Human Condition* (Cambridge, MA: MIT Press, 2011), 15–16.
21. Nick Bostrom and Toby Ord, 'The Reversal Test: Eliminating Status Quo Bias in Applied Ethics', *Ethics*, 116.
22. Bailey, 'Enframing the Flesh', 6.
23. First coined in 1960 by Manfred Clynes and Nathan S. Kline, the term cyborg refers to a *cyb*ernetic *org*anism, a being with both organic and biomechatronic body parts; Manfred Clynes and N. S. Kline. 'Cyborgs and Space', *Astronautics*, September (1960), 26–76.

24 Allenby and Sarewitz, *The Techno Human Condition*. Andy Clark, *Natural-Born Cyborgs: Minds, Technologies, and the Future of Human Intelligence* (New York: Oxford University Press, 2004); Donna J. Haraway, 'A Cyborg Manifesto. Science, Technology and Socialist-Feminism in the Late Twentieth Century', in *Manifestly Haraway* (Minneapolis: University of Minnesota Press, 2016).
25 Clark, *Natural-Born Cyborgs*, 7.
26 Bailey, 'Enframing the Flesh', 6.
27 Clark, *Natural-Born Cyborgs*, 175.
28 Bailey, 'Enframing the Flesh', 6.
29 Bailey 'Enframing the Flesh', 7.
30 Heidegger, *The Question Concerning Technology and Other Essays*, 27, emphasis added.
31 Martin Heidegger, *Being and Time*, trans. Joan Stambaugh (Albany: SUNY Press, 1996), 2-3.
32 Edmund Husserl, *Ideas Pertaining to a Pure Phenomenology and to a Phenomenological Philosophy – First Book: General Introduction to a Pure Phenomenology*, trans. F. Kersten (Dordrecht: Kluwer Academic Publishers, 1983).
33 Heidegger, *Being and Time*, 92.
34 N. Katherine Hayles, *How We Became Posthuman: Virtual Bodies in Cybernetics, Literature and Informatics* (London: University of Chicago Press, 1999), 3.
35 Heidegger, *The Question Concerning Technology and Other Essays*, 16.
36 Nick Bostrom, 'A History of Transhumanist Thought', *Journal of Evolution and Technology* 14, no. 1 (2005), 6.
37 Olivier Dard, 'Jean Coutrot', *Sciences Po History Center*. Available at: http://chsp.sciences-po.fr/en/fond-archive/coutrot-jean (Accessed on 5 August 2020).
38 Huxley, Julian, 'Transhumanism', in *New Bottles for New Wine: Essays* (London: Chatto & Windus, 1957), 13-17.
39 Steve Fuller and Veronika Lipinski, *The Proactionary Imperative: A Foundation for Transhumanism* (Basingstoke: Palgrave Macmillan, 2014), 87.
40 Fuller and Lipinski, *The Proactionary Imperative*, 25.
41 Fuller and Lipinski, *The Proactionary Imperative*, 26.
42 Fuller and Lipinski, *The Proactionary Imperative*, 37.
43 Parliament. House of Lords. *Ready for Ageing?* (HL 2012-13 (140)). (London: The Stationary Office, 2013), 7.
44 Aubrey De Grey and Michael Rae, *Ending Aging: The Rejuvenation Breakthroughs That Could Reverse Humans Aging in Our Lifetime* (New York: St Martins Press, 2008), 336; Nicholas Agar, *Humanity's End: Why We Should Reject Radical Enhancement* (London: MIT Press, 2010), 83-4.
45 To do this, proposals have been made to reconsider how we go about volunteer experimentation in licensed laboratories and design social insurance models, so as to give the same level of respect for the volunteers' protection and welfare that we afford to jury service and those serving in the military. See: Steve Fuller, *Humanity 2.0. What it Means to be Human Past, Present and Future* (Basingstoke: Palgrave Macmillan, 2011), 160; Fuller and Lipinski, *The Proactionary Imperative*, 109.
46 Lewis, 'The Abolition of Man', 419.

8

Deliver us from (artificial) evil

Are the generators of Artificial Intelligences morally accountable for the actions of those they generate?

Trevor Stammers

Artificial intelligence (AI) pioneers and the wider transhumanist community have long been characterized by their exuberant and largely unbridled optimism. Back in 1945, the father of cybernetics, US mathematician Norbert Wiener aimed to 'show that machines can learn and reproduce themselves'.[1] While some forms of machine learning have developed rapidly in the succeeding seventy-five years, machine self-reproduction is barely at an embryonic stage. Nevertheless, Wiener's predictions are comparatively modest in comparison to those of his successors.

The title of Ray Kurzweil's *The Age of Spiritual Machines: When Computers Exceed Human Intelligence*[2] contains two hubristic presumptions – when, not if, machines become smarter than their creators, they will also be spiritual beings. Similarly, with science writer Pamela McCorduck's *Machines Who Think*,[3] rather than *Machines That Think*, the assumption of the book is clear before the reader reaches the first page.

Such over-realized secular eschatology is also evident in the timescales for the advent of super-intelligence. In 1970, US roboticist Marvin Minsky prophesied, 'in three to eight years, we will have a machine with the general intelligence of an average human being'.[4] Hans Moravec, founder of the robotics centre at Carnegie Mellon University, predicted that by 2040, 'robots will displace humans from essential roles. Rather quickly they could displace us from existence'.[5] By 2000, Bill Joy, Chief Scientist at Sun Microsystems[6] was optimistic enough to advance Moravec's timescale by ten years, claiming, 'By 2030, we are likely to be able to build machines, in quantity, a million times as powerful as the personal computers of today – sufficient to implement the dreams of Kurzweil and Moravec.'

Dreams, however, can easily morph into nightmares. Wendell Wallach and Colin Allen,[7] US ethicists, imagine a hypothetical apocalyptic scenario in which financial transaction software bots engage in unethical transactions leading to a chain of events in which hospitals are shut down, patients die and planes collide. These authors believe it is imperative to develop *moral* machines to prevent such evils. No human could oversee all the possible consequences of such complex interacting hardware systems.

Therefore, human limitations constitute their argument for developing effective artificial moral agents. However, the possibility of artificial *immoral* agents, deliberately programmed for evil intent, is never raised.

This chapter then considers the nature of evil, focusing on concepts of 'artificial evil' and how the potential for evil relates to embodiment. It discusses the moral agency and accountability of AIs and the responsibilities of their generators.

The nature of evil

Moral and natural evil

Theologian John Kekes believes: 'The way in which we understand evil is crucial to our conception of morality, and if we misconstrue evil we shall advocate an unsatisfactory morality.'[8] However, Kekes' definition of evil as 'that which harms human beings',[9] though easily understandable, is arguably incomplete and itself misconstrues evil by excluding nonhumans as victims of evil. AIs were understandably not Kekes' priority in 1988 but more recently, Oxford philosopher Luciano Floridi[10] has discussed AIs and moral evil.

Floridi and Sanders consider that a moral action 'can be constructed as an information process, that is, a series of messages (M) initiated by an agent *a*, that brings about a transformation of states directly affecting a patient *p*, which may interactively respond to the messages with changes and/or other messages'.[11] They add two clarifications regarding the nature of evil:

1. 'Evil' is a second order predicate that qualifies primarily the messages.[12]
2. The interpretation of an agent covers all agents, both human and non-human (such as animals and natural disasters.) The former agents cause moral evil and the latter cause natural evil.[13]

Floridi then paves the way for his 'ethics of information' by proposing a third, more controversial clarification of the nature of evil:

3. The positive sense in which an action is evil (an agent's intentional harming) is parasitic on the privative sense in which the effect is evil (the decrease in patient's welfare).[14]

He claims that actions should *only* be evaluated as evil in respect of the harm they may cause to their patients, that is, evil as effect rather than cause. This is a variation of Augustine's[15] concept of evil as *privatio boni* – in which evil is the privation of good rather than substantive in itself. Floridi then suggests we replace what he considers to be the zoo-centric term 'harm', with the more neutral term 'damage', with annihilation being the most severe form of damage.[16] At a stroke then, he frees the definition of evil entirely from its biological connections with living matter. You can damage a corpse but you cannot harm it. Such a redefinition, however, enables

Floridi to transpose evil out of biology entirely and into machines – from mothers to motherboards.

This knight's move from 'harm' to 'damage' facilitates Floridi's redefining of evil action as 'one or more negative messages initiated by an agent that bring about a transformation of states that (can) damage a patient's welfare severely and unnecessarily; or more briefly *any patient-unfriendly message*'.[17]

Artificial evil

If natural evil is evil that humans do not initiate and cannot prevent or control, it follows that natural evils will inevitably diminish, as our ability to control nature increases. We see this trend at work already in public reaction to many 'natural' disasters to find out who might be humanly responsible. Any evil arising from AIs might then be considered the moral responsibility of their generators, just as the 2018 Italian Ponte Morandi bridge collapse in Genoa was seen as the responsibility of its construction company, rather than the heavy rainfall at the time.[18]

The 'ethics of information', however, blurs the boundaries between natural and moral evil. As Floridi and Sanders quip, 'the giver of a coin can hardly be held responsible for decisions made on the basis of tossing it, even if the coin is sold as a binary decision-making mechanism'[19]. They agree that moral evil is that 'produced by a *responsible* natural autonomous agent'[20] (such as persons) but they suggest using the term Artificial Evil (AE) for evil produced by *artificial* autonomous agents such as lethal autonomous weapons. Concerning such agents whose behaviour is partly or totally independent of their human generators, Floridi suggests that the relationship to those generators may be similar to that of children to their parents.[21]

Responsibility for actions usually depends on the agent's self-awareness of the nature of the action and their capacity to exercise autonomy, free from coercion. However, if autonomy is redefined to merely being *self-regulating* in terms of agency, then though evil actions can be caused by such autonomous agents, those agents cannot be held morally responsible for them. This puts AIs in a similar category to pets 'which can cause all imaginable evils, but which cannot be morally responsible for their behaviour'.[22] Owners, however, can be held liable for the actions of their pets.[23]

There is a sense in which it is plausible to say that autonomy is being self-regulating in terms of agency, However, both 'self-regulating' and 'agency' have very different nuances when applied to humans than when applied to computers. Computers can be 'self-regulating', but to conclude that this is an entirely univocal sense of 'self-regulating' such as that applied to humans seems to be stretching language too far.[24]

Floridi, however, stretches even further than this. Since AIs are continually acted upon as patients of other AIs, he considers computer viruses and webbot attacks as evil actions upon an AI *as a patient* and employs the notion of entropy as a measure of the degree of such evil. Using a form of digital Benthamite utilitarian calculus, Floridi notes an entropy structure is an ordering in cyberspace considered as a bad state of change, where the values of the entropy ordering of all data is greater after the change than before. However, 'Entropy in Information Ethics (IE) is *not* meant to refer to the thermodynamic concept. .

..It is a metaphysical term and means Non-Being, or Nothingness. Metaphysical entropy is increased when a Being, interpreted informationally, is annihilated or degraded'.[25]

Critics of IE, however, point to the untenable egalitarianism in its moral valuation of information objects. 'From the point of view of IE, a work of Shakespeare is as valuable as a piece of pulp fiction, and a human being as valuable as a vat of toxic waste.'[26] Floridi counters this accusation by endorsing what he terms 'the goodness of being', – a metaphysical position that claims 'all entities are at least *minimally and overridably* valuable in themselves'.[27] However, it remains unclear what, other than Floridi's fiat, gives all entities such intrinsic value and what ethical principles determine which entities are more overridable than others.

AIs as moral agents

If machines can be considered to act autonomously in moral situations, the question arises as to whether they can react adequately to normative problems. However, the advent of AIs changes the meaning of what to 'react adequately' entails. As we have seen one argument *for* an autonomous moral status of computers is that humans may not be capable of living up to new ethical standards in an age of AI and *only* computers are able to do so.[28] Furthermore, as we are simply not able to reduce machine actions to human actions, the technology scholar Bernd Stahl[29] contends that we should ascribe moral responsibility to computers as a purely pragmatic solution, irrespective of any other considerations.

The Moral Turing Test

The Moral Turing Test (MTT) was proposed in 2000.[30] The original Turing test relies on an 'imitation game' of whether or not a computer can be distinguished from a human person by an observer engaging in computer keyboard conversation with both of them. If the observer cannot tell the difference, Turing considered the machine should be given the status of a person.[31] The MTT uses a similar approach. It is difficult even for philosophers and theologians to agree on what constitutes appropriate ethics, so the chances of answering the question of whether computers can reflect ethically, seem moot. Instead, if computers' behaviour is tested to see whether they pass for moral beings in an independent observer's view, then this could constitute a criterion to consider them as autonomous moral agents. An MTT might then bypass any disagreements about ethical standards by restricting the standard Turing test to *conversations* about morality. If human 'interrogators' cannot identify the machine at above-chance accuracy, the machine should be considered as a moral agent.[32]

Information, morality and meaning

Information is usually part of a group of related terms such as data, or knowledge. A brief definition found in most textbooks on informatics is that information is 'data with meaning'. Data is itself defined as 'a set of discrete, objective facts about events'[33] and 'When "data" acquires context-dependent meaning and relevance, it becomes information.'[34]

'Meaning', however, is itself a complicated term interlinked with philosophy of mind, social and cognitive processes, metaphysics and epistemology. In the academic discipline of information systems, definitions may be neglected, because students tend to understand through *examples*. Computers may process, for instance, huge amounts of sales data and produce an understandable and 'meaningful' chart of information. For the purposes of the determining an artificial autonomous moral agent, however, the term 'meaning' would need clarification.

Swiss philosopher, Werner Ulrich, believes information science and technology (IT) appears to have it 'wrong philosophically speaking, from the start. Their conceptual and technical tools basically deal with the processing and transmission of signals (or messages, streams of signs) rather than with "information"'.[35] Stahl further argues that the moral quality of an action does not depend on any objective criteria but rather is a social construction that considers the relevant aspects of a situation.[36] In order for moral actors to participate in a social construct, they must understand the meaning of the situation to have a complete picture of the information at hand. This includes the capacity to decide which information is relevant and which is not. The ethical construction of an observer witnessing a boy push an elderly woman off the pavement into the road might be different if the boy turned out to be the woman's nephew due to inherit her fortune, rather than a total stranger who saw a child scooting on the pavement and about to knock the woman flying. There are no algorithms to decide *a priori* which data is relevant and which is not. Human beings are able to make that decision because they are in the situation and they create the relevant reality through interaction with it. Computers, however, do not know which part of the data they process is relevant for ethical evaluation because they are not aware of the context that gives it meaning.

A computer would need to understand the situation in question in order to participate competently in a dialogue about it in any Moral Turing Test that would allow the 'interrogator' to determine whether she is dealing with a moral agent. That means the machine would have to know the internal states of moral agents, the social process of constructing attribution of responsibility and the social background of accepted morality. These three aspects are closely connected and they are only accessible through an understanding of the entire situation.

Colin Allen maintains that computers can make moral statements[37], which implies that they understand moral meanings. Stahl's counterargument is based on Ludwig Wittgenstein's idea that 'the meaning of a word is in its use in the language'.[38] In order for a computer to be able to pass the MTT, it would have to understand a language, meaning it would have to be part of that language's use and development. This, for Stahl, is something of which computers are incapable.[39]

A key question then is how computers might progress from being data processors to real information processors; how can they access the meaning of the data they process? This same question applies to human beings. How do humans access the meaning of their sensory input?

The answer seems to be that humans grow into being moral agents by socialization, enculturation and learning. In order to understand the meaning, one has to be in the situation, to be 'in the world' in a Heideggerian sense,[40] to share a life-world with others. The life-world is the background of the understanding of meaning, the necessarily shared resource that allows communication, and that constitutes individual meaning acquired though social experience. This brings us again to the analogy of full moral AIs relationship with their generators being like that of children to parents. In order to acquire a life-world, an agent arguably needs to be embodied, to have emotions, and be able to connect with other participants in discourses on an equal level.

AIs, embodiment and evil

Monash University's Daniel Black raises the relationship of meaningful conceptions of harm being necessarily linked with embodiment. He argues that our behaviour towards other people is not primarily driven by a 'conscious belief in their possession of an invisible interior mental and emotional life, but rather by a pre-conscious affective response to their bodily exterior'.[41] This is seen, for example, in the emotional response of relatives to seeing a loved one who is brain dead, whose heart is still beating, and who is apparently breathing on a ventilator.

Black also raises the interesting possibility of a reverse Turing Test. In the original Turing Test, the machine's 'personhood' is attributed by independent observers to its responses to their questions. 'But if our belief in the personhood of any other body – human or machine – ultimately results from a subjective attribution arising from our perceptions, could exposure to a sufficiently human-like robot alter this attribution in such a way that we feel less empathy or shared humanity with real human beings?'[42] Rather than necessarily expanding the community of those considered deserving of human compassion and respect, 'such human-like robots could cause a shrinking of those boundaries, such that they no longer encompass even some human beings'.[43] Such an unintended potential for increased levels of evil directed at fellow human beings would surely be the responsibility of those generating such humanoid AIs?

What exactly constitutes the embodiment of AIs is contested among their generators; there is 'a perplexing diversity of notions of embodied cognition'.[44] While some regard the body as a sensorimotor interface enabling cognitive computational processes to engage with the environment,[45] others consider that human cognition is necessarily embedded in biological mechanisms. Such a 'multi-tiered affectively embodied view'[46] is very different from the interface view. Some roboticists maintain, 'current robotic technologies cannot have intentional states any more than is feasible within the sensorimotor variant of embodied cognition'.[47] This has marked implications for the current limits of robot autonomy and the accountability of its generators for its actions. Initiatives to link advances in cognitive science and synthetic biology (SB), such as the SB-AI workshops[48] may see an eventual merging of biological and mechanical systems but this is not yet a reality.

AIs, agency and accountability

The possibility of fully moral machines appears far less plausible in the light of evidence that moral perception is biologically based in both humans[49] and nonhuman animals.[50] The evolution of moral behaviours, such as nurturing and empathy, is also associated with the avoidance of pain and suffering, both of which are only possible with biological embodiment. Though a robot could be considered as damaged if one of its component parts were crushed, it would not suffer from such an injury as it is not 'truly embodied in the way that living creatures are'.[51] It is of course entirely possible that AIs could be programmed to react in a way that mimics visible bodily responses to pain and pleasure. However, the experience of either of these sensations, let alone to feel existential anguish and mental suffering, requires consciousness. Since we are still in the very earliest stages of understanding the nature of biological consciousness, the likelihood of replicating it into algorithms, even putting aside the ethical problems of so doing, is currently negligible.

In a 2018 TEDx talk,[52] UK bioethicist Calum MacKellar discusses whether an AI could ever experience suffering. He argues that though suffering is something we rightly seek to avoid as human beings, there are important capacities inextricably linked to the experience of suffering. These include the ability to empathize, as well as to feel and show compassion. He also suggests that other important moral intuitions and concepts, such as justice, punishment, trust, responsibility, free will and self-transcendence, either cannot exist or would become markedly attenuated in a world without suffering. This raises the moral dilemma that if it is unethical for an AI's generator to programme the ability to feel pain into it, could it ever feel compassion or behave compassionately? Arguably, without the ability to suffer, its capacity for evil might be completely unrestrained, as it has no understanding of empathy either.

Another reason for scepticism that AIs might ever become full moral agents is that they are intrinsically dependent upon their generators – 'tethered creatures',[53] as they have been aptly dubbed. Such dependency again recalls the analogy of the child–parent relation for the way autonomous artificial agents might relate to their generators. Recognizing the limitations of programming morality into an AI, 'the only way to expose them to the wealth of human moral situations and communicative interactions'[54] is to raise them within human families. It would be interesting to see how many scientists creating such AIs would be willing to 'volunteer' their own households for such a task.

While some assert, 'Robots with moral decision-making abilities will become a technological necessity'[55] or even that AI decision-making may be morally superior to that of humans,[56] such claims are open to several challenges. Brozek and Janik question whether AIs could ever be moral decision-makers at all. This is because in humans, 'the decisions in question would not result from applying . . . rules, but rather from the embodied moral intuitions, shaped over many years in social interactions'.[57] They touch on two key elements of morality here. Firstly, most moral decision-making is done subconsciously by emotionally linked intuitions[58] and secondly 'there is no morality without community'.[59] Human moral intuitions are inseparable from an internal emotional landscape moulded by decades of evaluation of experiences in varying contexts. Furthermore, moral rules are developed and negotiated by social engagement with other members of the moral community.

Even if AIs could become full moral agents, there is debate over whether they *should* be generated in this way. A recent paper[60] examines the most frequently advanced arguments for the creation of artificial moral agents – inevitability, prevention of harm to humans, complexity, public trust, prevention of immoral use, the superiority of machine moral reasoning over human morality and a better understanding of morals – and finds them all wanting. For example, with regard to the prevention of harm to humans, the authors categorize the issue at stake as one of safety, rather than moral agency of AIs. The roboticist Noel Sharkey crisply corroborates their point:

> This is not just being picky about semantics. Anthropomorphic terms like 'ethical' and 'humane', when applied to machines, lead us to making more and more false attributions about robots further down the line. They act as linguistic Trojan horses that smuggle in a rich interconnected web of human concepts that are not part of a computer system or how it operates.[61]

Even if we grant that AIs with full moral agency could and should be generated, issues around their accountability and how the law should treat them need to be resolved. US lawyer Gabriel Halevi makes some ingenious attempts to modify existing American law on sentencing humans, to apply to both individual and corporate AI crime.[62] For example, he equates capital punishment with system shutdown of an AI. Ensuring such shutdown AIs are not switched on again is, however, a far more difficult task than preventing resurrection from the dead for humans. Some of Halevi's other analogies stretch credibility even further. Though rightly acknowledging that imprisonment of AIs will achieve neither retribution nor deterrence since they neither suffer nor fear, he suggests that AIs can be deprived of their liberty and incapacitated 'by restricting their activities for a specified period of time and under strict supervision. During this time, the AI system may be repaired to prevent the commission of further offenses. Repair of the AI system may be more efficient if the system is incapacitated, especially if it is done under court order'.[63]

Other authors, however, are unconvinced by this and remain concerned about the existence of a responsibility gap, which cannot be filled by repairing an AI or shutting it down. In a detailed discussion of Automated Weapon Systems (AWS), Stanford ethicist Johannes Himmelreich concludes, 'Although AWS give rise to several serious moral quandaries, the responsibility gap is not one of them. When an AWS harms someone, the commander may be responsible – at least as far as this concerns the condition that the commander must be in control.'[64] Similarly, Sven Nyholm, though attributing some 'fairly sophisticated agency' to AIs, thinks, 'we ought not to regard them as acting on their own, independently of any human beings. Rather, the right way to understand the agency exercised by these machines is in terms of human–robot collaborations, where the humans involved initiate, supervise and manage the agency of their robotic collaborators'.[65] He concludes that rather than focusing on individual agency when AIs cause harm or death, we should turn to theory and law on collaborative agency where some agents are under the orders and supervision of others. Those who give and programme orders, bear overall responsibility for evil actions of their algorithmic offspring.

Conclusions

The predictions of would-be generators of transhuman and posthuman AIs, historically have been over-optimistic both about timescales and about what might be possible to achieve. While a limited form of agency in terms of self-regulation of AIs will continue to be developed, there are currently good reasons for doubt that AIs could have full moral agency. If this possibility did ever arise from ongoing research involving informatics and synthetic biology, *should* they be given it?

Embodiment involving some biological basis is almost certainly necessary for any AI to be accountable, and their generators would likely bear full or partial responsibility for evil actions carried out by such agents. Unintended harms, such as desensitization of people to violence, facilitated by faciality of humanoid robots, could lead to their generators being held morally, if not legally, accountable. Attempts by information ethicists to reconfigure the morality of actions and their agents into the currency of entropy have limited scope and application. Though AIs may or may not be capable of Artificial Evil, they are certainly capable of actual evil for which those who bring them into being will bear or share responsibility.

Notes

1. Norbert Wiener, *Cybernetics: Or Control and Communication in the Animal and the Machine*, 2nd edn (Cambridge, MA: MIT Press, 1961), 172.
2. Ray Kurzweil, *The Age of Spiritual Machines: When Computers Exceed Human Intelligence* (New York: Penguin Books, 2000).
3. Pamela McCorduck, *Machines Who Think* (Natick, MA: A K Peters, 2004).
4. Marvin Minsky, 'Interview with LIFE Magazine', 20 November 1970.
5. Hans Moravec, *Robot: Mere Machine to Transcendent Mind* (Oxford: Oxford University Press, 1998), 3.
6. Bill Joy, 'Why the Future Doesn't Need Us', *Wired*, 4 January 2000. https://www.wired.com/2000/04/joy-2/
7. Wendell Wallach and Colin Allen, *Moral Machines: Teaching Robots Right From Wrong* (Oxford: Oxford University Press, 2009).
8. John Kekes, 'Understanding Evil', *American Philosophical Quarterly* 25, no. 1 (1988), 13–24, 13.
9. Kekes, 'Understanding Evil', 13.
10. Luciano Floridi and J. W. Sanders, 'Artificial Evil and the Foundation of Computer Ethics 2000', https://uhra.herts.ac.uk/bitstream/handle/2299/1818/901811.pdf (Accessed on 31 January 2021).
11. Floridi and Sanders, 'Artificial Evil and the Foundation of Computer Ethics', 6.
12. Floridi and Sanders, 'Artificial Evil and the Foundation of Computer Ethics', 6.
13. Floridi and Sanders, 'Artificial Evil and the Foundation of Computer Ethics', 7.

14 Floridi and Sanders, 'Artificial Evil and the Foundation of Computer Ethics', 7.
15 Augustine, *The Enchridion*, Chapter 11. https://www.ccel.org/ccel/schaff/npnf103.iv.ii.xiii.html
16 Floridi and Sanders, 'Artificial Evil and the Foundation of Computer Ethics', 9.
17 Floridi and Sanders, 'Artificial Evil and the Foundation of Computer Ethics', 9, Italics mine.
18 Sabina Castelfranco, 'Inquiry into Genoa bridge Collapse Highlights Poor Maintenance, Design Flaws 2020', https://www.rfi.fr/en/europe/20201226-inquiry-into-genoa-bridge-collapse-highlights-poor-maintenance-design-flaws (Accessed on 30 January 2021).
19 Floridi and Sanders, 'Artificial Evil and the Foundation of Computer Ethics', 28.
20 Floridi and Sanders, 'Artificial Evil and the Foundation of Computer Ethics', 19, Italics in original. The authors do not define 'responsible'.
21 Floridi and Sanders, 'Artificial Evil and the Foundation of Computer Ethics', 20.
22 Floridi and Sanders, 'Artificial Evil and the Foundation of Computer Ethics', 20.
23 Rebecca J. Huss, 'Valuing Man's and Woman's Best Friend: The Moral and Legal Status of Companion', *Animals Marquette Law Review* 56 (2002), 48–105.
24 I am grateful to Dr Richard Playford for this point.
25 Luciano Floridi, 'Information Ethics: A Reappraisal', *Ethics and Information Technology* 10 (2008), 189–20, 200.
26 Philip Brey, 'Do We Have Moral Duties Towards Information Objects?' *Ethics and Information Technology* 10 (2008), 109–14, 112.
27 Floridi, 'Information Ethics: A Reappraisal', 194.
28 William Bechtel, 'Attributing Responsibility to Computer Systems', *Metaphilosophy* 16 (1985), 296–306.
29 Bernd Carsen Stahl, 'Information, Ethics, and Computers: The Problem of Autonomous Moral Agents', *Minds and Machines* 14 (2004), 67–83, 69.
30 Colin Allen et al., 'Prolegomena to Any Future Artificial Moral Agent', *Journal of Experimental and Theoretical Artificial Intelligence* 12 (2000), 251–61.
31 Alan M. Turing, 'Computing Machinery and Intelligence', *Mind* 59 (1950), 433–60.
32 Allen et al., 'Prolegomena to Any Future Artificial Moral Agent', 254.
33 T. H. Davenport and L. Prusak, *Working Knowledge: How Organizations Manage What They Know* (Boston, MA: Harvard Business School Press, 1998), 2.
34 Werner Ulrich, 'A Philosophical Staircase for Information Systems Definition, Design, and Development', *Journal of Information Technology Theory and Application* 3, no. 3 (2001), 55–84, 56.
35 Ulrich, 'A Philosophical Staircase for Information Systems Definition, Design, and Development', 59.
36 Stahl, 'Information, Ethics, and Computers: The Problem of Autonomous Moral Agents', 79.
37 Allen et al., 'Prolegomena to Any Future Artificial Moral Agent', 251–61.
38 Ludwig Wittgenstein, *Philosophical Investigations/Philosopische Untersuchungen*, trans. G. E. M. Anscombe, 3rd edn (Oxford: Blackwell, 2001), 18.
39 Stahl, 'Information, Ethics, and Computers: The Problem of Autonomous Moral Agents', 80.
40 Martin Heidegger, *Being and Time*, trans. John Macquarrie (Martino Fine Books, 2019).
41 Daniel Black, 'Machines with Faces: Robot Bodies and the Problem of Cruelty', *Body and Society* 25 (2019), 3–27, 4.

42 Black, 'Machines with Faces: Robot Bodies and the Problem of Cruelty', 5.
43 Ibid.
44 Tom ZImkie, 'The Body of Knowledge: On the Role of the Living Body in Grounding Embodied Cognition', *Biosystems* 148 (2016), 4–11, 4.
45 Rodney Brooks, 'The Engineering of Physical Grounding', in *Proceedings of The Fifteenth Annual Conference of the Cognitive Science Society* (Boulder, CO: Lawrence Erlbaum Associates, Inc, 1993), 153–4.
46 Jaak Panksepp, 'Affective Consciousness: Core Emotional Feelings in Animals and Humans', *Consciousness and Cognition* 14 (2005), 30–80.
47 Slawomir J. Nasuto and Yoshikatsu Hayashi, 'Anticipation: Beyond Synthetic Biology and Cognitive Robotics', *Biosystems* 148 (2016), 22–31, 22.
48 Pasquale Stano, Yutetsu Kuruma and Luisa Damiano, 'Synthetic Biology and (Embodied) Artificial Intelligence: Opportunities and Challenges', *Adaptive Behavior* 26 (2018), 41–4. The workshops began in 2016.
49 Patricia Churchland, *Braintrust: What Neuroscience Tells us About Morality* (Oxford: Princeton University Press, 2011).
50 Jessica Pierce and Marc Bekoff, 'Wild Justice Redux: What We Know About Social Justice in Animals and Why It Matters', *Social Justice Research* 25 (2012), 122–39.
51 Amanda Sharkey, 'Can Robots be Responsible Moral Agents? And Why Should We Care?' *Connection Science* 29 (2017), 210–16. https://doi.org/10.1080/09540091.2017.1313815
52 Calum Mackellar, 'The Suffering Robot', *TEDx Talk*, 2018. https://www.youtube.com/watch?v=nrUT7-qWo38
53 Deborah G. Johnson and Keith W. Miller, 'Un-Making Artificial Moral Agents', *Ethics and Information Technology* 10 (2008), 123–33.
54 Betram F. Malle and Matthias Scheutz, 'Moral Competence in Social Robots', in *Presented at the IEEE International Symposium on Ethics in Engineering, Science, and Technology*, Chicago, 2014, 30–5. https://ieeexplore.ieee.org/document/6893446
55 Wendell Wallach, 'Implementing Moral Decision-Making Faculties in Computers and Robots', *AI & Society* 22 (2007), 463–75. https://doi.org/10.1007/s00146-007-0093-6
56 Ronald C. Arkin, *Governing Lethal Behavior in Autonomous Robots* (Boca Raton, FL: Chapman and Hall, 2009).
57 Bartosz Brozek and Bartosz Janik, 'Can Artificial Intelligences be Moral Agents?' *New Ideas in Psychology* 54 (2019), 101–6, 103.
58 See for example Jonathan Haidt, 'The Emotional Dog and Its Rational Tail; a Social Intuitionalist Approach to Moral Judgement', *Psychological Review* 108 (2001), 814.
59 Brozek and Bartosz, 'Can Artificial Intelligences be Moral Agents?' 103.
60 Aimee van Wynsberghe and Scott Robbins, 'Critiquing the Reasons for Making Artificial Moral Agents', *Science and Engineering Ethics* 25 (2019), 719–35.
61 Noel Sharkey, 'The Inevitability of Autonomous Robot Warfare', *International Review of the Red Cross* 94, no. 886 (2012), 787–99. https://doi.org/10.1017/S1816383112000732
62 Gabriel Hallevi, *When Robots Kill: Artificial Intelligence Under Criminal Law* (Boston: Northeastern University Press, 2013). http://web.a.ebscohost.com.stmarys.idm.oclc.org/ehost/ebookviewer/ebook/ZTAwMHh3d19fNTU4Mjc1X19BTg2?sid=a556395f-a331-436b-985c-26e75017734e@sessionmgr4008&vid=0&format=EB&lpid=lp_156&rid=0
63 Hallevi, *When Robots Kill: Artificial Intelligence Under Criminal Law*, 168.

64 Johannes Himmelreich, 'Repsonsibility for Killer Robots', *Ethical Theory and Moral Practice* 22 (2019), 731–47. https://doi.org/10.1007/s10677-019-10007-9
65 Sven Nyholm, 'Attributing Agency to Automated Systems: Reflections on Human–Robot Collaborations and Responsibility Loci', *Science and Engineering Ethics* 24 (2018), 1201–19. https://doi.org/10.1007/s11948-017-9943-x

Part IV

Theological aspects in generating transhuman and posthuman persons

9

A Jewish outlook

A Jewish case study in creating transhuman and posthuman persons

Deborah Blausten

Introduction

The rabbi gazed fondly on his creature
And with some terror.
How (he asked himself)
Could I have engendered this grievous son,
And left off inaction, which is wisdom?

At the hour of anguish and vague light
He would rest his eyes on his Golem
Who can tell us what God felt,
As He gazed on His Rabbi in Prague?[1]

The legend of the Golem is a rabbinic thought experiment in the limits of human creativity that has acquired layers of legal, mystical and cultural significance over almost two millennia. Golem stories tell of a living creature created by humans, the most well-known of which is the legend of Rabbi Judah Loew's Golem, The Golem of Prague. It is this Golem, a creature that stories describe as being created to protect a community but which rampaged through the streets of Prague until it was finally subdued by its generator, that has become an archetypal cautionary tale in the generation of trans- or posthuman beings. When speaking at the unveiling of The Weizmann Institute's new computer in 1965 the Kabbalist and Golem scholar Gershom Scholem (1897–1982) recounted this version of the Golem story. Scholem remarked to the assembled audience that his advice to the computer, which he had suggested be known as Golem Aleph (a), was that it should 'develop peacefully and don't destroy the world'.[2] An example of moral behaviour that may be of interest to ethicists, since it represents a cautionary voice that speaks directly to the potential consequences of unleashing new beings into the world.

The Golem's literary existence is vast, and interest in the notion of a Golem has enjoyed significant resurgence in the biotech era. There is, however, a significant difference between the Golem of art, film and twentieth-century literature and the Golem of classical and religious Jewish texts. It is the latter, a creature which functions as a core idea in both *halachic* (Jewish legal) discussion around issues of bioethics and in a subset of *responsa* (rabbinic legal responses) that interrogate the Golem's legal responsibility and standing within a community, that is of interest in this piece. The rabbinic approach to the question of whether a novel being can be brought into existence, and what considerations apply to that generated being, is a unique case study of applied rabbinic decision-making and the way that legal and ethical considerations inform religious rulings about the status of such beings and their relation to their generator(s). In a field that deals in a large part with questions of the new and not-yet, classical texts like those pertaining to the Golem can help anchor religious reasoning and provide helpful historical and social context to contemporary ethical debates.

From Gavra to Golem – on creating and created beings

The Babylonian Rabbi Abba ben Joseph bar Ḥama (c. 280–352), who was known as 'Rava', created[3] a man, explains the narrative voice of the Talmud in Sanhedrin 65b, introducing a short narrative that underpins almost all Jewish religious conversation about the Golem.[4]

> Rava says: If the righteous wish, they can create a world, as it is stated (Isaiah 59:2): 'But your iniquities have separated between you and your God'. Rava created a man, and sent him before Rabbi Zeira. Rabbi Zeira would speak to him but he would not reply. Rabbi Zeira said to him: 'You were created by one of my colleagues.[5] Return to your dust.'

This third-century encounter, arguably the earliest example of the Turing test, appears to suggest that humans, should they be sufficiently righteous, can create a living being. Rava does not succeed, because his creation is lacking the power of speech and thus Rabbi Zeira deduces that he is not a man and destroys it; however, the text establishes the principle that should someone possess a sufficient degree of righteousness they would be able to bring another being into existence. The gemara (a layer of text within the Talmud)[6] continues to detail, in support of the idea that the righteous can create worlds, that the fourth-century Jewish scholars Rav Hanina and Rav Oshya would sit and read *Sefer Yetzirah* (The Book of Creation) on Shabbat, and as a result of their study, a calf would be created for them to eat.[7]

What these texts cannot tell a contemporary reader is whether these stories were originally told to set limits on human attempts to bring into existence new humanoid life, because if this was impossible for even the righteous Rava, then such a generation was certainly beyond the ability of an ordinary person, or whether they begin to offer a mystical blueprint for mirroring God's creative acts.[8]

This story in Sanhedrin does not use the word 'Golem', a word that is best translated in relation to its Hebrew root *g-l-m* as meaning unformed or unfinished, but instead *gavra*, which means man. The use of this term should be noted, and perhaps aid the contemporary reader in dismissing images of cartoon Golems or other artistic figures from their imagination when reading these texts. The *gavra* of Sanhedrin does not become formally associated with the term Golem until the twelfth century.[9] What is notable about this story in Sanhedrin is that it appears to be far from exceptional. It is apparently unproblematic in the eyes of the individuals involved that a person might generate another person, and the only necessary qualification is sufficient righteousness.

J. David Bleich, a much respected orthodox legal authority in the field of medical and bioethics, notes that a casual relationship with the boundaries of human creativity is something that marks Jewish tradition as distinct from other faith traditions, explaining:

There is no reflection in Jewish tradition of a doctrine that establishes a global prohibition forbidding man to tamper with known or presumed *teloi* of creation.... Man has been given license to apply his intellect, ingenuity and physical prowess in developing the world in which he has been placed subject only to limitations imposed by the laws of the Torah, including the general admonition not to do harm to other, as well as by the constraints imposed by good sense and considerations of prudence.[10]

In b Kiddushin 30b,[11] the sages recount that there are three partners in the generation of a person: the two parents and God. This text, and other similar Talmudic dicta that imagine humans as God's partners in the work of creation, function as part of a philosophical and legal ecosystem that allows for the generation of new beings by humans. Where Rava failed, a more worthy partner might not.[12]

Rather than an affront to God, the successful generation of another being by applied religious knowledge is a mark of devotion. The limits on that creativity are laws such as prohibitions regarding idol worship, which would allow for the bringing into existence of a being in the image of God or subject to earthly law, but not one generated to be viewed and treated as a deity. There is some suggestion that stories of the animation of the Golem have at times been created as a response to the animation of statues in other ancient near eastern cultures, and that the Golem's less than full human state in many stories is a commentary on parallel contemporary practices.[13]

Missing from the story of Rava's *gavra* is the method by which the man was created. The subsequent reference to *Sefer Yetzirah* with regard to the calf leads the medieval commentator Rashi to infer that it was through the methods contained within this text that the *gavra* was created.[14] *Sefer Yetzirah* is a mystical work that details the creative power of letter combinations. Words are 'God's instrument of creation' in the Genesis 1 creation story, and their use in this way functions as a permitted kind of magic.[15] The focus of discussions about the creative act is, however, not on the created being, but rather on the knowledge, mystical experience and status of its creator.

Whereas Rava's creation is known only as a man, Adam, the first human, is referred to as a Golem in midrash.[16] The account found in the Midrash Tanchuma manuscripts' rendering of the creation of Adam originally detailed in Genesis 2, gives a sense that Golem is an intermediate stage before the final full human is brought into existence.[17]

Adam is 'stood up' as a Golem in-between God's assembling of earth to create him, forming limbs and imbuing the creation with a soul. The model of creation, being formed from the earth, appears frequently in later Golem stories, but the detail of relevance in this discussion is the notion of a Golem as a fully formed being that has all the characteristics of a human except for a soul. In this way, the Golem stage of Adam's creation is much closer to the etymological meaning of the term Golem, even though the reference Golem for legal rulings appears to be the one generated by Rava.

The philosopher and scholar of Jewish mysticism Gershom Scholem produced the first comprehensive history of the development of the Golem from Talmudic ideas to then contemporary literature, work that was later expanded and critiqued by another scholar of Jewish mysticism, Moshe Idel. Both trace the development of the idea of a Golem from these earlier layers of rabbinic tradition to medieval writings in different parts of the Jewish world, where there are significant differences between the Ashkenazi and Sephardi traditions in their understanding of how a Golem was to be made, but these are largely mystical concerns focused on the methodology of Golem making. The term Golem might best be understood as a category in which we can group these various creative endeavours, even if those discussing them might not have chosen that particular vocabulary. That creating a Golem is permitted, and that several possible blueprints exist, is not debated, rather the texts are concerned with methodology, and whether anyone can sufficiently attain the levels of study and piety required to complete the task.

The ability to generate a Golem was an important measure of religious status. As Rabbi Byron Shwerin writes with regard to German Hasidim:

> One clear indication of having achieved piety, they believed, was the ability, inherent in the truly pious, to create life. Therefore among them, the creation of the Golem came to be viewed as a mystical rite of initiation. . . . By penetrating the mystery of creation, by becoming a creator, one came to experience the mystical rapture of oneness with *the* Creator. The creative experience thus became a conduit to mystical ecstasy'[18]

The foundational rabbinic layers of Golem stories are of relevance because of the importance they place on the state of mind and piety of the generator. They establish a principle that the bringing into existence of other beings is a question not just of the status and nature of those that are generated but also of the intent and characteristics of their generators. Classically, this related to their piety and religious observance, because the generation in question is one that is performed using religious tools. Should a new method for the bringing into existence of beings emerge, as humans discover new ways to interact with the raw materials given to us on this earth, then extrapolating from this tradition would be appropriate to raise parallel questions about the fitness of a generator to make use of those tools.

Golem making, in a sense that is relevant to the question at hand, entered Halakhic literature in the seventeenth century. It is at this point that the disparate traditions of man-made creatures converge into a cannon of legal texts that both ask questions about the Golem itself, and employ the Golem as a device in halachic reasoning. Both of these categories of responsa engage with fundamental ethical questions about the creation of trans- and posthuman beings. From rabbinic writings that engage with the Golem in this way, it is possible to gain a fuller perspective on the nature of Jewish ethical responses to this evolving field. Perhaps surprisingly, there is not significant divergence between Jewish denominations with regard to more recent religious rulings that engage with the Golem, particularly those that discuss cloning and definitions of humanity. Nevertheless, for completeness, where relevant I will note the denominational provenance.[19]

Halacha of the Golem

The Hacham Tzvi and his son Jacob Emden are two of the first rabbinic authorities to explore the halachic status of the Golem. Though these were largely theoretical discussions, the layers of engagement with the questions they raise are now transferable to other similar contexts made possible by scientific advancements.[20] Their questions related to the status of the Golem, and whether once created it could be counted in the number required to reach a *minyan*, a prayer quorum. The Hacham Tzvi's initial ruling was that just as the deeds of the righteous are considered their progeny, so the Golem, created by a righteous person, could be deemed progeny. However, because Rabbi Zeira turned the *gavra* back to dust, he infers that there must have been no benefit to keep him present in case of the need for a quorum. Thus, he cannot be counted in a minyan, and neither is there a concern about whether Rabbi Zeira had committed any infraction by turning the *gavra* to dust. The prohibition on shedding blood, according to the Hacham Tzvi, only refers to creatures formed within their mother's womb. As the *gavra* was not formed in this way, there is no prohibition in removing it from the world.[21] Emden continues his father's reasoning with regard to the Golem and why it cannot be counted in a minyan, placing it in the legal category of those who are not deemed to have capacity, and specifically intellect. He reasons that if the Golem possessed the faculty of hearing to the extent that it was able to receive instruction, it must also be worthy of the faculty of speech. This important detail suggests that Emden's ruling might have been different had he deduced that the *gavra* possessed the faculty of intellect.

The ruling that a Golem cannot count in a minyan is not a universal one, nor is the question of whether killing a Golem is without legal sanction. The challenge faced by the Rabbis in deducing the criteria that this semi-human being would need to fulfil in order to interpret proper and permitted conduct in relation to it, is indicative of the same kind of struggles facing present halakhists and Jewish ethicists when considering trans- and posthuman creations. The basis of the rulings to exclude the Golem is Rava's failed *gavra*, but in *Sidrei Tahorot*, a halachic collection by Rabbi Gersom Hanokh Leiner of the Izbiza Hasidim, a strong argument is made regarding the question of how the law would change should Rava have succeeded.[22] Just as the animals generated successfully by way of the methods in *Sefer Yetzirah* are considered halachically animal, he argues that this would be possible for a person as well. Leiner's line of argument is that should someone bring into existence a man through this method, and a man that was not deficient as in the case of the man that Rava generated, then this being would be counted in a minyan. The case in Sanhedrin is thus an imperfect proof text because it was an imperfect attempt. The American research biologist and bioethicist John Loike notes that Leiner is not alone in this argument, and a similar perspective is present in the commentary of Shmuel Eidels on the Sanhedrin text.[23]

With birth and death both discussed, it is perhaps unsurprising that the question of generating offspring with a Golem also appears in halachic literature. Rabbi Isaiah Horwitz, writing in the sixteenth century, imagines that it was a female Golem with whom Joseph's brothers were fornicating and that this was the substance of the evil report that he took to Jacob which annoyed his brothers.[24] Loike details a number of other halachic authorities who also contend that sex with a Golem is permissible, because the Golem is in a legal category of its own and thus not subject to any of the laws that govern interactions between humans and other humans or humans and animals.[25] This presumably still refers to a Golem that has not attained full human status, whereby they would be subject to the same laws and protections as a human being. These texts might well be ignored by others writing on the subject and perhaps avoided by religious leaders for fear of encouraging sexual immorality, but given the proportion of robots shown at events such as the Consumer Electronics Show each year that are devoted to sexual pleasure, there is doubtless scope for this to become a facet of ethical discussion as humans continue to generate humanoid beings to serve their needs.

The Golem in Halacha

The Golem and the halachic arguments surrounding its nature have become an important part of contemporary responsa that respond to some key questions around bioethics and Jewish law. In their 2003 work laying out the halachic criteria for defining human beings as a response to scientific advancement, John Loike and Rabbi Moshe Tendler employ the Golem and many of the aforementioned discussions as a central tool in understanding what makes a human in Jewish law. They explain that for much of history, the simple criteria of having been formed within a human being was enough to answer most questions about the nature of humans. In the twenty-first century, it is the Golem that enables them to formulate a new set of halachic criteria:

> Three criteria characterize the halachic definition of humans: a) being formed within or born from a woman, b) exhibiting da'at (moral intelligence), or c) exhibiting the capacity to produce progeny with another human being. However, an important issue is whether an organism requires one or all of these criteria to be classified as human. We propose from Talmudic and halachic sources that an organism has to possess at least one of three criteria to be defined as a human being and does not need all.[26]

This reasoning is deduced by way of the Golem literature. The Golem appeared human but was not made from human materials, and it was not formed from another person. It could not produce progeny, and yet as seen above from the arguments of Jacob Emden and others, should a Golem possess moral intelligence it would be considered human according to Halakha. This suggestion has enormous implications for the understanding of trans- and posthumans, and particularly their rights and responsibilities. It invites questions of how these beings, if understood to be human in this classification, might acquire their moral intelligence, and whether such a thing can be programmed. In his responsum for the Conservative movement's Committee on Law and Jewish Standards, Daniel Nevins applies the Golem to the question of Artificial Intelligence. He suggests that the idea that 'humans can create entities that mimic the physical and cognitive features of humanity has not exceeded the imagination of our halachic predecessors'. However, 'resemblance did not secure equal status'.[27] As AI and sophisticated neural networks continue to advance at pace, the question of whether this remains the case, and what the criteria for intelligence or cognition that reach the threshold of humanness are, becomes ever more important. Could a Golem's ethical reasoning be better than that of a human because its judgement is un-clouded by human emotion which is often unpredictable and irrational? Could they then become moral agents in halacha? There is clearly a need to develop the notion of moral intelligence, significantly, in order to be able to create a more substantive religious response to the question of what it means to understand something as a human in Jewish law in light of these evolving technological realities.

It has also been asked whether a human clone is classed as a Golem, given its nature as a living being generated by a human but not through sexual reproduction. In his survey of halachic arguments relating to cloning, Bleich explains the importance of the Golem literature in understanding the status of a cloned human and particularly in demonstrating the 'unassailability of the status of a cloned human as a human being'.[28] For Bleich, what makes a clone and a Golem different is that a Golem is generated from dust and lacks a human progenitor, whereas a clone does have a human progenitor. This precludes the categorization of the clone as a Golem, ensuring there is no doubt about its status as a human being. Doubt is halachically problematic, because it creates ambiguity with regard to religious law. Loike suggests that a stringent position would be to class a clone as *safek ish*, a human with doubtful status, but that it is not necessary because the discussion of the difference between a Golem and a clone ought to remove any ambiguity.[29]

When issues surrounding generation at the boundary of the human realm emerge in Jewish legal and ethical spheres, it is the Golem that forms the basis for argumentation and exploration. Without the extant literature, I think it is reasonable to question whether there would be such an open and relatively progressive religious definition of humanity as that produced by Loike and Tendler, or indeed the capacity to advocate from religious teachings for the idea that it may be possible to class a generated being as a human even if that being was not brought into existence from any human biological material. The notion that the status of person can be acquired through non-biological means, even if in their original texts those means are mystical, allows an adaptability in Jewish thought that might not otherwise be available to all streams of Jewish communities.

Nomos and narrative– the role of modern Golem legends in religious ethical debates

Rabbinic Judaism was, and in some ways still remains, an oral tradition. Talmud, or Oral Torah, is traditionally held to be revealed truth interpreted by scholars and written to preserve teachings as time passed and the volume of known material grew. Folk stories, legends and traditions concerning rituals and practice, all formed an important part of the oral tradition and the ideascape that Rava's *gavra* emerges from. The decision to demarcate the end of an era where the interpretation of religious thought, and the incorporation of new stories into the rabbinic cannon, is one that leaves a question as to the role of later stories or strands of tradition that emerge, and which become important narratives for extending our understanding of classical ideas. The stories of Rabbis and their Golems, which have resonance for their relevance in discussions of technical advancement and in understanding the contemporary historical experience of Jewish communities, pose a question for religious thought. What is the place of these stories? I have hitherto not engaged with the Golems of modern literature, film and art, because of this ambiguous position, but their relative novelty does not in my view preclude their inclusion in this discussion, as they reveal new and valuable lessons hidden within the Golem tradition. In particular, the Golem stories that are interwoven with the historical experiences of antisemitism at the start of the twentieth century, reveal important dimensions of motive for the generation of Golems. And the historical experience of Nazi science should also offer context to some Jewish reluctance to engage in trans- and posthumanist thought that appears to be similar to ideas of race and human improvement from the Nazi era.[30]

The Golem that Joseph Grimm encountered, and entered into the literary and folklore journal *Zeitung für Einsiedler* (Journal for Hermits), is the legendary Golem of Prague.[31] Before this, Golem stories centred on the Baal Shem Tov in Chelm. The Baal Shem Tov's Golem is the first to be described as running wild in the streets and was inactivated by his creator by tearing the paper laid upon it which contained the Hebrew letters that enabled its animation. Rabbi Judah Loew, also known as the Maharal of Prague, never spoke or wrote about Golems in his lifetime, but he is the Rabbi most associated with the Golem legend. This is likely due to a work of Rabbi Yudel Rosenberg, who included the story of the Prague Golem in his book about Loew. This story, of a Rabbi who created a Golem in response to attacks on the Jewish community of Prague, and whose Golem worked as a spy, communicating via hand signals to his master, gained great traction.[32] As is often the case with stories, the narrative around Loew's Golem grew, and the most well-known versions today often amalgamate Golem traditions, where the Prague Golem rampages through the city. Golems are found everywhere, from Pokemon animated characters to Marvel comics, and the Golem has become somewhat of an icon. This means that most contemporary Jews know nothing of the Golem literature of rabbinic tradition, or Rava's *gavra*, or the questions whether or not a Golem can be mistaken for a human. What import do these stories have in the lives and decision-making of modern Jews?

Rabbi Mark Washofsky, a prolific author of responsa who chaired the Central Conference of American Rabbis (reform) responsa committee, has argued for an integrated process of incorporating halacha and more contemporary sources into discussions of Jewish bioethics. Referencing the 'creative rapport between halacha and aggadah', where the stories of a community and its legal framework cannot be easily separated, he argues that there is no such thing as halachic formalism, and that every decision in the religious ecosystem is by virtue of its position in community, required to be in dialogue with its fullest context.[33]

When formulating their responsa outlining some broad guidelines for issues related to AI, and autonomous machines, the Conservative Committee on Jewish Law and Standards argued that though it is 'tempting to dismiss mystical texts in a discussion of contemporary halachah, we ought to resist this temptation'.[34] The Golem stories come from and involve many of the most important ethical and legal authorities of both mystical and legal scholarship. This is the approach taken by Rabbi Byron Sherwin in his volume about the role of the Golem in navigating the 'biotech century'. Sherwin spends little time on textual analysis of the stories themselves, but instead devotes himself to the applied ethical considerations that they present.[35] For Sherwin, there is no Golem without the later stories that animate him, and without the valuable lessons they offer about the complexities of the ability to generate other beings. Sherwin's conclusion is thus, 'whether our age will be the age of... Frankenstein and his monster or the age of Judah Loew and his Golem is up to us. As he protected the Jews of Prague long ago from their enemies, may the Golem protect us from ourselves'.[36]

As the potential for the generation of trans- and posthumans develops, the value of the Golem and its narrative moral is clear. Whether it is to suggest that there is a natural positivism towards science, or to emphasize the value of moral integrity in the objectives of the generators, a number of substantive lessons can be drawn from the Golem tradition. Nevertheless, the Golem is not the only tradition within Judaism that involves the generation of beings, and as technology changes and adapts, it is important that religious legal and ethical minds remain attuned to the wider textual landscape, and the creatures contained therein. As John Loike and Rabbi Moshe Tendler raise in their treatment of the halachic criteria for defining human beings, there are other creatures in Jewish tradition such as *dulphanim*, *adnei-ha-sadeh,* and the *bar nash de-tur*,[37] that though less studied, might reflect more appropriate categories for understanding how to approach particularly transhuman beings from a Jewish legal and ethical perspective, even if they do not have such a clear creation narrative as the Golem.[38] Though the Golem is an expansive category, and can refer to beings created in numerous ways, it is not necessarily an all-inclusive category.

Rabbi Elliott Dorff has outlined doctrinal principles for understanding the Jewish approach to transhumanism that refer primarily to the modification of existing human bodies. These include the notion that humans are mortal and ultimately human bodies belonging to God, that the lives of human beings created in the image of God have value, that the human being is an integrated partnership of body and soul, and that the body is morally neutral and potentially good. These principles are limited in that they extend only to those who fit within the halachic category of human. What the

Golem offers is the opportunity to infer a similar set of doctrinal principles for the not-yet extant being, that which exists in some way outside the framework that Dorff creates for humans.[39] Whereas for Dorff, there is no separation of body and soul (the consciousness that animates a body) in a human, this may not be the case for a posthuman creation, for instance, a virtual person or some other form of biological posthuman. Where these are concerned, the Golem offers a strong starting point for formulating a response. For instance, there is a symmetry in nature between digital beings or those that are the product of genetic engineering and the Golem because according to *Sefer Yetzirah* the Golem is brought into being through the combination of letters. This is noteworthy because the building blocks of both computer code and the genetic code on DNA strands are also, at their heart, a sequence of letters (although in all cases, the letters represent/embody much more than just a symbol). The presence of the Golem stories is a persistent reminder that religious thought is capable of developing a rich discourse around other forms of artificial anthropoids, and that it is not outside the capacity of our religious and ethical imaginations to develop a rich vocabulary for generating them.

At the heart of Rabbi Rava's failure to generate his *gavra* was the absence of righteousness, or צדק *tzedek*. This root, which also connotes justice, centres the importance of *kavanah*, intention, in any process of bringing into existence a being. It was not that Rava was not simply pious enough, but rather that the higher motive for the generation was not present. Perhaps this indicates that sending a messenger to fool a friend is not important enough to justify being able to access such creative power. While stories swirl in the medieval textual milieu about Rabbis who attempted, and succeeded in the generation of Golems, there remains no physical evidence or recorded instances of Golems beyond the folkloric and mystical literature. The Golem attributed to Loew, and the stories that were told about it, were desperately needed by a community that experienced a profound sense of vulnerability and a need to experience the feeling of protection, both divine but also physical and immediate. Though there is also no evidence of Loew's Golem, the strength of the story functions in such a way that it may almost be true.

In an age where science enables humans with the concrete abilities to contemplate that which many struggled to achieve with mysticism, the same charge that was put to Rava may now be directed to us. If the righteous so wish, they can generate a world. Golem stories are not just about the Golems, but about the virtues and motives of their generators which are an integral part of understanding the Golem tradition. While technology and the creative endeavour draws focus to the 'how?' of the generation of beings, Jewish tradition calls us back to the 'why?' and the 'what next?' Righteousness leads to the bringing into existence of worlds, but the creative endeavour must extend to ensuring that those creations do not become destructive forces. The centuries old framework for discussing the Golem's role in society offers a model for how the Jewish community might approach the integration of these beings into society. It forces us to confront not just the opportunity but also the responsibility, so that new creations are not returned to dust bringing their generators with them.

Notes

1. Jorge Luis Borges, *El otro, el mismo*.
2. National Library of Israel, 'The Maharal's Robot: The High-Tech Golem of Rehovot', (2018), https://blog.nli.org.il/en/scholem_Golem/ also Byron L. Sherwin, *Golems Among Us: How a Jewish Legend can Help us Navigate the Biotech Century* (Chicago: Ivan R Dee, 2004), 45.
3. The term בָּרָא bara used here is the same word used at the start of genesis when God creates the world בְּרֵאשִׁית, בָּרָא אֱלֹהִים. There is a linguistic parallel between the act of creation in Genesis and Rava's creation of man recounted in b Sanhedrin.
4. bSanhedrin 65b

   אמר רבא אי בעו צדיקי ברו עלמא שנאמר כי עונותיכם היו מבדילים וגו'. רבא ברא גברא שדריה לקמיה דר' זירא הוה קא משתעי בהדיה ולא הוה קא מהדר ליה אמר ליה מן חבריא את הדר לעפריך

5. Moshe Idel, *Golem: Jewish Magical and Mystical Traditions on the Artificial Antropoid* (New York: Ktav Publishing House, 2019), 28.

   Idel has suggested the term *chavraya* should be understood as pietists as opposed to magicians as others have indicated, noting that it appears in the Jerusalem Talmud with the context of a group of scholars in the Tiberian academy. See also Gershom Scholem, 'The Idea of the Golem', in *On the Kabbalah and Its Symbolism* (New York: Random House, 1996), 166.
6. The gemara is the term for the secondary layer of text within the Talmud. However, it is not really correct to say that the Talmud continues because it is gemara and not mishnah (the other layer - but they do form one contiguous text, just that mishnah is also found without gemara but gemara has mishnah woven into it).
7. Here, the root יצר is used to talk about creation, rather than ברא. יצר has the sense of being formed or fashioned, and is used in Genesis 2 in relation to the creation of man from earth אֶת־הָאָדָם אֲשֶׁר יָצָר (Gen 2.8).
8. Idel, *Golem*, 31.
9. John Loike, 'Is a Human Clone a Golem?' *The Torah U-Madda Journal* 9 (2000), 238, Moshe Idel has also explored this history in depth.
10. J. David Bleich, 'Survey of Recent Halakhic Periodical Literature: Cloning: Homologous Reproduction and Jewish Law', *Tradition: A Journal of Orthodox Jewish Thought* 32, no. 3 (1998), 53.
11. Kiddushin is a book of the Talmud. Talmudic references use the name of the tractate (folio), in this case Kiddushin, then the daf (page) and a/b indicating which page. The small b is a lettering convention that indicates it is the Babylonian Talmud rather than the Palestinian one, but it is not necessary as most people would assume a Talmud reference was Bavli, unless indicated otherwise with a y (for Yerushalmi).
12. Jacob Emden, (1884) She'eilat Yavetz. Lemberg. שאילת יעבץ חלק א-ב, עמדין, יעקב בן צבי (יעב"ץ) https://hebrewbooks.org/1408. Part 2 no. 82.
13. Idel, *Golem*, 28.
14. Rashi on Sanhedrin 65b:17. ברא גברא - ע"י ספר יצירה שלמדו צרוף אותיות של שם
15. Scholem, 'The Idea of the Golem', 166.
16. bereshit rabbah בְּשֵׁם רַבִּי אֶלְעָזָר אָמַר, בְּשָׁעָה שֶׁבָּרָא הַקָּדוֹשׁ בָּרוּךְ הוּא אֶת אָדָם הָרִאשׁוֹן גֹּלֶם בְּרָאוֹ 8:1
17. Midrash is a Jewish way of interpreting the Talmud. Midrash Tanchuma Buber, Shmini, Siman 12. Also found in Leviticus Rabbah.
18. Sherwin, *Golems Among Us*, 65.

19 It is also appropriate to acknowledge that the inclusion of non-orthodox voices in a discussion about legal rulings already indicates how this work is influenced by my own particular position within the Jewish community, although I am of the view that this is an area of religious life where there is cautious agreement and relatively little cause for disagreement.
20 Hacham Tzvi, Zevi Hirsch Ashkenazi (1660–1718), R. Jacob Emden (1697–1776).
21 Zevi Hirsch Ashkenazi (translated) in Byron Sherwin, *The Golem Legend: Origins and Implications* (Lanham, MD: University Press of America, 1985), 21–2.
22 Gersom Hanokh Leiner, Sidrei Tahorot, (1903), https://hebrewbooks.org/pdfpager.aspx?req=22096&pgnum=1
23 Loike, 'Is a Human Clone a Golem?', 240.
24 Idel, *Golem*, 15.
25 Loike, 'Is a Human Clone a Golem?', 239.
26 John Loike and Moshe Tendler, 'Ma Adam Va-teda-ehu: Halakhic Criteria for Defining Human Beings', *Tradition: A Journal of Orthodox Jewish Thought* 37, no. 2 (2003), 9.
27 Daniel Nevins, 'Halachic Responses to Artificial Intelligence and Autonomous Machines', *CLJS HM* 182, no. 1 (2019), 34.
28 Bleich, 'Survey of Recent Halakhic Periodical Literature', 67.
29 Loike, 'Is a Human Clone a Golem?', 242.
30 Hava Tirosh-Samuelson, '*Utopianism and Eschatology: Judaism engages Transhumanism*', in *Religion and Transhumanism: The Unknown Future of Human Enhancement*, eds. Calvin Mercer and Tracy Trothen (Santa Barbara, CA: Praeger, 2015), 161–80.
31 Edan Dekel and David Gantt Gurley, 'How the Golem Came to Prague', *The Jewish Quarterly Review* 103, no. 2 (2013), 242.
32 Sherwin, *Golems Among Us*, 23.
33 Mark Washofsky, 'Halacha, Aggadah, and Reform Jewish Bioethics: A Response', *CCAR Journal* (2006), 13.
34 Nevins, 'Halachic Responses to Artificial Intelligence and Autonomous Machines', 33.
35 Sherwin, *Golems Among Us*.
36 Sherwin, *Golems Among Us*, 212.
37 These are categories of being referred to in religious texts whose precise nature is debated but they are in various ways human/animal hybrids or semi-human creatures.
38 Loike and Tendler, 'Ma Adam Va-teda-ehu', 9–10.
39 Elliot N. Dorff, '*Judaism - The Body Belongs to God: Judaism and Transhumanism*', in *Transhumanism and the Body: The World Religions Speak*, eds. Calvin Mercer and Derek F. Maher (London: Palgrave Macmillan, 2014).

10

A Christian outlook

The rational body: A Thomistic perspective on parenthood and posthumanism

Michael Wee

Who will be the parents of posthumans? Or will posthumans be 'post-parents' as well? It is a striking feature of the literature surrounding posthuman aspirations for the future that the ethical questions surrounding the use of enhancement technologies are rarely framed with any explicit reference to the role that human or posthuman reproduction might play. Rather, the underlying assumption seems to be that the achievement of a posthuman condition is primarily an individual issue, concerning the limits of one's autonomy and capacity for self-creation.[1]

No doubt, reproduction is lurking somewhere in the background when posthumanism is spoken of as an evolutionary aim, for example, but it is not directly addressed. In discussions of germline genetic engineering – not in itself a posthuman proposal, but a cornerstone of potential techniques for enhancement – the significance of human reproduction is certainly more than implicit, given the safety concerns surrounding the passing down of genetically edited material to one's offspring (which does not occur with somatic gene-editing).[2] However, there is not always sufficient recognition that such techniques at times involve the generation of a new human being with specifically desired characteristics, as opposed to the genetic manipulation of a pre-existing person. The distinction is an important one, even if such genetic techniques are, for now, generally limited to addressing genetic diseases rather than aimed at creating so-called 'designer babies'. When there is a new being brought into existence, strictly speaking nobody is being cured.[3] Those who commission, create and bear the genetically edited child bear a moral responsibility that, arguably, must be evaluated through the prism of parenthood.

The absence of parenthood from the discourse surrounding posthumanism is perhaps itself symptomatic of the nature of certain posthuman aspirations, in particular those that envision a shift to a disembodied existence, for instance, in a computer. Posthumanity of this kind might be said to harbour a certain unease, not just with the human body as we know it, but with embodiment in general. If the aim is to reach a bodiless state, then parenthood becomes more of a metaphor thereafter. None of this ought to be terribly surprising, if posthumanism is seen as an exercise in self-creation. Much has been written elsewhere about how the idea – or myth – of the autonomous self has become a dominant paradigm in Western philosophy and theology, to the neglect of other aspects of the human condition such as relationality and dependence.[4] The very idea of being somehow 'constrained' by the fact of one's bodily origins, or by one's body at all, does not sit well with this paradigm.

The paradox facing us, therefore, is that just as parenthood is a potential vehicle for achieving a posthuman condition, it is also at risk of erasure from posthumanity. What resources do we have to overcome this somewhat functional view of parenthood, and question the very unease with embodiment that posthuman aspirations seem to carry? In this chapter, I will attempt to offer a response to this question by adopting a broadly Thomistic perspective – that is to say, one that is grounded in the work of the medieval Christian philosopher and theologian Thomas Aquinas, and the tradition of thought that has developed from it, and which continues to be the subject of much scholarship. Thomism offers, among other things, a rich history of dialogue and reflection on the human person as body *and* soul. Hence, I believe there is much to be gained from bringing it to bear on questions relating to posthumanity. Some of the thoughts that I will offer, as will become clear, also apply to already existing and largely accepted forms of reproductive technology. Perhaps the disconcerting conclusion that follows is that if ever there was any Rubicon in the way of an in-principle acceptance of posthuman technological dreams in our society, it has already been crossed.

Parenthood: A theological approach

What is parenthood? Words like 'parent', 'mother' and 'father' are used in many different ways, and not always literally – and not necessarily with a biological connection in mind. From a metaphysical point-of-view, at least, is there a primary sense of 'parenthood'?

It helps to consider something of a counter-example, in the first place. In 2018, the *Daily Mail* reported on some remarks that the UK's most senior Anglican cleric, Justin Welby, had made on God and gender. The headline read: '"God is not male . . . OR female": Archbishop of Canterbury says "the Father" cannot be defined by human gender'.[5] Why this was newsworthy almost certainly had less to do with its theological content and more to do with contemporary controversies about gender that are outside the scope of this chapter. But suffice to say, this is not news as far as Christian theology is concerned – the Scriptures remind us that 'God is a spirit' (Jn 4.24),[6] and Aquinas writing in the thirteenth-century states unequivocally near the beginning of the *Summa Theologica* that 'God is not a body'.[7] In fact, God whose very essence is existence is a being of absolute simplicity, who neither has parts (ST I, q. 3, a. 7, co.) nor can be contained in any category (ST I, q. 3, a. 5, co.). Sexual differentiation, on a Thomistic view, is primarily a matter of the body,[8] so it follows that God, who has no body parts, cannot be male or female.

Nevertheless, the BBC television programme *Newsnight* took up this story for one of its broadcasts, with the programme host introducing the discussion by stating that the language of God as 'Father' was 'the language of religion based on and embodying a patriarchy'.[9] The suggestion here is that the notion of God as Father is really just the projection of the limited experience of social structures in *men*'s minds onto a transcendent, divine reality – our perception of which has been sullied by our inept human language. Justin Welby is reported to have also said, 'All human language about God is inadequate and to some degree metaphorical', and this might have been taken as further support of that position.[10] Terms like 'the Father', on such a view, could be explained away by sociolinguistics.

How might a Thomist respond to this claim? To be sure, human language and the inherent limitations of human experience, from which we draw analogies, can indeed sully our perceptions of God. But this general point is not incompatible with a more specific and longstanding contention of Christianity, which is that the fatherhood of God is a matter of God's self-revelation about his identity and his relation to us. It is true that many of the names with which we speak of God can only apply to him metaphorically; they are predicated primarily of creatures and applied to God on account of some degree of similitude – with the caveat that God is ultimately more different from the primary analogate than he is similar. 'The Lord is my shepherd' (Ps. 23.1)[11] is one such example, and perhaps most of the words we use to speak of God are of this kind; we find other references in the Bible to God as a rock, or as a refiner's fire. But, citing the authority of Scripture, Aquinas contends that fatherhood involves a different kind of predication (ST I, q. 13, a. 6): God is the Father, '[o]f whom all paternity in heaven and earth is named' (Eph. 3.15). On the one hand, we learn the word 'father' from common human experience – that is to say, from biological fatherhood – before we learnt to apply it to God, and in this respect it is similar to 'shepherd'. But unlike the metaphor of 'shepherd', the perfection signified by 'fatherhood' belongs primarily and exclusively to God, and is applied to humans only secondarily. Comparatively few names are of this kind; other examples include knowledge, beauty and goodness. Again, we first learn these concepts from their imperfect instantiations in human life, but it is in God alone that their perfection – beauty *as such*, or goodness *as such* – is found.[12]

If this understanding is right, then it means that our words have a deeper significance that we do not, and could never, fully comprehend. Yet we can try our best to make sense of what it means to say that the perfection of fatherhood resides in God. As has already been mentioned, God the Father is not a biological entity, so this must be a rather different kind of paternity – although ours surely still resembles it in some crucial way, since it stands in an analogical relationship to God's fatherhood. Here, it is worth clarifying that this should not be taken to mean that biological fatherhood is therefore just a metaphor, a kind of figurative description; it remains, on a Thomistic view, a literal description, even though it participates somewhat imperfectly in the fatherhood that is properly ascribed to God, which is its primary reference point.

At this stage, we can make two crucial points in relation to the task of understanding the fatherhood of God: First, 'paternity', according to this theological understanding of the term, refers a particular mode of relationship, of which biological fatherhood is only one kind. Hence, in the language of the Nicene Creed, which is widely used in Catholic, Orthodox and Anglican, worship, Christ is 'born of the Father before all ages', even before he 'was incarnate of the Virgin Mary, and became man'.[13] Second, in a similar vein to reasoning from an effect to a cause, we can reflect on our biological experience of paternity – and perhaps parenthood more generally – in order to better understand that particular mode of relationship, which otherwise seems rather ethereal when attributed to God.

Yet on that latter point, even before we turn to address any implications of parenthood for posthumanism, we must come face-to-face with a practical problem: it should be immediately apparent that biological parenthood is already the scene of great cultural contestation. How will this shed any light on the divine fatherhood? After all, there is an undoubtedly widespread attitude towards the facts of biology in contemporary Western society that can be summarized in this way: There is no ultimate explanation for these facts, other than evolutionary processes, and they carry no intrinsic value whatsoever. An obvious practical consequence of this has been the broad acceptance of various forms of assisted reproductive technologies in many societies today, where natural sexual reproduction is not seen as any more valuable in and of itself than, say, in vitro fertilization (IVF) for achieving parenthood; it might be an aesthetic preference but not necessarily a moral one. Even genetic ties to future offspring can be dispensed with if necessary, through egg or sperm donation – the only barrier that stands in the way is the need for consent of all parties involved prior to conception.

Such attitudes reveal an unmistakeably dualistic anthropology of the human person. Rationality is something added on top of the sub-rational body, like icing upon a cake. What is otherwise brute, faceless matter is given its individual character and meaning by the presence of the mind. Consent is what opens the door to technological manipulation of our reproductive potential because it is the rational mind, the seat of the autonomous self, that is the primary creator of value and the final arbiter of moral choice concerning one's body. Human reproduction, though it is invested with all kinds of social significance, is at its core a material process – babies are made, not begotten.[14]

To this perspective we must ask: In our day-to-day lives, is it not extraordinarily difficult to actually convince ourselves of all that, especially in the way we live? Despite the legal frameworks that allow for the fracturing of biological parenthood by consent, our common human experience of parenthood stands in protest to that. We experience genetic ties precisely as relationship-*constituting* – parental relationships do not seem merely incidental to these ties. When I look at my parents with the knowledge that 50 per cent of my DNA comes from each of them, I do not think this to be a cold, clinical fact. I am, instead, given a basic picture of the world, one which is not value-free. This is particularly evident with those who experience the phenomenon known as genealogical bewilderment[15] and who search for their genetic parents, after having been separated from them either through adoption or donor conception. This in turn points to a certain irony about the practice of donor conception. The purpose of donor conception in many cases, it seems, is precisely that 'one would-be parent is trying to ensure for him or herself a genetic *and* social connection with a child – while at the same time denying the child any social connection to the donor parent'.[16] If biological ties did not matter all that much, there would be no reason to resort to this.

Contrast our experience of parenthood with merely material processes of production. To give a slightly facetious example,[17] suppose you tell me that your mobile phone was made in the same production line as mine, with its metals taken from the same sources, and so on. It would be either silly, or else metaphorical, to say that there thus existed a familial relationship between them. The mere sharing of material and origins in such a case does not lead me to conclude that this establishes a nexus of rights and duties – that I am obliged, for example, to share my phone's batteries with yours as a matter of course. Figurative language cannot carry one so far.

With human biology, by contrast, poetry becomes lived reality. The material facts of reproduction on their own seem unable to account for this, while at the same time making it clear that biological similitude matters. The ancient utterance of Adam to Eve, 'This now is bone of my bones, and flesh of my flesh' (Gen. 2.23), could well be said by a parent to their child. In a way this expression is echoed by what some of the most poetic lines of the Nicene Creed, which capture the essence of the relationship of Christ to the Father – a relation not founded on genetic ties, yet one of similitude and derivation:

> God from God, Light from Light,
> True God from true God,
> begotten, not made, consubstantial with the Father.[18]

As one theologian puts it, 'The derivation of the Son (the Radiance) from the Father (the Light), far from implying any Arian-style subordination, conveyed their unity and equality',[19] with reference to the fourth-century Church Father Athanasius of Alexandria's 'analogy of the light and its brightness, which, while distinguishable as two, are one and the same substance.'[20]

Flesh coming from flesh could not, given its finite material nature, carry the total unity of substance implied by Light coming from uncreated Light. Nonetheless we begin to see some similarities between biological and divine paternity – namely, a gratuitous giving or sharing of one's substance, and by virtue of that a radical equality of dignity. Biological parenthood, which seems to be constituted at least in part by the gift of genetic and other biological material, is for this reason an image of the perfection contained in the Father's begetting of the Son. But why does the gift of biological material constitute parenthood in a way that the sharing of inanimate matter between artefacts does not?

To respond to that question, it is worth considering the natural phenomenon of identical twinning at the embryonic stage, sometimes called embryo-splitting. If, as some believe, the original embryo survives as one of the two resulting twins,[21] why do we not consider that embryo the parent of the other? Surely, based on the above, this seems to resemble even more closely the relationship of 'Light from Light' than the fusion of gametes from two different individuals to produce a third individual human being. Samuel Condic and Maureen Condic, however, in their philosophical study of the embryo, reject the idea that twinning results in a parental relationship. For a couple who may not want to have children at the point of intercourse, their natural sexual relations are still 'intrinsically or naturally ordered' to procreation, Condic and Condic argue, and so they are acting for the end of reproduction nonetheless. The same cannot be said of biological matter that is simply 'susceptible' to twinning – the effect of twinning is incidental to the embryo's nature, and not a result of the embryo somehow acting for a reproductive end.[22] Hence, even though embryo twinning comes closer to the reality of parenthood than a mere artefact sharing inanimate matter with another object, its sharing of biological matter on its own does not qualify it as a parent.

To put it in another way, parenthood in a corporeal sense must be the result of some form of rational ordering of the body, towards the sharing and giving of one's substance in the formation of new life. The mere transfer of material, biological or otherwise, between living things does not constitute familial ties – kidney donors and their recipients do not become siblings. This condition, as it were, of parenthood mirrors the more perfect though non-bodily parenthood of God the Father, whose eternally begotten Son is also called the Word (*Logos*) of God (Jn 1.1) – the very term signifying a relationship constituted by an innate rational ordering in the divine substance. Of course, we speak of other forms of incorporeal parenthood, often in a much more figurative way – we speak of godparents and spiritual children, fatherly or motherly figures, the parenthood of ideas and institutions. These uses similarly indicate the importance of rational purpose – which is distinct from conscious awareness or choice – in the concept of parenthood. The founder of a new political ideology may not know the full extent of those who consider themselves 'children' of the resulting movement, yet they result from a rational process of dissemination and fertilization of ideas.

So, to refine our initial observation of human parenthood, biological similitude matters, but in the specific context of a rational ordering of the body to the end of reproduction. Such relationships turn the poetry of kinship into literal reality. And yet, this idea of rational ordering in the body is not entirely straightforward. Biological parenthood, in this way, points us towards the mystery of the human person as a figure of embodied rationality. A brief excursus on this subject is therefore necessary.

Embodied rationality

Embodied rationality is a paradox we must pass through in order to properly grasp the implications of human parenthood. But how can rationality, in the sense of our 'capacity to acquire intellectual abilities'[23] and which transcends material boundaries, somehow be 'encased' in a physical body? Is not the idea of a 'rational body' a contradiction in terms?

This is the paradox of human persons, made 'a little less than the angels' (Ps. 8.6), but higher than non-rational animals. In Thomistic terms at least, matter is almost by definition that which is subject to change and decay, while the immaterial is precisely not so, yet in the human person the two are held together in a hylomorphic union – that is, composed of form (the immaterial soul, which is the source of our rationality) and matter (the body).[24] This particular language of form and matter, with which Thomists understand body–soul union, comes from Aristotle's metaphysics and is not intuitive to the modern reader. The folk understanding that we have become used to in contemporary society is often some form of Cartesian dualism, where mind and body are seen as separate substances altogether. The mind, invariably, becomes associated with consciousness in particular, the surest sign of one's existence as a 'thinking thing'.[25]

A problem with such a mentalistic understanding, so to speak, of rational thought is that it essentially takes the mind to be comprehensible in analogy to matter. The assumption is that just as you can understand matter in such-and-such ways, the mind is just like another kind of matter, only an immaterial kind (and that is a proper contradiction in terms), a kind of 'refined ethereal medium' in which thinking takes place.[26] But as Sir Anthony Kenny reminds us in *The Metaphysics of Mind*, the human mind is first and foremost 'a capacity, not an activity'[27] – a capacity for language, for interpersonal relations, for moral action, just to name a few things. Rationality is a quality that infuses the whole body, not an activity that goes on somewhere in my head. That is why even certain activities that we might do 'without thinking' – that is, without conscious mental effort – like making a cup of tea are truly rational and intentional acts. A Cartesian view, it seems to me, does not sufficiently appreciate how the exercise of our rationality is so deeply *embodied* in everyday life.

And the reality of the rational body, though it sounds mysterious in character, is made clear precisely by those everyday moments that remind us how matter is never the full story or the full truth of human life.[28] One need not look to mystical experience – I have in mind fairly mundane things here. Ludwig Wittgenstein, one of the most important philosophers of the twentieth century, once posed a deceptively simple question: How could someone point to the shape of something, *as opposed to* its colour? This distinction cannot be found in behaviour alone. But nor is it to be explained by some kind of inner thought or phenomenological experience.[29] We do not have to perform an 'inner pointing', by some act of the mind, towards shape but not colour in order to make such a distinction clear to ourselves and to others; such a meaning of one's finger-pointing could be conveyed by language, or perhaps by the context. So also the mystery of the human body resists understanding when we have the wrong conception of words like 'rationality' or 'thought' – those signs of the immaterial soul. Post-Descartes, we are fixated with consciousness as the sign and bearer of our rationality, and have a great tendency to think of thought as signifying a mental event or mental state. Although as Elizabeth Anscombe pointed out in her study of the concept of intention, which has become one of the classics of contemporary philosophy, when somebody says, 'A penny for your thoughts', they are not actually asking for a report of your mental goings-on.[30] When we share our thoughts with somebody, we are not simply telling them words that have appeared in our minds.

In fact, we quite literally think with our bodies as well, which again demonstrates how deficient the Cartesian understanding of 'thought' is. I do not mean communicating symbols via certain hand gestures, as with sign language, but cases where intentional bodily movements are themselves the expression of a particular thought. Anscombe offers an example of someone doing a jigsaw puzzle, moving a piece about in such a way that we might interpret his behaviour as *embodying* the following thought: 'Perhaps it'll fit in *this* place, but the other way round.'[31] Such is not a claim about what is going on in his mind while he is acting (he may well have been thinking about supper – or about Cartesian philosophy); instead, it is a claim about what kind of thought the act *is*.

So we can begin to make sense of the Thomistic notion that the rational soul is not like a motor that activates a machine, but is the form of the body, and *present in every part* (ST I, q. 76, a. 8, co.). Form in this case signifies a kind of intrinsic rather than accidental shape – the life principle that directs the body's growth from within. That is, in essence, the idea of the rational body – contrary to the prevailing worldview today, there is no 'sub-rational' matter in the human body on this view. So long as rationality continues to be thought of, principally, as the workings of consciousness – mental 'activity' – then the idea of rational ordering in the body will continue to baffle us. The Aristotelian language of form and matter, by contrast, presents us with a veritable model for understanding the relationship of immaterial rationality to material realities.

We can, on this account, begin to distinguish between three types of rational activity. First, there is the Cartesian sort of thinking, the mental goings-on we can report or describe, which relates to terms such as *qualia* or consciousness. Second, there is intentional action that is rational, in that it can be explained by a rational purpose upon further reflection, such as Anscombe's puzzle-solver, but which is not accompanied by conscious mental acts. Many more actions than we realize fall into this category, such as when we speak at ordinary pace (without stopping to think about each word carefully, as we might in some situations) or ride a bicycle (unless we are a novice). These two categories of rational activity, I take it, are less controversial – and less dependent on a wholesale acceptance of a Thomistic anthropology of the human person. But I would suggest that there is a third kind, which relates to our earlier discussion of the ordering of natural sexual relations towards procreation and parenthood. These are actions which involve an intentional choice on some level, but which have an ordering towards an end independent of the acting person's will or motives.[32] For example, we might think to put food in our mouths for all kinds of subjective reasons such as for social reasons, without concern for the nourishing purpose of eating, yet our digestive system does continue to nourish us as it breaks down and facilitates the absorption of our food into the bloodstream. As a rational agent, we have acted for the end of nourishing ourselves in this way, cooperating thus with the natural ordering of the body through our free choice. These actions of the body, too, are rational inasmuch as they pertain to the teleological orientation of the body and are, ordinarily speaking, initiated by free choice – although one can be force fed, in which case the resulting action of the body still retains its rational character and orientation but not without suffering a certain moral injury.

Sexual reproduction, it seems to me, falls into this third category of rational activity. Like the nourishing of the body via digestion, it is meant to be initiated by free choice, and it can take on a variety of other meanings at a social or subjective level. But the sexual act itself retains its teleological ordering as a reproductive-type act regardless of the individual couple's motivations.[33] A resulting pregnancy may be unintended, but it is not accidental to the nature of sexual union. This picture of human sexuality is, perhaps, difficult to accept unless we have a conception of the body itself as rational, owing to its hylomorphic union with the soul. It is not so much that rationality is constrained by the body; rather the body's biological realities and the inclinations that flow from them, such as that to food or to sex, form a starting point and a frame of reference for rational choice.

Begetting the posthuman?

How do these foregoing considerations relate to posthumanism and the role of parenthood in its endeavours? First of all, the potential tension between objective, teleological ordering in the body and subjective motivations of agents is what makes biology so culturally contested on various different fronts, including parenthood. Soul and body sometimes appear to be at war with one another; the rational mind's grasp of the objective realities of the body is sometimes obscured by external influences. Second, as we have seen from our reflections on parenthood, biological ties of kinship matter precisely because of the rational nature that we embody. To recapitulate the point, biological similitude is an image of the perfect begetting of God the Son from the Father, who share one and the same substance. But in the case of biological parenthood, it is not simply the sharing of genetic or other matter that constitutes ties of kinship. Parenthood is also about a rational relationship, the capacity for which is already present in the teleological orientation of our bodies.

At the same time, it would be inaccurate to focus too exclusively on the objective ordering of the body's sexual faculties to reproduction, if we wish to explore more fully the rational character of parenthood, and how it matters for posthumanist aspirations. It is worth reflecting on the fact that just as sexual relations are referred to as knowledge in the Biblical sense – 'Adam knew Eve' (Gen. 4.1) – it is also commonplace in the Christian tradition to think of the begetting of the Son (the *Logos*) from the Father as the result of God's self-knowledge – an idea which comes down to us from Augustine of Hippo, one of the pre-eminent Church Fathers.[34] Mortal man and mortal woman, each on their own, carry the image of God only imperfectly, but there are moments where the significance of the image of God is more readily apparent. By their sexual relations, man and woman can be said to come to a deeper knowledge of themselves and of the other, with whom they are one flesh by the bond of marriage. The gratuitous gift of self, of one's substance, to one's potential offspring is thereby mediated by the gift of self to one's spouse in the marital act, and this is an image of God's self-knowledge which underpins the begetting of the Son from the Father. This mutual knowledge between man and woman is rational in its character, not in the sense of cold, clinical calculation, but in the sense that it engages with the source of each person's being, their intellects and wills facing one another in a spiritual and bodily embrace, and in so doing exemplifying their identity as husband and wife who have pledged their lives to each other. In a similar vein, the rational relationship of parenthood, before it involves any specific activities of nurturing and rearing, at its fundamental level concerns the self-knowledge of both the parent and the child, and their capacity for mutual recognition of their relational identity as flesh coming from flesh, as self who has come from another self.

And thus even for the couple who so desperately want children, human sexuality is such that intercourse can never quite be experienced as purely reproductive.

While being physiologically similar to that of many other animals, the human sexual act is transformed by our rational nature into an act that also has the character of interpersonal communication and union – an interpersonal knowing. Just as the physical act of jigsaw puzzle-making can embody different thoughts, so can the physical acts of lovemaking. The rational character of human sexual intercourse, it seems to me, is accentuated by the fact that the sexual act is always at a certain remove from the moment of fertilization – though reproductive in its biological orientation, the sexual act itself is not the direct process that generates new life. In fact, it cannot ever guarantee such an outcome on its own. There is an in-built serendipity to begetting.

This is why the phrase 'making babies' is, in truth, not an accurate description of natural sexual reproduction. Rather, intercourse involves a partnership, indisputably biological and also deeply rational. As the contemporary natural law theorist John Finnis writes in his essay 'C.S. Lewis and Test-tube Babies', sexual intercourse has a 'physical and emotional structure making it inherently apt to be experienced by each partner as a giving of self and receiving of the other, a giving which may be complemented by the gift of a child'.[35] This is one of the crucial differences between sex and reproductive technologies like IVF by which children are conceived through acts of technical mastery and production. In its natural form, then, human reproduction cannot be reduced to a purely material process of insemination and fertilization. For Finnis, the implication for parenthood is that the child is not thereby a 'product' but a *'partner* in the familial enterprise', radically equal to his or her parents.[36] Processes of manufacture do not, however, he argues, reflect this equality but instead suggest subordination as a creature to its creator.

So, to pose the question point-blank to ourselves, why are technical, material processes – as opposed to biological reproduction – inapt for generating new human, or indeed posthuman, beings?

To put it simply, our origins matter for our sense of identity. The peculiarity of the rational mind, I believe, is that it is not content with tracing the origins of its being to mere making. One recalls the haunting words of Frankenstein's monster in Mary Shelley's novel: 'At length the thought of you crossed my mind. I learned from your papers that you were my father, my creator.'[37] Despite there not being any biological relationship, the language of parenthood surfaces here in order to fill what we might think of as an instinctual void.

This has something to do, I think, with the way in which rational beings live their lives in narrative form. We order our experiences through the intelligibility of narrative forms, examining histories, motives, sub-plots and resolutions in our lives. Narratives have explanatory value – they are means of understanding or bringing to light hidden causal relations in our lives. A couple look back on why their relationship has broken down; a nation at the crossroads looks at the historical forces underlying its present crisis. We are, in a word, story-telling animals.[38]

Our inclination to narrative, however, falters when we try to explain the existence of a new rational being in purely efficient or material causal terms. With matter one can look to material explanations – to prior matter that gave rise to, or was manipulated to form, a new material object or series or objects, as with mobile phones on the same production line. But each rational person is like a whole new universe, and it is more difficult to understand a time when *I was not*. The asymmetry between existence and non-existence is stark. Our rational nature is such that mere matter seems to be deeply insufficient as an explanation for our being. Aristotle saw this when he wrote in *On the Generation of Animals*, 'Reason alone enters in, as an additional factor, from outside',[39] unknowingly anticipating the Christian doctrine that the human soul is always created directly by God 'from outside' as it could not ever be the result of physical causation.

What I therefore want to suggest here is that the difference between natural sexual congress and technological forms of reproduction that replace the sexual act, such as IVF and cloning, is that in the case of the former, because what is being done is an act of the rational body, there is a continuity of narrative. The body is, as it were, telling a story – a story so profound that it manifests itself in a whole new person, a brand new rational soul in union with a body. Acts of manufacture, by contrast, represent a break in the intelligibility of the narrative-making with which we shape our lives. To trace one's origins back to a technical act rather than to the mutual self-knowledge of a couple does not seem befitting for the figure of embodied rationality, who is neither begotten purely of the flesh nor purely of the immaterial soul. The self-gift of one's substance is only present in truncated form where it comes under the power of a technical mastery.

But why cannot manufacture be part of a narrative – is manufacture not an act of immense human creativity and, indeed, rationality? There is analogy here with the direct creation versus the reproduction of art. Walter Benjamin, the Marxist philosopher, saw quite clearly in his landmark essay, 'The Work of Art in the Age of Mechanical Reproduction', that artworks lost their 'aura' – their authenticity, and presence in space and time – when they became subject to mechanical reproduction.[40] Benjamin did not, however, unequivocally lament this fact, seeing it as bringing about the emancipation of art from ritual. Yet his insight contains something transferable to the domain of human reproduction. Mechanical methods of human reproduction take the potential for the generation of new life out of the bodily centres of history of the human person, out of rational flesh and into the domain of mechanical matter. The gratuitous gift of one's own bodily substance is disrupted by the requirements of manufacture. Worse, if genetic material is enhanced for the purpose of posthumanist qualities, this cannot be said to be a genuine sharing of one's substance for the generation of new life. No longer is it 'flesh of my flesh'.

Conclusion

Parenthood is, in summary, not a mere process but a rational relationship, understood in the context of the teleological ordering of our bodies. Posthumanism, it seems to me, is willing to take the logic of assisted reproduction to its more radical conclusions in order to objectify the body, treating as sub-rational matter, to be re-used, reprogrammed for other purposes. Ironically, although it is premised on expanding the potential of the body, it involves in actual fact a thoroughgoing rejection of the body as a centre of rationality and personal history.

It has been observed that creation myths vary from culture to culture, and motif of 'deus faber' – God the craftsman – is particularly associated with advanced technical cultures.[41] An interesting hypothetical question is: If our culture today had its own creation myth, given our present state of technological advancement, what would it be? In its rejection of the body and its spiritual significance, has our culture replaced a creation-of-the-world myth with a creation-of-the-individual myth: the idea that each being comes from a technical process, which can be done 'inefficiently' and 'randomly' or in a more technical and controlled manner? Man is both creator and creature on this view, ever-increasing his technical manipulation of biological 'raw materials'.

This myth, I think, lies at the bottom of many posthumanist aspirations. In order to provide a corrective, technical efficiency – which in our contemporary society has the appearance of 'neutrality' and 'objectivity' – must be critiqued and called out for its rejection, in its extreme forms, of the human spirit. By that term, I do not mean some romanticized pre-technological past, or a luddite preference for old-fashioned ways. Rather, I mean the rationality of the natural order – the rationality of our deepest intuitions which perceive that biology matters, that parenthood matters and matter is never the full story.

Notes

1. For a helpful discussion of autonomy in the context of transhumanism and posthumanism, see Ciano Aydin, 'The Posthuman as Hollow Idol: A Nietzschean Critique of Human Enhancement', *The Journal of Medicine and Philosophy* 42, no. 1 (2017): 304–27.
2. See, for instance, Nuffield Council on Bioethics, *Genome Editing and Human Reproduction: Social and Ethical Issues* (London: Nuffield Council on Bioethics, 2018).
3. Robert Andorno et al., 'Geneva Statement on Heritable Human Genome Editing: The Need for Course Correction', *Trends in Biotechnology* 38, no. 4 (2020): 352; Tina Rulli, 'Reproductive CRISPR Does Not Cure Disease', *Bioethics* 33, no. 9 (2019): 1072–82.
4. See, for instance, Alasdair MacIntyre, *Dependent Rational Animals: Why Human Beings Need the Virtues* (Chicago: Open Court, 1999).
5. Zoie O'Brien, '"God Is Not Male . . . OR Female": Archbishop of Canterbury Says "The Father" Cannot be Defined by Human Gender', *MailOnline*, 21 November 2018, https://www.dailymail.co.uk/news/article-6412481/God-not-male-female-Archbishop-Canterbury-says-Christian-deitys-gender.html (Accessed on 30 September 2020).
6. All biblical quotations are, unless otherwise stated, taken from the Douay-Rheims 1899 American Edition, https://www.biblegateway.com/versions/Douay-Rheims-1899-American-Edition-DRA-Bible/ (Accessed on 2 October 2020).
7. Thomas Aquinas, *The 'Summa Theologica' of St Thomas Aquinas*, trans. Fathers of the English Dominican Province (London: Burns, Oates and Washbourne, 1920), I, q. 3, a. 1, co. Hereafter ST.
8. Paul Gondreau, 'The Natural Ordering to Marriage as Foundation and Norm for Sacramental Marriage', *The Thomist* 77, no. 1 (2013): 42.
9. *Newsnight*, 'Does God Have a Gender?', aired 22 November 2018 on BBC Two, https://www.bbc.co.uk/programmes/p06sjxfz.
10. O'Brien, 'God Is Not Male'.

11 This is the rendering in most English translations, but not in the Douay-Rheims.
12 Battista Mondin, *The Principle of Analogy in Protestant and Catholic Theology* (The Hague: Martinus Nijhoff, 1963), 93–8.
13 *The Roman Missal* (London: Catholic Truth Society, 2011), trans. International Commission on English in the Liturgy Corporation, 562.
14 Near the beginning of his well-known book on reproductive technology, *Begotten or Made?* (Oxford: Clarendon Press, 1984), 1, Oliver O'Donovan speaks of the difference between begetting and making. The former concerns being, not will; we do not, he contends, 'determine what our offspring is, except by ourselves being that very thing which our offspring is to become'. To make, by contrast, is to fashion 'the product of our own free determination'.
15 One of the earliest uses of the term, which predates donor conception, is H. J. Sants, 'Genealogical Bewilderment in Children with Substitute Parents', *British Journal of Medical Psychology* 37, no. 2 (1964): 133–41. For a more recent study of donor-conceived adults, which mentions genealogical bewilderment, see A. J. Turner and A. Coyle, 'What Does It Mean to be a Donor Offspring? The Identity Experiences of Adults Conceived by Donor Insemination and the Implications for Counselling and Therapy', *Human Reproduction* 15, no. 9 (2000): 2041–51.
16 Helen Watt, 'Parenthood, Filiation, Corporeality', in *Accompanying Life: New Responsibilities in the Technological Era*, eds. Vincenzo Paglia and Renzo Pegoraro (Rome: Pontifical Academy for Life, 2018), 62.
17 It is only 'slightly' facetious because, regrettably, when mitochondrial donation (also known as 'three-parent IVF') was being debated in the UK's House of Commons, media reports frequently described the process as being akin to changing the batteries of an ovum. See David Albert Jones, 'The Other Woman: Evaluating the Language of "Three Parent" Embryos', *Clinical Ethics* 10, no. 4 (2015): 97–106, for why this is a fundamental misrepresentation of the technique.
18 *The Roman Missal*, 562.
19 S. J. Gerald O'Collins, *The Beauty of Jesus Christ: Filling out a Scheme of St Augustine* (Oxford: Oxford University Press, 2020), 40. 'Arian-style subordination' refers to the fourth-century heresy of Arianism, which denied both that Christ was divine and that he existed from eternity with God the Father.
20 J. N. D. Kelly, *Early Christian Doctrines*, 5th edn (London: A. and C. Black, 1977), 130, quoted in ibid.
21 See, for instance, Jason T. Eberl, *Thomistic Principles and Bioethics* (Abingdon: Routledge, 2006), 38.
22 Samuel B. Condic and Maureen L. Condic, *Human Embryos, Human Beings: A Scientific and Philosophical Approach* (Washington, D.C.: The Catholic University of America Press, 2018), 98–100.
23 Anthony Kenny, *The Metaphysics of Mind* (Oxford: Oxford University Press, 1989), 20.
24 Jones, *Approaching the End: A Theological Exploration of Death and Dying* (Oxford: Oxford University Press, 2007), Ch. 5, 'In One Way Natural, in Another Unnatural: Death in the Thought of Thomas Aquinas', 90–143.
25 Gary Hatfield, 'René Descartes', *The Stanford Encyclopedia of Philosophy* (2018), ed. Edward N. Zalta, https://plato.stanford.edu/archives/sum2018/entries/descartes/ (Accessed on 30 September 2020).
26 G. E. M. Anscombe, 'Analytical Philosophy and the Spirituality of Man', in *Human Life, Action and Ethics: Essays by G.E.M. Anscombe*, eds. Mary Geach and Luke Gormally (Exeter: Imprint Academic, 2005), 10.

27 Kenny, *The Metaphysics of Mind*, 20.
28 The following two paragraphs are adapted from an earlier essay of mine, 'Elizabeth Anscombe's Philosophy of the Human Person', originally published in *Public Discourse: The Journal of the Witherspoon Institute*, 17 March 2019, https://www.thepublicdiscourse.com/2019/03/50333/ (Accessed on 30 September 2020), and reproduced with permission.
29 Anscombe, 'Analytical Philosophy', 7–8.
30 Anscombe, *Intention*, 2nd edn (Oxford: Basil Blackwell, 1976), §2.
31 Anscombe, 'Analytical Philosophy', 14.
32 These are actions distinct from those that take place without any conscious choice at all, such as the beating of the heart or the fighting off of an infection. These are not rational acts, although they might be called acts of the body *qua* rational. Though they may go on in a seemingly mechanical fashion, just like in non-rational animals, in our case they are ordered towards the sustaining of life that is rational in character.
33 I develop this further in relation to the institution of marriage in 'Natural Family Planning and the Myth of Catholic Contraception', *Church Life Journal*, 12 March 2018, https://churchlifejournal.nd.edu/articles/natural-family-planning-and-the-myth-of-catholic-contraception/ (Accessed on 2 October 2020).
34 S. J. Gerald O'Collins and S. J. Mario Farrugia, *Catholicism: The Story of Catholic Christianity*, 2nd edn (Oxford: Oxford University Press, 2015), 150.
35 John Finnis, 'C.S. Lewis and Test-Tube Babies', in *Human Rights and Common Good: Collected Essays: Volume III* (Oxford: Oxford University Press, 2011), 278.
36 Ibid.
37 Mary Shelley, *Frankenstein, Or, The Modern Prometheus* (Oxford: Oxford University Press, 2018), 102.
38 Alasdair MacIntyre develops the notion of narrativity in *After Virtue: A Study in Moral Theory*, 3rd edn (London: Bristol Classical Press, 2007), Ch. 15: 'The Virtues, the Unity of a Human Life and the Concept of Tradition', 204–25. Somewhat delightfully, he also observes here that one of the great ironies of Jean-Paul Sartre's work was that he tried to explain the meaninglessness of life being using narratives!
39 David Albert Jones, *The Soul of the Embryo: An Inquiry into the Status of the Human Embryo in the Christian Tradition* (London: Continuum, 2004), 81.
40 Walter Benjamin, 'The Work of Art in the Age of Mechanical Reproduction', in *Illuminations: Essays and Reflections*, ed. Hannah Arendt, trans. Harry Zohn (Boston: Mariner Books, 2019), 166–95.
41 Marie-Louise von Franz, *Creation Myths*, rev. edn (Boston: Shambhala, 1995), 139.

11

An Islamic outlook

Islamic perspectives on the ethics of bringing transhuman and posthuman persons into existence

Mehrunisha Suleman

Introduction

On scope

As a species, humans excel at innovation and industry. Our ability to constantly invent and transform environments is what sets us apart from other species.[1] Such activity led to the Anthropocene, an era in which human activity has dominant and unprecedented influence on the global climate.[2] Yet recent developments in artificial intelligence, genomics and neuroscience are heralding a new frontier in which we can potentially alter and manipulate ourselves. This transformation of ourselves as chief engineers of our environments to ones where we turn our tools of innovation on ourselves is unprecedented, and unsurprisingly has prompted growing dialogue and concerns about potential risks and consequences. The other significant concern is about how such endeavours may be influencing our understanding of ourselves 'as instruments to be engineered, optimized, and programmed, as if our minds and bodies were themselves nothing more than technologies'.[3] Arguably, forms of cognitive enhancement are already present such as smart phone technologies, increasingly omniscient computer databases and networks. These are, however, presently external to us despite becoming more integral to all of our daily lives.

Proponents of human enhancement reason that the pursuit of new capacities and the need to overcome limitations to human life, originated at the birth of our species.[4] The Swedish-born philosopher Nick Bostrom explains that transforming or transcending our physical nature is central to the transhumanist view. This considers:

> [H]uman nature as a work-in-progress a half-baked beginning that we can learn to remould in desirable ways. Current humanity need not be the endpoint of evolution. Transhumanists hope that by responsible use of science, technology, and other rational means we shall eventually manage to become posthuman, beings with vastly greater capacities than present human beings have.[5]

This desire to acquire greater capacities and the process through which such an enterprise ought to be borne out is explored in this chapter. In particular, it will focus on why, if at all, we should embark on such an undertaking and whether there is an ethical manner to bringing new kinds of persons into existence, and if so what the parameters of such a process ought to be.[6]

Need for diverse accounts

The account presented here will provide an analysis of theological, ethical and historical accounts within the Islamic tradition pertaining to bringing transhuman and posthuman persons into existence, including references to the *Qur'an*, traditions of the Prophet Muhammad (*hadith pl. ahadith*) as well as jurisprudence (*fiqh*) and scholarly edicts (*fatwah pl. fatawah*). Given that calls for enhancement impact the future of the human species, it is critical that diverse voices contribute to the debate and in particular religious and cultural traditions that are to date underrepresented in this discourse. The Islamic tradition is replete with teachings about the nature and purpose of humankind as well as offering detailed scriptural accounts of the story of creation. Nevertheless, very little is known about the normative tradition and the practices and views of Muslims on the moral implications of bringing transhuman and posthuman persons into existence. I hope that the discussion offered here will contribute to addressing this knowledge gap and act as a stimulus for much needed further discussion within the interdisciplinary Islamic scholarship from traditional seminaries to academia.

Brief background on the sources of the Islamic tradition

Islam as a civilization, a body of thought and religious practices comprises myriad traditions. At its origins, it is defined as a 'way of life' received by the Prophet Muhammad through revelation (*Qur'an*). Muslims rely on understandings of the *Qur'an* as well as *hadith* to formulate their worldview. From its nascent period, Islam began to emerge not as a monolith but a discursive tradition involving deliberations and disagreements about scriptural interpretation, succession of the Prophet as well as the role of reason and revelation in theological and ethico-legal analyses. A critical departure from the original Muslim community occurred immediately after the Prophet's death with disagreements about who ought to succeed him. Those who pledged allegiance with Abu Bakr, the Prophet's closest friend and confidant formed a sub-group of believers known as *Sunni*. Others who considered the Prophet's cousin, Ali, as the legitimate successor are known as *Shi'a*. The schism that occurred forming *Sunni* and *Shi'i* communities was not only political but also religious, where *Sunnis*, after the Prophet's death, placed their authority in the *Sunnah* (Prophetic tradition, transmitted through *hadith* or narrations of the Prophet) and the community (*jama'a*). The *Shi'a* in contrast placed authority in the Prophet and also the descendants of Ali or the infallible imam. The divergent sources of religious authority led to a plurality in theology and philosophy between the two groups. *Shi'i* philosophy and theology are heavily influenced by *Mu'tazili* theology, which emphasizes free will and the role of reason in the interpretation of the *Qur'an* and *Hadith*. Furthermore, *Mu'tazili* theology relies on metaphorical and symbolic interpretations of the *Qur'an*, whereas that preferred by *Sunnis*, the *Asha'ari* School,[7] relies on a more orthodox and less allegorical method of interpretation of the *Qur'an*.[8] Given the predominance of Sunni believers throughout Islamic history, it is the *Asha'ari* School that has dominated throughout the Islamic world. The detailed differences between Islam's two schools of theology is beyond the remit of this chapter, their mention here is to highlight the prevalence of plurality within the tradition that is pertinent to subsequent sections.

Diverse views are not limited to theology. As the *Qur'an* and *Ahadith* do not offer distinctive guidance on emerging ethico-legal problems, such as transhumanism and posthumanism, religious experts are called on to analyse and interpret the textual sources. In the *Sunni* tradition this is primarily through consensus (*Ijma*) and analogy (*Qiyas*) and in the *Shi'i* school (which does not rely on *Qiyas*), through the implementation of individual and/or collective reasoning (*ijtihad*). The result of such scholarly reasoning, through the ages, is the formation of Islamic jurisprudence (*fiqh*). The latter involves meticulous attention to the primary sources and underlying values of the tradition to determine the rightness and wrongness of the matter under consideration. Deliberative tools employed by Islamic scholars include *fatawah* or non-binding ethico-legal Islamic opinions that can inform views and actions of the lay Muslim community. This chapter includes references to such sources and views to provide an analysis of Islamic scholarly opinions and lay Muslim views about the ethico-legal and theological considerations around the possibility and process of bringing into existence novel sapient beings.

It is important to highlight here that there is yet to be a collaborative effort or enquiry through traditional Islamic scholarly deliberation or systematic academic analysis that provides comprehensive insight into this topic, namely the Islamic tradition's response to transhumanist and posthumanist visions. There are, however, book chapters,[9] academic articles[10] and most recently a volume titled 'Muslim and Supermuslim'[11] looking at Muslim philosophical accounts pertaining to transhumanism. Although I make references to some of these contributions, this chapter relies primarily on my analysis of Quranic and Prophetic accounts to offer novel insights on whether and how to ethically bring into existence transhuman and posthuman persons.

Section 1

On terminology: Theological and linguistic analyses on whether we are 'playing God'

A challenge that emerged from the outset of this project[12] was the identification and use of correct terminology. Does the activity of, for example, 'bringing forth', 'creating', 'co-creating', 'giving birth to' and 'bringing into existence' carry synonymous weight linguistically and theologically when we envisage novel sapient beings? Within the Islamic tradition, there has been dedicated scholarship iterating what is central to Islamic theology and the Prophetic message, that of monotheism. The latter is a distinctive commitment to belief in One God and the attributes that God assigns to Himself as revealed in the *Qur'an*. Given the emphasis of monotheism in Islam, I will briefly review some of these attributes and in particular those that refer to God's manifestation as Creator. Delineating God's attributes will provide a better understanding and language of what the human endeavour of designing, shaping and engineering novel capacities is and is not.

Quranic account of God's attributes (*sifat*)

There is a detailed account within Islamic theology of discussions and disagreements between *Mu'tazili* and *Asha'ari* scholars on how to understand God's *sifat*, the divine attributes described by His 'most beautiful names' (*asma al-husna*). Concerns in particular were raised about the dangers of anthropormorphizing the divine attributes. Also, apprehensions about undermining God's transcendence meant that *Mu'tazili's* concluded that the *Qur'an* is created. Although God's word, it cannot be coeternal with God as this would challenge His unity. *Ashari's* and *Sunnis* have disagreed with this and despite their concerns about how to conceive of divinity, they argue that the attributes outlined in the *Qur'an* ought not to be passively acknowledged and that although human understanding is limited this should not prevent reasonable analysis.[13] Although the intricacies of these scholarly developments is beyond the scope of this chapter, I am keen to emphasize the challenge of extracting and understanding God's *sifat*, as detailed in the *Qur'an*. Here I make a tentative survey to try and demarcate transcendence from human capacities.

Of the ninety-nine names, which explicate God's attributes (*sifat*), there are at least twelve that illuminate God as Creator.[14] I have surveyed Quranic terms related to God's attributes as Creator through a careful review of the *asma al-husna*, a published account on creation[15] and a survey of Quranic verses corresponding to the relevant *sifat*. Table 11.1 displays these terms, their associated translations and reference in the *Qur'an*. *Al-Khaliq* was found to be the most prevalent term for God's attribute as Creator.

The survey offers three key insights pertinent to the human endeavour of designing, shaping and engineering novel capacities. The first is that the numerous *sifat* provide an indication of the singular nature and complexity of God's ability and process of creation. That these terms are only used in the *Qur'an* in reference to God Himself is indicative of the delineation between God's actions and that of humankind.

Second, the table includes references to God as *al-Ba'ith* (The Resurrector) and *al-Muhyi* (The Restorer), both referring to God as the Returner of life after death. In a verse outlining miracles performed by Jesus, the restoration of the dead is referred to by the term *tukh'riju* (you bring forth) (The Holy *Qur'an* Chapter 5 Verse 110).[17] The terminology used by God for the action carried out by Jesus is thus distinctive to the attributes defining God's role as Restorer. *Tukh'riju* (you bring forth), the word describing the action of Jesus, originates from the root word *kharaja* (to leave, to go

Table 11.1 Attributes Illuminating God as Creator

Sifat	Translation	References of Qur'anic verses mentioning term
al-Khaliq*	The Creator	(6:102) (13:16) (15:86) (35:3) (23:14) (37:125) (36:81) (38:71) (39:62) (40:62) (52:35) (56:59) (59:24)[16]
al-Ba'ith	The Resurrector, The Infuser of new life, The Reviver, The Raiser	(2:56) (16:84) (16:89)
al-Badi*	The Originator, Absolute Cause	(2:117) (6:101)
al-Bari'*	The Producer, The Inventor, The Evolver	(2:54) (59:24)
al-Fatir	The Creator, The Originator	(6:14) (12:101) (14:10) (35:1) (39:46) (42:11)
al-Mubdi*	The Beginner, The Originator	(7:29) (29:19) (29:20) (32:7) (85:13)
al-Mueed	The Restorer, The Reproducer	(17:51)
al-Muhyi	The Maintainer, The Restorer, The Giver of Life	(30:50) (41:39)
al-Musawwir*	The Fashioner, The Former, The Shaper	(59:24)
al-Muqtadir*	The All Powerful, The All Able	(18:45) (43:42) (54:42) (54:55)**
al-Qadir*	The Omnipotent, All Powerful	(18:45) (43:42) (54:42) (54:55)**
al-Qahhar*	The Dominant, The All Prevailing One, The Subjugator	(6:18) (6:61) (7:127)

*From: David B, Burrell, in Burrell DB (2008) Creation. In: Winter, Tim, ed. *The Cambridge companion to classical Islamic theology*. Cambridge University Press, 2008. Page 141.
** al-Muqtadir and al-Qadir both stem from the root word qadara so reference verses are the same.

out). This is linguistically distinct to, for example, references made to God bringing forth (*nabra-aha*[18]), where *nabra-aha* stems from the root word ba-ra-aa whose active participle is *Bari* or God's *sifat* as The Evolver.

The account of Jesus's actions provides us with a Quranic understanding of the delineation between God's actions and attributes and that of humankind. It also provides a syntactical offering of suitable terminology when considering bringing into existence novel sapient beings. Using linguistic guidance from the *Qur'an*, the term(s) that can be used when referring to the process of bringing forth transhuman and posthuman beings include: bring forth, bring into being, bring into existence and/or phrases morphologically similar to these. This analysis also provides, through the root word *kharaja*, suitable terminology for scholars seeking to carry out similar research in Arabic, which takes account of Quranic understandings of processes considered in the purview of God and those of humans.

Finally, the above verse also provides Quranic reference to a critical feature of Islamic theology, namely that the concept of humans 'playing God' is implausible. This is because all of humankind's actions occur through God's permission. That we are capable of doing means that such actions occur through God's will (*qadar* or divine decree) and not in spite of it. For example, the eminent Persian theologian and Sufi thinker Abu Hamid al-Ghazali (d. 505/1111) on 'Faith in Divine Unity and Truth in Divine Providence' book 35 in his work *Revival of the Religious Sciences* (*Ihya Ulum al-din*) states that: 'Oh linguist, you have posited the term "agent" to signify the one who originates, but [in that sense] there is no agent but God, so the term belongs to Him.'[19] The Catholic scholar David Burrell explains that Ghazali's grammatical sense of the term 'acting' in reference to being an 'agent' encompasses 'originating' or 'creating' where he emphasizes that such capacity is the purview of God alone.[20]

Thus, Islamic theology differs from some Christian theological interpretations that may consider procedures that bring into existence novel beings as inappropriate due to their being synonymous to 'playing God'.[21] As the above analysis has shown, both in terms of God's *sifat* and that of the capabilities or processes borne out by humans, through the example of Jesus, bringing into existence novel beings is not an anathema. This is because such an enterprise would not be synonymous with that of God's attributes as Creator, rather it would resemble, for example, the actions of Jesus bringing forth the dead with God's permission.

Creation ex nihilo

God as described in the *Qur'an* creates *ex nihilo*.[22] That any transhuman or posthuman enterprise will be materially demarcated differentiates this process with that of God's. Furthermore, the *Qur'an* provides repeated mention of God's transcendence as marked by His being the Creator.[23] The Quranic account of the creation story also details how God created the Prophets such as Adam and Jesus and indeed all of humankind in a manner similar to other matter, through Divine Will:

> Indeed, the example of Jesus to God is like that of Adam. He created Him from dust; then He said to him, 'Be,' and he was. (The Holy *Qur'an* Chapter 3 Verse 59)

Although we will return to accounts of the creation story in subsequent sections about the nature and purpose of humankind, this brief mention is to offer the Quranic distinction of God's creative power and that of the human endeavour of designing, shaping and engineering novel capacities.

On human embryology, reproduction and 'biological hacking'

Human embryology, reproduction and ensoulment

Another concern about the potential of altering humankind is the process through which this may occur. Bringing into existence novel beings through genetic manipulation, neuroscientific or cybernetic enhancement would differ markedly from the model we currently have. Fertilization, implantation, early embryonic development, the milestones of pregnancy and birth are the processes through which human persons, so far, have come into existence. I will briefly present pertinent Islamic theological and ethico-legal perspectives that offer insight into whether concerns around altering or circumventing such processes are valid.

In the *Qur'an*, there are several verses that describe human embryology[24] and there is also a tradition of the Prophet that offers further detail on gestation and ensoulment (40 hadith of Nawawi – Hadith number 4).[25] The verses outline the intricate detail with which the *Qur'an* depicts early human development, growth and maturation. It describes both the process of implantation and embryonic development. The *hadith* adds further detail about the modular nature of human development and how material development is accompanied, at a prescribed time, by an immaterial soul.

How transhuman and posthuman beings will be understood in terms of their material and immaterial components and if there will be an immaterial component does require further study. Will the electromagnetic wave composite that may be derived from processes/pulses through biological and/or silicon-based circuitry resemble the human soul? Or will such beings simply differ from our human selves with regards to their being without a soul? If so, what impact would that have on their sense of self and also their moral status as beings? Do these questions and concerns around ensoulment mean that engaging in transhuman and posthuman endeavours is counter to Islamic theological teachings? There is yet to be a definitive answer on the latter, though some work has been done on the importance of the soul in Islamic theological and ethico-legal understandings of human nature.[26] Although subsequent sections deal, in more detail, with issues around human form and human nature as being divine, here I am trying to raise possible questions and concerns that may stimulate further normative theological and ethico-legal scholarship on the process of gestation and pregnancy in particular.

Having raised the above problems about human embryology and human nature, it is important to briefly highlight existing exceptions and, in particular, rapid acceptance and uptake of assisted reproductive technologies among Muslim societies. If the 'natural way' in which humans have always been conceived, carried and been borne was sacred, then there would be an inability to embrace emerging methods of correcting or enhancing reproductive processes. Analysis of the last two decades of Islamic ethico-legal scholarship[27] and anthropological accounts of Muslim societies[28] offers evidence on the tradition not only accepting but readily embracing such methods and Muslims themselves becoming increasingly reliant on such techniques to fulfil what they consider both religious and cultural commitments, that of procreating and having a family.

Furthermore, given the prevalence of genetic diseases in Muslim societies, there has been a concerted Islamic scholarly effort to review emerging biomedical interventions that could offer potential solutions. For example, research shows that in countries like Saudi Arabia up to 25 per cent of marriages occur between first cousins where resulting conceptions carry a 5 per cent higher risk of genetic disease.[29] Interventions such as genetic screening, counselling, testing and preimplantation genetic diagnosis

(PGD) have all been carefully and repeatedly reviewed by bodies of theological and ethico-legal scholars around the Muslim world. There is resounding consensus that not only would such technology and/or interventions be acceptable but that they ought to be encouraged on the basis of protecting one's progeny. Additionally, terminating a pregnancy due to genetic defects has undergone careful scholarly review. Again, there is broad consensus that such termination is acceptable if the condition is severe, untreatable and unmanageable and if conducted prior to 120 days of gestation.[30] Moreover, the permissibility of somatic therapy was advocated by the Islamic Jurisprudence Council, of the Islamic World League (Organization of Islamic Countries – OIC) in 1998.[31]

That a departure from what is considered 'natural' has been successfully negotiated within the Islamic ethico-legal tradition through the development and issuing of *fatawah*,[32] pertaining to assisted reproductive technologies (ART), genetic testing, PGD and somatic therapy means arguably that a legal and moral precedent exists for the possibility of bringing into existence transhuman and posthuman beings through novel means. Through the aforementioned procedures, humans have modified their chances and methods of having children, the risk of disease these children may experience or in extreme cases whether or not to have a child based on the likelihood of a disorder. The evidence suggests that we have already gone considerably beyond what our forbearers would have considered the 'natural order' and/or the state of unconditionally accepting our procreated children.

There are, however, still outstanding questions in relation to this. Firstly, are ARTs distinct in that they still rely on cellular precursors (ova and sperm), which means that the procedures are, overall, still considered natural? It is important to mention here that more scholarship is needed to take into consideration the procedures through which novel beings would be brought into existence and whether and to what extent they would differ from existing and accepted innovations to the processes of fertilization, implantation, pregnancy and birth.

The miracle of Jesus's birth: An example of 'biological hacking'?

Given what has just been mentioned about the potential importance of cellular precursors defining the natural parameters of human reproduction, it is necessary to review an account in the *Qur'an* that provides further insight into human conception. When we look at our prevailing biological paradigm, we understand conception as being the result of a fusion between an egg and sperm cell. The *Qur'an* (and other sacred texts), however, describe how in the case of Mary's seclusion the conventional process of conceiving does not occur (The Holy *Qur'an* Chapter 3 Verse 47).[33]

There are of course limitations in our understandings of the miracle of Jesus's birth. The miracle of conception is described, Mary's pregnancy ensues and is followed by Jesus's birth. Yet, what occurs physically at the onset of her pregnancy is unknown. Does God provide this example as another instance of His transcendence? Or does He offer an illustration of how nature need not be limited? Is the cellular process of fertilization sacred or does Jesus's birth offer a reasonable exception to allow processes of conception to be carried out that are unconventional? Is God providing a model of 'biological hacking' that can offer potential insights for transhuman and posthuman endeavours?

The evidence and associated unresolved questions reveal that concerns around altering or circumventing the processes of human reproduction are not in themselves conclusive in enabling us to reject novel approaches in bringing into existence transhuman and posthuman persons. The discussion here is not advocating such endeavours rather it seeks to highlight the need for rigorous and systematic Islamic ethico-legal, theological and anthropological scholarship on such issues.

On human form: Nature and status of the body

In Mercer and Maher's volume titled *Transhumanism and the Body*,[34] perspectives from the major world religions are considered, particularly in relation to how understandings about the body may inform an ethics of bringing into existence new kinds of persons. The Islamic scholar, Hamid Mavani,[35] describes Islamic perspectives on the status, role and function of the body. He posits that a guide to understanding the status of the human body within the Islamic paradigm is by assessing its prominence not just in life but also in death, once the soul has departed. It is critical to point out here that Islamic perspectives on the status, role and function of the body is illustrated in beliefs about an individual's spiritual and physical rootedness manifested through the body. It means that it is not just the immaterial self that matters, but the body through which one intends, acts and witnesses, which is crucial. The body acting and existing impacts both physical and metaphysical existences. This is because there is a lack of distinction made, within many Islamic ethico-legal traditions, between the sanctity of the living and dead body. Mavani,[36] for example, explains that the dead body retains its living status and spiritual connection such that faculties like awareness and pain, which are often ascribed to the soul, are still manifest within the dead body. The practical implications of such understandings are marked by Muslim moral commitments to ensuring respect for the dead body, its handling to prevent physical harm, and resistance towards scientific and/or medical intervention including post-mortem examination and/or research, organ retrieval and cremation.

Perspectives from faith traditions in Mercer and Maher's[37] volume share in their respect for the human body but also that it is good for humans to improve themselves and attain a deeper level of life, beyond their biological needs. They share in their beliefs around humans seeking to better their life, though they may differ in what 'better' means. Buddhism, for example, emphasizes training of the mind, not to abandon or glorify the body but to reach enhanced states of awareness. The final point is to attain a state of being beyond physical cycles of rebirth, such that bodily longevity in and of itself would serve no purpose. In Islam, by contrast, spiritual and moral enhancement is achieved through a bodily existence and not outside of it. Faith traditions may thus differ in their consideration of human ontology – whether we are unitary beings experiencing life at several levels (physical, moral, spiritual), or whether we are a composite of two or more ontologically different realities (e.g. body and soul), which may function as a unity or also separately.

What influence would such beliefs have on bringing into existence transhuman and posthuman persons? Mavani explains that from Islamic perspectives, if we consider transhumans as beings who have a body, which is recognizably human, then bringing such forms into existence would require similar ethical injunctions to those deemed necessary for existing humans.[38] Are genetic interventions that reduce or ameliorate human suffering acceptable despite the possibility that they may transgress what would be natural? The latter speaks to intentions, motivations as well as ends, and, Mavani argues, most Islamic perspectives would support interventions to address/limit human physical suffering. If addressing disorders means a realization of beings who were dissimilar to us in such a regard (for example, immune from known diseases) and are still recognizably human, then the bringing into existence of such beings ought to involve the same ethical injunctions as those which are already present for humans. He does, however, emphasize that such a project ought to occur within God's permission of seeking cures and as with some other faith traditions 'maintaining an organic and recognizably human body'.

Mavani's account, however, means that such an ethics of generation falls short of embracing posthuman forms of existence. The majority of current and historical Islamic perspectives are rooted in respecting the creation of the body and soul as a composite, such that a translocation of one's memory and consciousness to attain digital immortality would be counter to accepted Islamic theological commitments to birth, death, resurrection and the afterlife. Other than a resistance to bringing into existence posthumans, where the transformation of existence is such that it forever sunders the rootedness of the body and soul, Islamic perspectives are yet to offer a way of thinking about the generation of such entities.

There is a notable exception to this widely held Islamic perspective on the status of the body, which is the view of the Persian physician and philosopher Abu Bakr ar Razi (854–925). Though, he was one of the greatest physicians during the medieval period, some of his religious views made him infamous among his contemporary Muslim scholars. His reputation may thus have impacted the uptake of his philosophical ideas. Razi posited that the whole body, including the brain, 'is simply the instrument and implement of the rational soul'.[39] Furthermore, he suggested that within its earthly existence, the soul is entangled with the body, and that 'if the rational soul would make perfect and complete use of its rationality it would liberate itself from the body in which it is enmeshed'.[40] Although a minority perspective, further research on Razi's account and his interpretations of Platonic analyses on the soul may offer novel Islamic perspectives on the possibilities and ethics of bringing posthuman persons into existence.

So far in this discussion, we have been primarily concerned with the question of 'what are we doing?' when we are thinking about bringing into existence transhuman and posthuman persons. The above analysis summarizes Islamic theological and ethico-legal accounts of whether the 'what' of the process raises concerns about 'playing God' or deviating from the 'natural order' of procreation and birth. Furthermore, the section looks at the implications of potentially altering or replacing altogether the human body as the form through which one can exist. The 'what' is but one aspect of analysis relevant to the Islamic tradition. Key to any Muslim endeavour is the purpose for which an action is undertaken, the so-called 'why are we doing this?' aspect of the transhumanist vision. The following sections deal with the 'why' focusing on Islamic metaphysical understandings of the nature and purpose of creation, and a worldview which posits, 'that we can does not necessarily mean we should'.

Section 2

On the nature and purpose of creation

As mentioned above, the transhumanist vision is committed to the idea of 'human nature as a work-in-progress', where we can potentially become 'posthuman, beings with vastly greater capacities than present human beings have'.[41] Two questions emerge from this which require an analysis of Islam's foundational texts. The first is: what is said about human nature and is it considered 'a work-in-progress'? If so, one could extrapolate that the foundational Islamic texts are congruent with the transhumanist vision. The second question is about why we would begin such an undertaking and what do the *Qur'an* and *Ahadith* say about the possibility of acquiring greater capacities.

Quranic perspectives on human nature and purpose: Relationship between the Creator and the created

Both the *Qur'an* and *Ahadith* are replete with teachings pertinent to our discussion on whether we should seek to generate transhuman and posthuman persons. Foundational to the Islamic worldview is having an understanding of the purpose of all creation. God emphasizes in the *Qur'an* that our existence and the existence of the universe is not without purpose (The Holy *Qur'an* Chapter 3 Verse 191) [42] (The Holy *Qur'an* Chapter 38 Verse 27).[43] Furthermore, God stipulates clearly the purpose of creation is solely to worship Him (The Holy *Qur'an* Chapter 51 verse 56).[44]

What the *Qur'an* describes, through these verses, is our responsibility and accountability before God, where humankind's primary purpose is worship (*ibadah*). Furthermore, Muslims are committed to an understanding of *ibadah* as not just ritual worship, but submission to God, where all of one's actions align with God's will. This submission, within the Islamic tradition does not just apply to this physical earthly existence. The *Qur'an* describes how ontologically our being on this earth was preceded by each of us assembling as a primordial gathering of souls (The Holy *Qur'an* Chapter 7 verse 172).[45] That there is a spiritual and/or physical continuum between our pre-earthly, earthly and post-earthly existence influences our purpose and accountability on earth. Muslims thus consider it spiritually crucial to ensure that each action is carried out in alignment with God's will. Such a commitment would reinforce the belief in God's oneness and humankind's purpose to bear witness to God through each action

Determining God's will, however, has occupied theologians, ethicists and legal experts across the ages, nevertheless, there is a vital message in the *Qur'an* about the nature of humankind that is pertinent for transhuman and posthuman endeavours. God describes Adam and all of humankind as the best of creation, honoured through the prostration of all of the Angels in the heavens (The Holy *Qur'an* Chapter 17 Verse 70).[46] Furthermore, God describes giving Adam form and stature (The Holy *Qur'an* Chapter 7 Verse 11)[47] and the *Qur'an* also mentions how humankind has been created in the best of moulds (The Holy *Qur'an* Chapter 95 Verse 4).[48]

This stature and honour afforded to Adam and all of humankind suggests that a Quranic view is markedly different to that of the transhumanist view. Being created in the 'best of moulds' intimates a stark difference to a 'work-in-progress'. However, it is important to consider in what capacity God is referring humankind as the best of moulds. Is it our physical state or our spiritual distinction from other creatures? Or is it both? Does 'best of moulds' imply optimal potential or optimal state? The latter is crucial when considering the Prophetic mission that complements the Quranic message.

Lessons from the *Qur'an* and Ahadith on moral striving: Interhuman/transhuman relationships

The Prophet Muhammad explained that he had been sent to 'perfect good character'.[49] *Adab* (virtue) and *akhlaq* (proper conduct) are thus integral to the Islamic worldview and commitment of Muslims. The Islamic tradition is abounding with scholarship on *adab* and *akhlaq*. For example, during the medieval period when the translation movement of Greek texts into Arabic was taking place, Greek virtue ethics were incorporated into the Islamic civilization by scholars such as the Arab philosopher and physician al-Kindi (801–873) as well as the Persian philosophers al-Farabi (c. 872–c. 951) and Ibn Miskawayh (932–1030).[50] That the forming of good character is a striving emphasized by the Prophet suggests that Islam's view of humankind is of a being of optimal potential and not optimal state. Such a striving is not only borne out by an individual in isolation, the *Qur'an* mentions how those created ought to assist one another in moral pursuits (The Holy *Qur'an* Chapter 3 Verse 104)[51] (The Holy *Qur'an* Chapter 103 Verses 1-3).[52]

Such verses reveal what is integral in the Islamic moral tradition about interhuman relationships: that humankind ought to strive not just for one's individual commitment to God but to support such an undertaking by everyone. Believers may do this through teaching, for example, of ritual obligations. An illustration of this, relevant to our discussion on transhuman and posthuman endeavours, is of a novel intervention by a teacher in Iran, who adopted robotics in the Islamic studies classroom to teach his students how to offer the five obligatory daily prayer.[53] Such advancements reveal an interest in Muslim societies of employing technologies that resemble or mimic human capabilities to facilitate spiritual and/or moral endeavours. This does raise the question of whether a transhumanist endeavour that potentially seeks to enhance moral capabilities would comply with Islam's worldview of humankind's nature and purpose?

A related question would be what the telos or ends of such an endeavour would be. Are we seeking to generate perfectly moral beings? The above discussion may seem to suggest an answer in the affirmative.

However, the *Qur'an*, through the example of Adam (The Holy *Qur'an* Chapter 77 Verse 22)[54] absolves humankind of such expectation. The account of the fall of humankind reveals that erring is a part of human nature. Furthermore, theologically, it is pertinent to consider whether the undertaking of moral enhancement and/or moral perfection is feasible. God's *sifat* of *Al Ghaffar* (The Forgiver), *Al Gafoor* (The All Forgiving) and *Al Afuww* (The Pardoner) mean that the manifestation of these attributes of forgiveness point to perpetual erring by humankind.

The *Qur'an* designates clearly the purpose of creation and sapient beings. If transhuman and posthuman beings are human, that is, they are synonymous to us in moral capacity and consciousness then they ought to be conferred the same rights and responsibilities as us. What does that mean for them in terms of Islam's moral and legal framework? By endowing novel beings with greater capacities, are we burdening them with greater accountability? Also, the Prophetic endeavour of perfecting moral character was centred on overcoming one's moral shortcomings. However, as individuals and a collective community, by 'biologically hacking' our physical and psychological parameters, are we spiritually and morally cheating? If beings are brought into existence to be 'better than us', do their actions represent goodness and striving as described by the Prophet, or is such moral enhancement an example of moral mimicry and not true morality? Moral mimicry originates from human prosociality,[55] where good rapport leads to mirroring of moral behaviour. Duffy & Chartrand[56] explain in their 2017 book entitled *From mimicry to morality* that prosocial cognition (feeling the same) increases the likelihood of prosocial behaviour (behaving the same). Would the neural programming or genetic editing of new beings who are more virtuous, resemble a mirroring of expectations that we are coding or transcribing? Or are we really enabling a choice of moral striving and good action? The Prophet Muhammad explained that intentions are crucial to the Islamic moral tradition (Sahih Bukahri Book 1 Hadith 1).[57] In the case of transhuman and/or posthuman persons that are simply programmed to do good without the choice or intention of doing so, what would be the moral status of their actions? Additionally, prosociality is crucial in the development and maintenance of moral behaviour. Given such a psycho-social paradigm, what would the introduction of morally enhanced beings do to our interhuman/transhuman relationships? Duffy & Chartrand[58] explain that prosocial affect depends on trust. If beings are acting in a good way but not actually *intending* good, would that erode prosocial trust? Would that mean that although overall there would be more beings acting virtuously, the collective would be morally poorer? More research is needed to elucidate moral psychology from Islamic perspectives and the impact of such views in bringing novel sapient beings into existence.

On relatedness and relationships

Although previous sections dealt with the biological implications of potentially circumventing conventional processes of conception, implantation, gestation and delivery, I will now briefly present the potential impact of bypassing such processes. Within the creation story, relatedness is imbedded. God mentions in the *Qur'an* how He created humankind from clay and breathed into humankind 'from His soul' (The Holy *Qur'an*, Chapter 32 verses 7-9).[59] That we are endowed with a proportion of divinity means we are conferred dignity, status and love. Furthermore, God Himself offers humankind relief against perfection by delineating our erring and His transcendence. This Creator–creation relationship symbolizes God's mercy and the Islamic understanding of all of God's creation being worthy of being accepted. A relationship of mercy between the Creator and the created offers insights into whether there is an ethical manner to bring transhuman/posthuman persons into existence. The aforementioned verses and Islamic understandings of the vulnerability, needs and dependencies of sapient beings outline virtues of mercy and love being crucial. These are central to Islamic teachings around family and parenthood.

Through the emotional and practical commitments of seeking parenthood, humans presently invest in a deep and multifaceted way when embarking on pursuing a pregnancy and having a child. Conception is often imbued with love which parents hope will envelope the life of their child. Within the Islamic tradition, pregnancy, nursing and motherhood are deeply respected and are considered the cornerstone of families and society. The bonds of love and interdependency represented by mother and child are morally significant in Islam. Children are expected to be loved, cared for and protected, and parents have the responsibility to nurture them physically and spiritually. Need and dependency through childhood builds bonds of trust and love. Interdependency is thus the fabric upon which families and societies are woven within Islamic contexts.

Pregnancy in particular holds a special status within the Islamic tradition. The word for womb, *rahm*, in Arabic originates from the same root as *Rahmah* or mercy/compassion. This linguistic synergy points to an understanding within the Islamic tradition of the love and compassion a mother has towards her children.[60] Being cared for in childhood, nevertheless, carries responsibility in adulthood. Muslims are instructed to respect and care for parents and elderly relatives who showed compassion to them when they were young and vulnerable. Mothers, in particular, are conferred an elevated status in Islam where the Prophet described that 'paradise is beneath her feet'.[61] Muslims are thus committed to caring for their parents and their mothers in particular, both to acknowledge the care they previously received but to also honour their status as parents.

The Islamic worldview is thus centred on relatedness and interdependency that evokes compassion, acceptance, a duty to care and protect. Were we to render such relationships redundant from conception, what impact would this have on new individual beings and society more broadly? Families and communities are currently bound through physical, spiritual and moral ties. Our interdependency marks not our vulnerability but collective strength. If novel beings are brought into existence outside of such a context will they be devoid of interrelatedness and relationships? Or will their coming to being bring into existence new relationships?

Furthermore, if we bring into existence beings that are resilient, independent, invulnerable to ageing, disease, or the environment what does that mean in terms of their ability to form relationships that are built on mutual need and trust that form society? Is a telos of hyper-independence and invincibility leading us to procedures of 'generation without care'? Such a world would mean that the new beings would be vulnerable to isolation and loneliness. Additionally, despite these new persons being morally capable, their self-sufficiency would be challenged by an inability to enact virtues of compassion and care. Moreover, they would be unable to overlook or be merciful to the foibles and weaknesses that draw us together and make us human. Thus, maybe we ought to ensure that such beings have the luxury of imperfection and the capacity to embody moral character and not just moral action.

Notes

1 Brett Frischmann and Evan Selinger, *Re-engineering Humanity* (Cambridge: Cambridge University Press, 2018), xi.
2 Francesca Ferrando, 'Leveling the Posthuman Playing Field', *Theology and Science* 18, no. 1 (2020), 1–6.
3 Frischmann and Selinger, *Re-engineering Humanity*, xi.
4 Nick Bostrom, 'A History of Transhumanist Thought', *Journal of Evolution and Technology* 14, no. 1 (2005), 1–25.
5 Nick Bostrom, 'Transhumanist Values', *Journal of Philosophical Research* 30, Issue Supplement (2005), 3–14.
6 The chapter will not include deliberations about whether or not such novel beings are persons.
7 It is important to highlight here, that although the *Asha'ari* School is the dominant theological school in Sunni Islam, it is by no means the only one. The *Maturidi* school, which has close historical ties with the *Hanafi* school, is also very important to Sunni Islam. However, the focus here is on the *Asha'ari* School given its overall predominance.
8 Tim Winter, ed., *The Cambridge Companion to Classical Islamic Theology* (Cambridge: Cambridge University Press, 2008), 1–14.
9 Farzad Mahootian, 'Ideals of Human Perfection: A Comparison of Sufism and Transhumanism', in *Building Better Humans? Refocusing the Debate on Transhumanism*, eds. Hava Tirosh-Samuelson and Kenneth L. Mossman (Frankfurt: Peter Lang, 2012), 133–57; Hamid Mavani, 'Islam – God's Deputy: Islam and Transhumanism', in *Transhumanism and the Body: The World Religions Speak*, eds. Calvin Mercer and Derek F. Maher (New York: Palgrave Macmillan, 2014), 67–83.
10 Sara Hejazi, '"Humankind. The Best of Molds" – Islam Confronting Transhumanism', *Sophia* 58, no. 4 (2019), 677–88; Anke Sandra Bouzenita, '"The Most Dangerous Idea?" Islamic Deliberations on Transhumanism', *Darulfunun ilahiyat* 29, no. 2 (2018), 201–28.
11 Roy Jackson, *Muslim and Supermuslim: The Quest for the Perfect Being and Beyond* (Cham, Switzerland: Palgrave Macmillan, 2020).
12 The author would like to thank and acknowledge Dr Calum MacKellar and the Scottish Council on Human Bioethics for initiating and supporting this project.
13 El-Bizri, 'God: Essence and Attributes', in *The Cambridge Companion to Classical Islamic Theology*, ed. Tim Winter (Cambridge: Cambridge University Press, 2008), 1–14.

14. Although I have attempted to make this list as comprehensive as possible and have added four further attributes to the eight proposed by David B. Burrell (in David B Burrell, 'Creation', in *The Cambridge Companion to Classical Islamic Theology*, ed. Tim Winter (Cambridge: Cambridge University Press, 2008), 141), this compilation is likely to still be incomplete.
15. Burrell, 'Creation', 141.
16. Although there are 203 references in the *Qur'an* of terms originating from the root word Kh-la-qa, here reference is made in particular to the Active participle in reference in God. Please see: http://corpus.quran.com/qurandictionary.jsp?q=xlq (Retrieved 5 June 2020). The author would like to thank and acknowledge Corpus Quran for their database and search facility.
17. The Holy *Qur'an* Chapter 5 Verse 110: '[The Day] when Allah will say, 'O Jesus, Son of Mary, remember My favour upon you and upon your mother when I supported you with the Pure Spirit and you spoke to the people in the cradle and in maturity; and [remember] when I taught you writing and wisdom and the Torah and the Gospel; and when you designed from clay [what was] like the form of a bird with My permission, then you breathed into it, and it became a bird with My permission; and you healed the blind and the leper with My permission; and *when you brought forth the dead with My permission*; and when I restrained the Children of Israel from [killing] you when you came to them with clear proofs and those who disbelieved among them said, "This is not but obvious magic."'
18. Translation: We bring into being, bring into existence, bring forth.
19. Al-Ghazali on Faith in Divine Unity and Trust in Divine Providence. Translated by: David B. Burrell (Fons Vitae, 2002).
20. Burrell, 'Creation', 155.
21. Edgar Dahl et al., 'Attitudes towards Preconception Sex Selection: A Representative Survey from Germany', *Reproductive BioMedicine* 9, no. 6 (2004), 600–3.
22. The Holy *Qur'an* Chapter 40 Verse 68: 'It is He Who gives Life and Death; and when He decrees a matter, He but says to it: "Be" and it is.'; The Holy *Qur'an* Chapter 16 Verse 40: 'Indeed, when We will something to happen We but say to it, "Be", and it is.'
23. The Holy *Qur'an* Chapter 7 Verse 191: 'Do they associate with Him those who create nothing and they are [themselves] created?'.
24. See: 'And certainly did We create humankind from an extract of clay. Then We placed him as a sperm-drop in a firm lodging. Then We made the sperm-drop into a clinging clot, and We made the clot into a lump [of flesh], and We made [from] the lump, bones, and We covered the bones with flesh; then We developed him into another creation. So blessed is Allah, the best of creators' (The Holy *Qur'an*, Chapter 23 verses 12–14). 'O People, if you should be in doubt about the Resurrection, then [consider that] indeed, We created you from dust, then from a sperm-drop, then from a clinging clot, and then from a lump of flesh, formed and unformed – that We may show you. And We settle in the wombs whom We will for a specified term, then We bring you out as a child, and then [We develop you] that you may reach your [time of] maturity' (The Holy *Qur'an*, Chapter 22 verse 5).

'Who perfected everything which He created and began the creation of man from clay. Then He made his posterity out of the extract of a liquid disdained. Then He proportioned him and breathed into him from His [created] soul and made for you hearing and vision and hearts ...' (The Holy *Qur'an*, Chapter 32 verses 7–9).

25 40 hadith of Nawawi – Hadith number 4:

> On the authority of Abdullah ibn Masud, who said: 'The Messenger of Allah, and he is the truthful, the believed, narrated to us, "Verily the creation of each one of you is brought together in his mother's womb for forty days in the form of a *nutfah* (a drop), then he becomes an alaqah (clot of blood) for a like period, then a *mudghah* (morsel of flesh) for a like period, then there is sent to him the angel who blows his soul into him and who is commanded with four matters: to write down his *rizq* (sustenance), his life span, his actions, and whether he will be happy or unhappy (i.e., whether or not he will enter Paradise)"'.

26 Arzoo Ahmed and Mehrunisha Suleman, 'Islamic Perspectives on the Genome and the Human Person: Why the Soul Matters', in *Islamic Ethics and the Genome Question*, ed. Mohammed Ghaly (the Netherlands: Brill, 2018), 139–68.
27 Gamal I. Serour, 'Islamic Perspectives in Human Reproduction', *Reprod Biomed Online* 17, Suppl 3 (2008), 34–8.
28 Marcia C. Inhorn and Soraya Tremayne, eds., *Islam and Assisted Reproductive Technologies: Sunni and Shia Perspectives*, vol. 23 (Oxford and New York: Berghahn Books, 2012).
29 Mohammed A. Albar, 'Ethical Considerations in the Prevention and Management of Genetic Disorders with Special Emphasis on Religious Considerations', *Saudi Medical Journal* 23, no. 6 (2002), 627–32.
30 The Islamic Jurisprudence Council of the Islamic World League of the Islamic Organisations of Islamic Countries, 1990. In its 15th session where it was decided that: '(1) (it is permissible) to use genetic engineering for disease prevention, treatment, or amelioration on the condition that such use do not cause further damage; (2) to forbid the use of genetic engineering for evil and criminal uses or what is forbidden religiously; (3) to forbid using genetic engineering and its tools to change human personality and responsibility, or interfering with genes to improve the human race; (4) to forbid doing any research or therapy of human genes except in extreme need, after critical evaluation of its benefits and dangers and after an official consent of the concerned, respecting the extreme confidentiality of the information and human rights and dignity as dictated by Islamic Shariah . . .'.
31 Aida I Al-Aqeel, 'Ethical Guidelines in Genetics and Genomics: An Islamic Perspective', *Saudi Medical Journal* 26, no. 12 (2005), 1862–70.
32 Marcia C. Inhorn, *Local Babies, Global Science: Gender, Religion and In Vitro Fertilization in Egypt* (New York: Routledge, 2012).
33 The Holy *Qur'an* Chapter 3 Verse 47: 'She said, "My Lord, how will I have a child when no man has touched me?" [The angel] said, "Such is Allah; He creates what He wills. When He decrees a matter, He only says to it, "Be," and it is.'
34 Mercer and Maher, *Transhumanism and the Body*.
35 Mavani, 'Islam – God's Deputy: Islam and Transhumanism', 67–83.
36 Mavani, 'Islam – God's Deputy: Islam and Transhumanism', 67–83.
37 Mercer and Maher, *Transhumanism and the Body*.
38 Mavani, 'Islam – God's Deputy: Islam and Transhumanism', 67–83.
39 Thérèse-Anne Druart, 'Al-Razi's Conception of the Soul: Psychological Background to His Ethics', *Medieval Philosophy & Theology* 5, no. 2 (1996), 245–63, 248.
40 Druart, 'Al-Razi's Conception of the Soul: Psychological Background to His Ethics', 249.
41 Bostrom, 'Transhumanist Values'.
42 The Holy *Qur'an* Chapter 3 Verse 191: 'Our Lord, You did not create this in vain (aimlessly); exalted are You'.

43 The Holy *Qur'an* Chapter 38 Verse 27: 'And We did not create the heaven and the earth and that between them in vain (aimlessly).'
44 The Holy *Qur'an* Chapter 51 verse 56: 'And I have not created jinn and humankind except to worship me'.
45 The Holy *Qur'an* Chapter 7 verse 172: 'And [mention] when your Lord took from the children of Adam - from their loins - their descendants and made them testify of themselves, [saying to them], "Am I not your Lord?" They said, "Yes, we have testified." [This] – lest you should say on the day of Resurrection, "Indeed, we were of this unaware."'
46 The Holy *Qur'an* Chapter 17 Verse 70: 'And We have certainly honoured the children of Adam and carried them on the land and sea and provided for them of the good things and preferred them over much of what We have created, with [definite] preference.'
47 The Holy *Qur'an* Chapter 7 Verse 11: 'And We have certainly created you, [O Mankind], and given you [human] form. Then We said to the angels, "Prostrate to Adam"; so they prostrated . . .'.
48 The Holy *Qur'an* Chapter 95 Verse 4: 'We have indeed created humankind in the best of moulds (stature)'.
49 Muwatta Book 47, Number 47.1.8 'Narrated / Authority of: Malik: Yahya related to me from Malik that he had heard that the Messenger of Allah, may Allah bless him and grant him peace, said, 'I was sent to perfect good character'. http://ahadith.co.uk/chapter.php?cid=97 (Retrieved 9 June 2020).
50 Majid Fakhry, *Islamic Philosophy: A Beginner's Guide* (Oxford: Oneworld Publications, 2009).
51 The Holy *Qur'an* Chapter 3 Verse 104: 'And let there be [arising] from you a nation inviting to [all that is] good, enjoining what is right and forbidding what is wrong, and those will be the successful.'
52 The Holy *Qur'an* Chapter 103 Verses 1–3: 'By time, indeed humankind is surely in loss. Except those who believe, and do good deeds, and enjoin (each other) to the truth and enjoin (each other) to steadfastness'.
53 Anonymous, 'Iranian Teacher Builds Robot to Teach Prayer', *PhysOrg*, 25 February 2014, https://phys.org/news/2014-02-iranian-teacher-robot-prayer.html (Retrieved 9 June 2020).
54 The Holy *Qur'an* Chapter 77 Verse 22: 'So he (Satan) made them fall, through deception. And when they tasted of the tree, their private parts became apparent to them, and they began to fasten together over themselves from the leaves of Paradise. And their Lord called to them, "Did I not forbid you from that tree and tell you that Satan is to you a clear enemy?"'
55 Korrina A. Duffy and Tanya L. Chartrand, 'From Mimicry to Morality: The Role of Prosociality', in *Moral Psychology: Virtue and Character*, eds. Walter Sinnott-Armstrong and Christian B. Miller (Cambridge: The MIT Press, 2017).
56 Duffy and Chartrand, 'From Mimicry to Morality: The Role of Prosociality', 439–64.
57 Sahih Bukahri Book 1 Hadith 1: 'The reward of deeds depends upon the intentions and every person will get the reward according to what he has intended.'
58 Duffy and Chartrand, 'From Mimicry to Morality: The Role of Prosociality'.
59 'Who perfected everything which He created and began the creation of man from clay. Then He made his posterity out of the extract of a liquid disdained. Then He

proportioned him and breathed into him from His [created] soul and made for you hearing and vision and hearts...' (The Holy *Qur'an*, Chapter 32 verses 7-9).
60 Asghar Ali Engineer, 'On the Concept of Compassion in Islam', *Centre for the Study of Society and Secularism, Mumbai. IslamiCity* (2001).
61 Sunan an-Nasa'I, Book 25, Hadith 20: He (the Prophet) said: 'Do you have a mother?" He said: "Yes." He said: "Then stay with her, for Paradise is beneath her feet.'

Part V

Ethical aspects in generating transhuman and posthuman persons

12

Procreating transhuman and posthuman persons

Calum MacKellar

Introduction

Human beings generally consider the possibility of having children in a very positive light. Why they take this view still needs to be fully understood but many different reasons are likely, including a biological instinct or even a search for meaning in existence. In an ideal situation to which many (though maybe not all) aspire, this generation (bringing into existence) takes place in the context of unconditional love and acceptance between a man and a woman – a normative perspective, which can be seen as an important aspect of the particular act of procreation (in contrast to other acts of generation, such as reproduction or manufacture which are discussed later). In this regard, *pro* in Latin means 'on behalf of' or 'for'; thus, children are procreated 'for' the parents but also 'for' the child's sake.[1]

However, children may also be procreated 'for' others in a community so that they can unconditionally love, and be loved by, these others. The American theologian and bioethicist Brent Waters develops this idea, indicating: 'A child is not the outcome of a reproductive project, but exhibits an unfolding familial love. Thus, a child is not a means of self-fulfilment, but the impetus of an expansive and loving fellowship.'[2] In the procreation of a child, therefore, an act of 'begetting' takes place because he or she is recognized as having the same moral status, worth and nature as those who brought him or her into existence. Another American theologian and bioethicist Gilbert Meilaender explains:

> In begetting we give rise to one like us, one with whom we share a nature equal in being and dignity. Since we do not transcend the child we have begotten, we do not give it worth and significance any more than we understand ourselves to have been given dignity by our progenitors.[3]

Thus, children are procreated by their parents 'like from like'[4] and can never be considered merely from a consumerist perspective as objects or products because they are as precious in value and in worth as their parents. The question then arises, however, whether it is ever possible to specifically procreate transhuman or posthuman persons. But before this is examined, it is necessary to enquire what kinds of preconditions are generally seen as a being necessary for an act of procreation to occur.

The requirements of procreation

Interestingly, there is no single definition of the concept of procreation, but the word usually presupposes an idealistic and traditional manner of generating children. In other words, it assumes that two human parents are involved in the act of begetting through an exclusive and unconditional loving relationship. As Meilaender again explains: '[I]n distinctively human procreation the child is not simply a product of the will or choice of its progenitor. It is, instead, the internal fruition of an act of marital love.'[5]

Similarly, the American bioethicist Leon Kass indicates: 'How does begetting differ from making? In natural procreation, human beings come together, complementarily male and female, to give existence to another being who is formed, exactly as we were.'[6] This means that a number of preconditions may need to be fulfilled for persons to procreate and beget new persons – requirements which have generally been recognized as being valuable and important (even normative) in the past. Thus, for procreation to occur, it may be suggested that the generation should take place from:

- persons with full inherent value and worth;
- selfless, unconditional and faithful love;
- the complementary gendered love of the generators;
- the exclusive relationship of love of the generators; and
- the bodies of the generators.

In the context of the possibility of generating new transhuman or posthuman persons, however, it will be necessary to examine, in more detail, these procreative requirements.

Procreation from persons

Generally, only persons with full inherent value and worth can generate other persons. This means that persons do not just appear spontaneously out of nothing and that nonpersons cannot beget persons by themselves. For example, nonhuman animals cannot bring a person into existence by themselves without the input of another person such as a biologist who may, for example, modify the genome of a nonhuman offspring so that it is generated as a person.

This also means that in bringing new transhuman and posthuman persons into existence, it is necessary that some present or past person with full inherent value and worth must have taken part, in some way, in this generation. Accordingly, a person, such as a human engineer or scientist or even another transhuman or posthuman person must participate in some form in the generation of the new beings, if these are to be considered as persons. In other words, for a being to be a member of the family of persons, this individual must have at least one forebearer who was a person.

Until now, this has generally been recognized in that persons have been classified as belonging to a single community of common descent, namely those who came from the *Homo sapiens* original species. Interestingly, however, these *Homo sapiens* ancestors seemed to have also generated offspring with other *Homo* species, including the *Neanderthals*[7] – offspring who may represent the first Trans-original-*Homo sapiens*.

In this regard, the American biomedical ethicist, Maxwell Mehlman, explains:

> Modern humans . . . are descended from a long line of species that no longer exist . . . . [T]here is general agreement that before (and possibly alongside) *Homo sapiens* there were a number of other species of the genus *Homo*, preceded by species belonging to other homini genera . . .
>
> In fact, the transhumanist vision of a future in which evolutionary engineering creates a more advanced species of *Homo*, or, for that matter, a species belonging to an entirely new hominid genus, is perfectly consistent with the succession of species in the past.[8]

In addition, for a specific act of procreation to take place, it may be suggested that only persons with full inherent personal value and worth (and no other beings) actually take part in this procreation. And, as will be seen, only two persons can, in fact, be involved.

Procreation out of selfless, unconditional and faithful love

Having noted that only persons with full inherent value and worth can generate other persons, another important aspect of procreation is the intentional selfless, unconditional and faithful love that should be present between the generating persons.[9] One way of expressing this love between procreators is represented as a willing disposition (and not just a transient feeling) to put the other first and to give freely to another without any thought of reciprocity, which also means demonstrating a total and unconditional acceptance of the other. Thus, to be completely accepted and to be completely loved may be an expression of the same relationship. That is to say, the deep meaning of love must always involve other persons because selfless and faithful love is about giving from oneself to the other. Only through the existence of an 'other' can a human being love the 'other'. In this regard, there is also a uniting experience in the love of the procreators which can be characterized as a willingness to become one with the other through mutual and complete acceptance.

In addition, the very willingness to procreate is generally considered to originate from the love between the two prospective parents – a love which expresses a mysterious willingness to multiply in the procreation of a child. In short, the bringing into existence of a new child creates a possible new relationship of love towards this child, which arises from the deep love between the original parents.

Thus, when a couple procreates a child, it is both persons unified by the relationship of love between them who procreate. This means that procreation occurs when both (1) two persons exist and (2) a relationship of love between the parents exists which expands onto the resulting child. As Meilaender explains:

> In begetting, we ... give of ourselves and thereby form another, who, though other, shares our nature and is equal to us in dignity. If, by contrast, we come to think of the child as a product of our reason and will, we have lost the deepest ground of human equality – and, perhaps as important, have missed the meaning of the human act of love.[10]

It follows that when unconditional love and acceptance are not present between the generators of a new person, the specific act of procreation (in contrast to other acts of generation, such as acts of reproduction) cannot take place. In view of this, and because it is unlikely that any relationship of love would, or even can, exist between the generators of new transhuman and posthuman persons, it is very improbable that such a generation can be seen as an act of procreation. For example, if (in a thought experiment) a human person were to produce a transhuman child through a sexual relationship with a nonhuman animal, then no intentional and unconditional love would exist between the two beings generating the child, meaning that procreation in the sense outlined earlier does not occur.

Procreation out of complementary gendered love of the procreators

The gender of a human person is the range of characteristics pertaining to, and differentiating between, masculinity and femininity. Interestingly, the expression has its origin in the Latin *genus*, which characterizes birth or family (as in 'generating') though it also includes the reality that different genders may be necessary to generate.

When a man and a woman form a couple, the complementary genders of their personal identities in their mutual self-giving love as a couple usually complement each other in all their different characters and embodied qualities.[11] As a result, when a man and a woman come together in an exclusive relationship of love, their genders form a very deep complementary unity and completeness.

However, it is not only the gender of the personal identities of the couple that may form and express this unity but also the manner in which both partners love each other. Indeed, the very way the man loves the woman may be seen as quite different (but complementary) to the way the woman loves the man, though the intensity of these loves is usually similar. A very strong complementarity in communion may thus exist between the masculine and feminine personal identities in the couple but also of the masculine and feminine manner in which their love towards each other may be expressed.

But in the case of generating new transhuman and posthuman persons, it may be impossible for this physical and loving complementary to exist between the masculinity and femininity of the generators. For example, if it ever became possible for a human person to generate a child with a robot, even if a kind of love could exist between the two beings, it is very unlikely that this physical and relational love would be a complementary love between masculine and feminine beings as in the love between a man and woman. In other words, the generation may not be the result of gendered complementarity.

There may also be a real problem if the generated transhuman or posthuman persons are asexual and non-gendered. A completely non-binary situation may then exist where these new persons cannot even identify or recognize themselves as having any masculine or feminine identity in society. In a world where every person is gendered in some way, being a non-gendered individual could even mean having no place in society. Indeed, to exist as some kind of sexless, genderless third non-binary being is an element of the very definition of a certain form of posthumanism.

Interestingly, in the gothic novel *Frankenstein* published in 1818, English novelist Mary Shelley tells the story of a monster, generated by a scientist named Victor Frankenstein, who at first is simply portrayed as a sexless lifeless body. Indeed, it is only ascribed masculinity for the first time in the novel when it becomes alive. Frankenstein recounts:

> I started from my sleep with horror; a cold dew covered my forehead, my teeth chattered, and every limb became convulsed; when, by the dim and yellow light of the moon ... I beheld the wretch – the miserable monster whom I had created. *He* held up the curtain of the bed; and *his* eyes, if eyes they may be called, were fixed on me.[12]

In the book, Frankenstein does not seem to consider generating a being with any specific gender or place in society. He does not even anticipate the monster's desire to generate its own children. It is only when it exists, as a living being, that Frankenstein is then confronted with the monster's own wishes to generate offspring. In this regard, questions can also be asked whether the generators of new transhuman and posthuman persons will ever be able to adequately bring into existence gendered beings. A requirement which, as already indicated, is seen as necessary for procreation to occur.

Procreation and the exclusive relationship of the procreators

Having noted that unconditional love should exist between the persons seeking to procreate a new living being, it may also be accepted that this relationship of love should be exclusive. This means that it is a relationship between two and only two partners (of complementary gender) – hence it is a love that is different from all other loves, such as between parents and their children or between siblings. Each person in the couple gives themselves completely to the other without division in the act of procreation, which would be impossible if three or more persons were participating in the generation of a child. This is because a person cannot give himself or herself wholly and completely to two or more persons at the same time. Thus, for procreation to occur, only the two parents should generate the child and other actors should not take part in any significant way.

In the case of the generation of a new transhuman and posthuman person, however, it may be the case that a multitude of different generators may be necessary to bring such persons into existence. For example, a whole laboratory of engineers and scientists may be required to generate a robotic transhuman person. But this would then mean that the new generated person was not brought into existence from the exclusive love of its generators.[13] In other words, this person cannot be considered as having been procreated.

Procreation from the bodies of the procreators

As already indicated, for the specific act of procreation to take place between two gendered persons, unconditional love and acceptance should exist between these persons. This is very important since persons are always embodied minds and en-minded bodies and not just 'virtual' or 'imaginary' beings. Thus, when two gendered persons express their love, this does not just take place through their minds but also through their physical bodies (including their brains). Usually, this results in a physical relationship between a man and a woman through which the sperm cell, representing the whole man, and the egg cell, representing the whole woman, physically unite thereby procreating a physical child.[14]

In this regard, what is taking place in sexual intercourse is not just a 'physical' act but is an expression and a manifestation of the whole persons in an exclusive complementary relationship with each other. It is a whole gendered person that has sexual intercourse with another whole gendered person. This is also expressed in that the man's body does indeed become, in a very real and expressive way, one-flesh with that of the woman – the woman then also becoming one-flesh with the man. Moreover, a one-flesh union ideally reflects a lot more than just a sexual and physical intercourse. It expresses the relationships of embodied love of a couple in loyalty and exchange. With such a love, the couple then truly becomes 'one flesh' from a physical perspective, which can be seen as an image or metaphor for the closeness, unity, and exclusivity of the partnership.

Interestingly, a one-flesh relationship can even exist without a sexual physical connexion such as when one or both partners have a severe disability which makes sexual union impossible. This means that it is the important exclusive relationship which exists between two whole embodied persons that is central and not just the sexual act. In other words, the concept of one-flesh, though certainly involving physical intimacy, goes beyond the physical alone by including emotional unity, thereby expressing a oneness between the partners, of which the physical is a part.[15] The English theologian, Peter Bristow, explains that the communion between spouses is more than just a relationship of bodies. It is a communion of will, minds, and hearts: 'It must be unconditional in time and exclusive of all others, otherwise it is not a total commitment of the whole person in their spiritual and bodily nature by which the couple become "one flesh".[16]

What is significant, moreover, is that it is only from the exclusive and embodied one-flesh relationship in the couple that a one-flesh child can be procreated. This means, for example, that other body parts from other embodied persons should not participate in the bringing into existence of a child. The couple are the only persons who can actually procreate together though they could, if necessary, use the assistance of technology as long as this does not involve body parts of a third person.

Furthermore, in a similar manner to the way the love of the parents should expand onto the child, the bodies of these parents also expand into the body of the child. In other words, the one-flesh relationship existing in a couple expands through procreation into a one-flesh embodied child. This form of faithful and exclusive relationship in the couple is, as the American ethicist Paul Ramsey (1913-88) indicates, a 'covenant whose matter is the giving and the receiving of acts which tend both to the unique one-flesh unity between the partners and to the unique one flesh of the child beyond them'.[17] Thus, the one-flesh relationship and embodied oneness of the parents is expressed and expands, in the procreative process, into and onto the embodied one-flesh of the child. As a result, a one-flesh family and a single embodied social community is formed, which includes the child.

Accordingly, procreation expresses the giving of the embodied parents to each other and to the child. As the American biologist and bioethics commentator Lee Silver indicates:

> [W]hat most happily bonded couples have always wanted to do – and always will want to do – is to produce a child that represents the ultimate consummation of their love for each other: a child that comes not from one parent or the other, but one that mixes together both their heritages.[18]

However, in the bringing into existence of a new transhuman and posthuman child, it may be impossible to generate such a child through a one-flesh relationship. As Kass observes:

> But life in the laboratory also allows other people – including those ... who will prefer to have their children rationally manufactured entirely in the laboratory – to declare themselves independent of their bodies, in this ultimate liberation. For them the body is a mere tool, ideally an instrument of the conscious will, the sole repository of human dignity. Yet this blind assertion of will against our bodily nature – in contradiction of the meaning of the human generation it seeks to control – can only lead to self-degradation and dehumanization.[19]

As a result, in the generation of new transhuman and posthuman persons, a similar situation may arise in which the body may no longer matter – a model which may not come as a surprise since many transhumanist values are similar to those found in the religious movement of Gnosticism, which originated in the late first century, where followers rejected the material world to only concentrate on what is spiritual. [20] In response, Saint Irenaeus, a second-century Christian bishop of Lyon (central France), argued that the gnostic despising of the body led to two conflicting ethical positions. Firstly, a moral stance of liberty to physical experiences could develop because human bodies were no longer considered as an important part of a person, meaning that it did not really matter what a person did with it. The second position was one in which a person could demonstrate the meaninglessness and insignificance of his or her body through neglecting it or by expressing extreme austerity towards his or her physical nature.

Once again, it may be queried whether the generators of possible future transhuman or posthuman persons will ever use, or even consider, their own bodies in bringing into existence these new beings. As a result, a kind of gnostic generation may be taking place without any one-flesh relationship between the generators. Interestingly, this may also happen if these new transhuman or posthuman persons want to generate their own offspring. For example, it may be very difficult for a posthuman person existing in a computer to be able to have a one-flesh relationship with a human person (or a completely different kind of posthuman).[21]

The sense of belonging between generators and their children

As already indicated, there is very often an experience of mutual belonging, communion and deep bonding between a personal procreator and the children brought forth through procreation. Thus, those who are procreated by their parents in this way generally recognize that, but for their procreators, they would not exist. In other words, it is important for these procreated persons to acknowledge the source of oneness from which they originated in the love of their procreators and be unconditionally loved by this source which gives them a sense of belonging, a place, an identity and a meaning in existence.

Ideally, the two partners in procreation may then acknowledge, together, that their love has expanded into and upon a child who can then love his or her parents in return, thereby enabling, through the specific act of procreation, a multiplication of the relationships of love. This is what generally causes the unity and oneness of mutual belonging originating in the profound oneness of procreators. The deep love of parents towards their biological child, and the longing for this child to somehow be reunited to them, knowing all the time that he or she will now be forever 'other', is an expression of the profound love and sense of belonging between parents and their child. As Waters explains:

> The birth of a child does not simply entail the creation of a parallel relationship; a family is not merely a container for its separate spousal, parental, filial and fraternal relationships. Rather, they are related aspects of larger loyalty, mutual belonging and common love.[22]

Generating persons outside of procreation

When procreative love does not exist in the bringing into existence of a transhuman or posthuman person, then other terms for such a generation can generally be used including the term 'production'. This entails generating 'on behalf of' or 'for' the producers. For example, the act of producing may be a form of reproduction or of manufacture whereby something (or someone) new is brought into existence.

Manufacture

The concept of manufacture reflects a bringing together of raw materials by hand or by machinery and is not usually used in the generation of persons. Thus, manufacturing may occur when procreation is impossible because no selfless faithful love exists between the personal generators. When such an act of generation happens, Kass explains that the products can sometimes be reduced to only having an economic commercial value. He indicates: 'And procreation dehumanized into manufacture is further degraded by commodification, a virtually inescapable result of allowing babymaking to proceed under the banner of commerce.'[23] In other words, the granting of property rights to transhuman and posthuman children by their manufacturers may have significant ethical consequences for these children. These include the risk of endangering such children to:

1. Objectification – the treatment of a being as a thing or an object, disregarding its personality as well as inherent value and worth. It means that the individual becomes something whose own experience and feelings do not need to be taken into account.[24]
2. Instrumentalization – the transformation of a being into a mere means to an end. The being or entity then becomes the instrument of another person.[25]
3. Commodification – the treatment of a being as an interchangeable marketable commodity which can give rise to commerce. This implies fungibility whereby the commodified individual has a price and can be replaced by money or other objects having an equal market value.[26]

What is disturbing, therefore, about the manufacture of beings such as transhuman and posthuman persons is that the subject is instrumentalized to fulfil the needs or desires of another person. Furthermore, the commodification of a being by the generators may make this individual susceptible to being objectified and/or commodified by others who may then just see this being as the sum total of its (his or her) marketable parts.[27]

Reproduction

Reproduction is the process by which a new subject or object is generated from existing subject(s) or object(s) who/which have similar characteristics. As the British anthropologist Dame Marilyn Strathern indicates: 'Reproduction commonly means to bring into existence something that already exists in another form.'[28] Thus, in reproduction there is generally something of the original in the product with a special kind of relationship often arising between the reproducer(s) and the reproduced subject or object because of their similarities. For example, an artistic reproduction is a copy but motorcars are not reproduced but manufactured.[29]

It was only in 1748 that the term 'reproduction' was introduced into the life sciences by the French naturalist, mathematician and encyclopédiste, Georges-Louis Leclerc, Comte de Buffon (1707–1788). In so doing, it is believed that he borrowed the word from discussions in theology, at the time, where it meant 'resurrection'. Thus, applied to the life sciences, the word 'reproduction' in its initial usage reflected a kind of reconstitution from component parts.[30]

Interestingly, the first time the term 'reproduction' was apparently mentioned in relation to human beings in the English language occurred in 1782 when the English theologian John Wesley (1703–91) objected to its use by de Buffon. Indeed, he was unhappy that the plain word for generation was being replaced by reproduction which, to him, brought humankind down not only to the level of beasts but also to vegetables such as onions. Thus, it was argued at the time, that human beings cannot just be considered as copies (as in reproduction) but, instead, are brought into existence as individual persons, meaning that they have the same nature and moral status as all other persons.[31]

The concern that human children are only being generated through reproduction may also be reflected in modern society where the concepts of individualism, autonomy and the freedom to do what one wants are increasingly emphasized. Because of this, bringing children into existence has increasingly become something to be controlled by prospective parents. As Meilaender explains: 'The shift from "procreation" to "reproduction" is in part a manifestation of human freedom to master and reshape our world.'[32] In the light of this, it seems very likely that most cases of generation of new transhuman and posthuman persons may, unfortunately, be cases of reproduction, at best, but may even be cases of manufacture.

The generation of transhuman and posthuman offspring from transhuman and posthuman generators

The question now arises whether it would ever be possible for transhuman and posthuman persons to procreate their own offspring. Of course, this may be extremely difficult to accomplish, if at all, since as already mentioned for procreation to occur, these new persons should be able to express their exclusive, selfless, unconditional and faithful embodied gendered love for each other.

Clearly then, if they cannot fulfil these requirements, the eventual human generators of these transhuman and posthuman persons (who may want to generate their own offspring) should seriously consider why they are bringing such beings into existence in the first place. Here again, Shelley's novel *Frankenstein* can act as a warning when it portrays the complex relationship of Victor Frankenstein with his monster, especially when it asks him to generate a partner:

> The being [Monster] finished speaking and fixed his looks upon me in the expectation of a reply. But I was bewildered, perplexed, and unable to arrange my ideas sufficiently to understand the full extent of his proposition. He continued, 'You must create a female for me with whom I can live in the interchange of those sympathies necessary for my being. This you alone can do, and I demand it of you as a right which you must not refuse to concede.'[33]

But when Frankenstein reflects about the demands of his monster and the possible future his dæmon may have with his eventual female partner, he becomes alarmed, indicating:

> Even if they were to leave Europe, and inhabit the deserts of the new world, yet one of the first results of those sympathies for which the dæmon thirsted would be children, and a race of devils would be propagated upon the earth, who might make the very existence of the species of man a condition precarious and full of terror. Had I a right, for my own benefit, to inflict this curse upon everlasting generations?
>
> I had before been moved by the sophisms of the being I had created I had been struck senseless by his fiendish threats; but now, for the first time, the wickedness of my promise burst upon me;
>
> I shuddered to think that future ages might curse me as their pest, whose selfishness had not hesitated to buy its own peace at the price perhaps of the existence of the whole human race.[34]

As a result, Frankenstein refuses to generate a female companion. However, it is possible to ask whether future generators of transhuman or posthuman persons would enable them to generate their own offspring. And, if this happened, whether these new persons would be able to actually procreate in love or just generate more misery.

Conclusion

For the specific act of procreation to occur, which can be considered as both idealistic and normative, it is generally accepted that two persons of complementary gender generate children from their exclusive, selfless, unconditional and faithful embodied love for one another. A love that is then embodied in the resulting children, which enables these children to know that they were procreated by love, to be loved, thereby confirming that they have a rightful place in existence. In other words, that their very existence is unconditionally welcomed – that they do not have to ask why they exist or fulfil certain preconditions for their acceptance. This also means that because children should be brought into existence through the one-flesh unity love of their parents, they cannot be seen as their possessions. Instead, children and their parents belong together as a family of equals. As Meilaender notes:

> A child who is thus begotten, not made, embodies the union of his father and mother. They have not simply reproduced themselves, nor are they merely a cause of which the child is an effect. Rather, the power of their mutual love has given rise to another who, though different from them and equal in dignity to them, manifests in his person the love that unites them. Their love-giving has been life-giving; it is truly procreation. The act of love that overcame their separation and united them in 'one flesh', that direct them out of themselves and toward each other, creates in the child a still larger community.[35]

In this context, the story of Frankenstein can be used as a warning to those seeking to bring transhuman and posthuman persons into existence.[36] Accordingly, the US-based bioethicist Josephine Johnston indicates:

> In a straightforward – even didactic – way, the novel [*Frankenstein*] chronicles the devastating consequences for an inventor and those he loves of his utter failure to anticipate the harm that can result from raw, unchecked scientific curiosity.[37]

In a similar fashion, the generators of new transhuman and posthuman persons may not comprehend what they are really doing or what it means to bring a new person into existence. They may not even understand all the possible grave future consequences of their acts. For example, Frankenstein looks forward with excitement, at first, to the day when his new being would come into existence: 'A new species would bless me as its creator and source; many happy and excellent natures would owe their being to me. No father could claim the gratitude of his child so completely as I should deserve their's.'[38] But he soon discovers how mistaken he was when the monster indicts him with all his suffering and loneliness:

> Unfeeling, heartless creator! You had endowed me with perceptions and passions, and then cast me abroad an object for the scorn and horror of mankind. But on you only had I any claim for pity and redress, and from you I determined to seek that justice which I vainly attempted to gain from any other being that wore the human form.[39]

In a similar way, it is very likely that future transhuman and posthuman persons will feel angry and bewildered if they are not procreated from the embodied love of their parents. Again, this is movingly illustrated by Frankenstein's creature and its search for identity. Though Frankenstein had intended his creature to be attractive, the experiment is a disaster and results in a monster who he then completely rejects and abandons. But the nameless creature goes in search for his generator since he realizes that Frankenstein is the real origin and cause of his very existence and life, and that he must therefore be the answer to his deep existential angst. The monster, in a way, is looking for answers as to why he was generated while seeking to understand the deep sense of rejection and abandonment he experiences. His anguish and distress are deeply moving in his exclamation: 'My person was hideous and my stature gigantic. What did this mean? Who was I? What was I? Whence did I come? What was my destination? These questions continually recurred, but I was unable to solve them.'[40]

Likewise, it is possible that new transhuman and posthuman persons generated outside of procreation will feel completely lost in their very existence and identity. Indeed, it is difficult to see how the generation of such new beings could ever be possible without them experiencing deep anguish and suffering, making their generation completely unethical. The American science-fiction author, Elizabeth Bear, indicates:

> There is a strong link between Victor [Frankenstein]'s failure of empathy for his creature and the particular kind of hubris that allows for the discarding of other people's lives in service to an ambition. This failure of empathy is closely connected to the moral cowardice of refusing to take responsibility for one's actions or for the outcomes derived from one's research.[41]

As Bear explains in the case of Frankenstein: 'He undertakes his research in a spirit of self-aggrandizement: it's not knowledge he seeks but power and renown, and this ambition leads him to become far more of a monster than the creature he creates.'[42] In this respect, it is difficult not to see a similar outcome for anyone who may seek to generate new transhuman or posthuman persons outside of procreation.

Notes

1. Of course, in one sense, a child cannot be procreated for his or her own sake because he or she does not pre-exist his or her own conception. See: Christine Overall, *Why Have Children? The Ethical Debate* (Cambridge, MA: The MIT Press, 2012), 87. However, children do generally value their own lives once they are aware of their existence and seek to avoid death.
2. Brent Waters, *Reproductive Technology* (London: Darton, Longman and Todd, 2001), 51.
3. Gilbert Meilaender, *Bioethics: A Primer for Christians*, 3rd edn (Grand Rapids, MI: Eedermans Publishing Co, 2013), 20.
4. St. John of Damascus, 'An Exposition of the Orthodox Faith, Book I, Chapter 8', in *New Advent*, http://www.newadvent.org/fathers/33041.htm (Accessed on 13 December 2007).
5. Gilbert Meilaender, 'Human Dignity and Public Bioethics', *The New Atlantis* 17 (2007): 33–52.
6. Leon R. Kass, 'The Wisdom of Repugnance', *New Republic* 216, no. 22 (1997).
7. Adam C. Estes, 'It Wasn't Just Neanderthals: Ancient Humans Had Sex with Other Hominids - New Research Shows the Extent to Which Our Ancestors Interbred', *The Atlantic*, 6 September 2011.
8. Maxwell J. Mehlman, *Transhumanist Drams and Dystopian Nightmares: The Promises and Peril of Genetic Engineering, Maryland* (Baltimore: The Johns Hopkins University Press, 2012), 106.

9. This may be reflected as a kind of covenant.
10. Gilbert Meilaender, *Bioethics: A Primer for Christians* (Grand Rapids, MI: Eerdmans, 1996), 14–15.
11. This is a very general statement and different definitions of what 'complementary' means may exist and be critiqued. For a supporter of some kind of complementarity between genders see: Mohammadreza Hojat, *Empathy in Health Professions Education and Patient Care* (New York: Springer, 2016), 169–87.
12. David H. Guston, Ed Finn and Jason Scott Robert, eds., *Mary Shelley, Frankenstein, Annotated for Scientists, Engineers, and Creators of All Kinds* (Cambridge, MA: The MIT Press, 2017), 43 (my emphasis).
13. Leon Kass indicates: 'Does Not the Scientist-Partner Produce a Triangle that Somehow Subverts the Meaning of "Two"?' in *Life, Liberty and the Defense of Dignity: The Challenge for Bioethics*, ed. Leon R. Kass (California, San Francisco: Encounter Books, 2002), 101.
14. Calum MacKellar, 'Representative Aspects of Some Synthetic Gametes', *The New Bioethics* 21, no. 2 (2015): 105–16.
15. Scott B. Rae and D. Joy Riley, *Outside the Womb: Moral Guidance for Assisted Reproduction* (Chicago: Moody Publishers, 2011), 41.
16. Peter Bristow, *Christian Ethics and the Human Person* (Oxford: Family Publication, 2009), 317–18.
17. Paul Ramsey, *One Flesh: A Christian View of Sex Within, Outside and Before Marriage* (Bramcote: Grove Books, 1975), 4.
18. Lee M. Silver, *Remaking Eden* (London: Orion Books, 1999), 137.
19. Kass, *Life, Liberty and the Defense of Dignity: The Challenge for Bioethics*, 100.
20. For a discussion about Gnosticism and Transhumanism, see: Lee A. Johnson, 'Return of the Corporeal Battle: How Second-Century Christology Struggles Inform the Transhuman Debate', in *Religion and Transhumanism: The Unknown Future of Human Enhancement*, eds. Calvin Mercer and Tracy Trothen (Santa Barbara, CA: Praeger, 2015), 273–90.
21. In this regard, the term 'kinds' is more commonly used in folk-taxonomy than in modern biology. Indeed, from a biological perspective, living organisms are not classified into kinds but into species (that is, into groups which do not normally interbreed).

    It may also be possible that transhuman or posthuman persons to have reproductive cells that do not represent them. Thus, some human-nonhuman interspecies animals already produce human gametes which do not represent the animal itself.
22. Waters, *Reproductive Technology*, 46.
23. Kass, 'The Wisdom of Repugnance'.
24. See also: Donna Dickenson, *Body Shopping: Converting Body Parts to Profit* (Oxford: Oneworld, 2009), 23–7.
25. Will Kymlicka. 'Rethinking the Family', *Philosophy and Public Affairs* 20, no. 1 (1991): 77–97.
26. Another way in which the concept of commodification can be used is when an entity is not only bought, sold or rented but considered in discussions or the way it is seen in transactions, Margaret Jane Radin, 'Market-Inalienability', *Harvard Law Review* 100, no. 8 (1987): 1849–937; Elisa Garcia and Henk Jochemsen, 'Ethics of Stem Cell Research', in *Human Stem Cells*, ed. Henk Jochemsen (Prof. Dr. Lindenboom Institute and Business Ethics Center of Jerusalem, 2005), 97; Scott Altman, '(Com)modifying Experience', *Southern California Law Review* 65, no. 1 (1991): 293–340.

27 Paige C. Cunningham, 'Is It Right or Is It Useful? Patenting of the Human Gene, Lokean Property Rights and the Erosion of the Imago Dei', *Ethics & Medicine* 19, no. 2 (2003): 85–98.
28 Marilyn Strathern, 'Displacing Knowledge: Technology and the Consequences for Kinship', in *Conceiving the New World Order: The Global Politics of Reproduction*, eds. D. Ginsburg and R. Rapp (Berkeley, Los Angeles and London: University of California Press, 1995), 354.
29 A subject or object can also reproduce without any conscious intervention such as with bacteria.
30 Staffan Müller-Wille and Hans-Jörg Rheinberger, *A Cultural History of Heredity* (Chicago: University of Chicago Press, 2012), 15, quoted in Denis Alexander, *Genes, Determinism and God* (Cambridge: Cambridge University Press, 2017), 27.
31 Michael Banner, *Christian Ethics and Contemporary Moral Problems* (Cambridge: Cambridge University Press, 1999), 226.
32 Meilaender, *Bioethics: A Primer for Christians*, 3rd edn, 11.
33 Guston, Finn and Robert, eds., *Mary Shelley, Frankenstein, Annotated for Scientists, Engineers, and Creators of All Kinds*, 120.
34 Guston, Finn and Robert, eds., *Mary Shelley, Frankenstein, Annotated for Scientists, Engineers, and Creators of All Kinds*, 139–40.
35 Meilaender, *Bioethics: A Primer for Christians*, 3rd edn, 15.
36 For a discussion relating to how Frankenstein can be discussed from a transhuman perspective, see: Marcus Rockoff, 'Literature', in *Post- and Transhumanism: An Introduction*, eds Robert Ranisch and Stefan Lorenz Sorgner (Frankfurt am Main: Peter Lang, 2014), 251–70, 257–9.
37 Josephine Johnston, 'Traumatic Responsibility: Victor Frankenstein as Creator and Casualty', in *Mary Shelley, Frankenstein, Annotated for Scientists, Engineers, and Creators of All Kinds*, eds. Guston, Finn and Robert, 201.
38 Guston, Finn and Robert, eds., *Mary Shelley, Frankenstein, Annotated for Scientists, Engineers, and Creators of All Kinds*, 37.
39 Guston, Finn and Robert, eds., *Mary Shelley, Frankenstein, Annotated for Scientists, Engineers, and Creators of All Kinds*, 116.
40 Mary Shelley, *Frankenstein* (London: Penguin Popular Classics, 1994), 124.
41 Elizabeth Bear, 'Frankenstein Reframed; or The Trouble with Prometheus', in *Mary Shelley, Frankenstein, Annotated for Scientists, Engineers, and Creators of All Kinds*, eds. Guston, Finn and Robert, 231.
42 Bear, 'Frankenstein Reframed; or The Trouble with Prometheus', 231.

Posthuman children

Questions of identity

Gillian Wright

Realise this (said the Cabinet-maker, the King and the Engineer together) *conker cannot be made, however you ask it, whatever word or tool you use, regardless of decree. Only one thing can conjure Conker – and that thing is tree.*[1]

Introduction

The generation of a posthuman person would be no mean feat. To make a person from scratch requires a certain magic: a mix of unique consciousness, morality and distinctively free will. A posthuman person is one whose 'capacities so radically exceed those of present humans as to be no longer unambiguously human'.[2] To generate such a posthuman would be a truly remarkable act of bioengineering. Yet, with each year that passes, remarkable scientific milestones *are* being passed. The generation of a posthuman life becomes ever more possible. However, the task at hand is to establish whether there is an ethical way to do so. Earlier chapters have considered who posthuman persons are from a human perspective. Now let us turn to the way in which posthumans might consider their own generation and try to understand their perspective. Let us walk in their (virtual) shoes. We shall postulate some posthuman psychology – how they might feel about their identity and how they might feel about those who made them. In addition, we must consider what responsibilities parents should have to the posthumans they generate.

'Who am I?' is the most fundamental question of personal identity. It affects our life choices, our relationships, our mental health, our spiritual or existential searching. It is often followed by a cascade of further questions: 'Where did I come from?', 'Why was I brought into existence' and 'Who are my family?' We seem to have an innate sense of belonging to others and to seek out community. Finally, the troubling question 'Ought I have been made at all?' can be asked. We will consider these dilemmas with a posthuman hue – in particular, the sense of identity and questions of relationship of posthumans to their parents or kinship. We will consider if it is possible to harm posthuman persons by the way in which we generate them. There will also be a caveat as to the validity of the methods we might use in such generation.

What does it mean 'to generate ethically'?

The idea of generating a posthuman person is a challenge of a new frontier. Why did humans reach the moon, scale Everest or split the atom? This desire to conquer and explore permeates science in all its forms - bioengineering is no exception. However, should it be unrestrained? Are there reasons to restrain scientific autonomy for the good of the wider community?

Clarifying the terms of reference will give boundaries to the arguments ahead. The term we have chosen in this volume for 'to bring into existence a posthuman person' is 'to generate'. However, 'to generate' has overtones of machinery and uniformity. It seems difficult to rationalize those with the value and worth of human life. Nevertheless, the process *is* mechanical. It involves computer circuitry and biological processing. It adds to the basic process of reproduction and so the term 'to generate' is technically accurate. Notwithstanding, to generate a person must involve a moral dimension not present when building a greenhouse or knitting a sock. To generate ethically is to assume moral as well as mechanical responsibility for the actions taken in making a new posthuman being.

What is a posthuman person?

The literature on the nature of human–machine complexes (often called cyborgs) is remarkably confusing. The medical ethicist Grant Gillett illustrates the spectrum of change from human to transhuman in his 2005 paper 'Moral Identity of Cyborgs'.[3] He describes different scenarios to help our understanding of the differences between human and transhuman. I will propose a final modification of one of these scenarios to illustrate the concept of a posthuman.

Gillett's first imagined case in the paper is Hansie, a severely brain-injured baby who is given experimental treatment involving growth factors and micro-electrical stimulation which restores his brain to a functioning state. As we would consider this restoration rather than enhancement, Hansie would be still 'human'. Gillett asks, 'Should they be allowed to think of this child as still being Hansie and does our ethical attitude to what they (his parents) are doing depend on how we answer that question?' He then answers these questions: 'I would say that they can, and that it does not, even though some theories of personal identity would render both of these stands problematic.'[4]

The second case is another baby, Henri-Charles, who is also severely brain-injured, and whose brain is replaced with 'a set of regularly modular microchips with the capacity to respond to biological signals generated by cell membranes'.[5] As a result, Gillett describes Henri-Charles' responses as automated: 'Our intuitions are thrown, however, by the fact that some of the human reactions and responses that Henri-Charles will come to exhibit may be cold, calculating and robotic in ways that disengage him from the moral community at important points.'[6]

If I now further postulate that Henri-Charles has a photographic memory and astonishingly accurate mental arithmetic, transhuman would be a good description of the melding of human and machine. But what would a posthuman be? If I may extend Gillett's example, when Henri-Charles' body fails, his modular microchips could be maintained. This data could then be uploaded to a computer. Henri-Charles could still be a person, albeit 'living' in a computer. He would be a posthuman person. How would Henri-Charles perceive himself? To answer this question, we must consider some issues surrounding identity.

Personal identity

Although there is little consensus on definitions of identity itself, it is generally understood as the way persons define themselves in the world and how the world defines them.[7] The UK's Nuffield Council on Bioethics defines personal identity as, 'a highly elastic concept which is used to encompass many different ideas, how a person sees him or herself, how society sees that person and how we distinguish between individuals'.[8]

There are different interpretations of identities. These are socially constructed and complex with some paradoxical themes.[9] There is continuity of identity over time and place enabling a person to remain the same person though circumstances change. Though Frank might retire as a firefighter and become a volunteer tram driver, he remains the same person. But if there is a fire in the old tram works and Frank helps to put out the fire, who is he then? Can Frank be considered two persons – a firefighter and a tram driver? If Frank's mind is replicated and multiple versions exist in the fire service computer system, are there multiple Franks or should they all be given new posthuman names?

Identity may be affected by multiple factors. It may be shaped by a person's biological characteristics, their psychology and the cultural context. One individual may have multiple identities, which overlap, and can change over time or in different circumstances. Kate may be a daughter at home, but a dentist at work and a Karate teacher on Thursdays. People have a total identity, the sum of many different aspects about themselves. Together these give them a fundamental sense of meaning in their lives.

Social identity

Social identity is our sense of who we are because we belong to a certain group. The Polish social psychologist Henri Tajfel (1919–82) described social identity theory as having the underlying premise that 'individuals define their own identities with regard to social groups and that such identifications work to protect and bolster self-identity'.[10]

Tajfel proposed that the groups such as social class, family or team were an important source of pride and self-esteem. Self-esteem rises when your football team wins a crucial goal; national honour is at stake in the Olympics. Individual pride arises from group achievements. Groups give us a sense of social identity: a sense of belonging to the social world. However, it also gives rise to rejection of those who do not belong to our group and to 'in-groups' and 'out-groups'.[11] 'Otherness' is not a new-fangled phenomenon. The Danish author, Hans Christian Anderson, captured it in his timeless fable of 'The Ugly Duckling' in 1843. A shabby cygnet hatches in a nest of preening ducklings and they run him out of town. He does not look like them, sound like them or act like them. It could be an analogy for any civil war, departmental struggle or inter-racial marriage, when there has been strife because of difference. Yet the beauty of the eventually arising swan remains a salutary lesson.

Any source of difference can effectively create two groups. Humans and posthumans will likely be no different. The interesting question will be if posthumans will be the in-group or the out-group? If the posthuman has highly developed cognitive function and physical strength, it is more likely to be the in-group and the antiquated human will be side-lined. The relationship between the two groups is intriguing. Will there be a kinship bond between the progenitor and the generated?

Kinship

Kinship is not easy to define but easier to recognize. A dictionary definition is 'a blood relationship or the state of having common characteristics or a common origin'.[12] However, this seems to neglect two key aspects: social relationship and mutual responsibility. Kinship implies more than mere genetic relatedness, although this may vary with culture and history.[13] The warmth of the African proverb 'It takes a whole village to raise a child' contrasts with Western individualism. Will humans have a sense of kinship towards the posthumans they generate? Will biological relatedness, social closeness and moral responsibility exist? How will posthumans reciprocate? We will examine these three aspects of kinship in turn.

Biological kinship

In many cultures, blood has a meaning of close biological relatedness, with the sharing of blood reflecting the sharing of life. Societies, in the past, honoured the blood ties of the Pharaohs of Egypt and the Emperors of Rome. The bloodline expressed a biological understanding of procreation and of life. The sociologist Eviatar Zerubavel noted:

> Yet as implicit in our notion of 'blood ties' (and of being 'related by blood') and of our vision of lineages as blood lines, we had already biologized and thereby essentialised ancestry and kinship long before we discovered genetics.[14]

There is a recurrent yearning to express connection in a physical form. The Nuffield Council on Human Bioethics highlights the modern equivalent interest in genetic connections. It quotes the UK-based moral and social philosopher Brenda Almond, who argued that: 'People are increasingly concerned to understand their own complex genetic inheritance and to have access to the world of their genetic relations.'[15]

Modern society prizes genetic tests very highly. Paternity tests establish legal rights and responsibilities. However, the concept of genetic identity is still not clearly defined.[16] When searching for identity, it is not the genetic code itself that is significant. Instead, its significance lies in that it establishes a connection with another person.[17] The American Social Work Professor Brené Brown, whose TED talk resonates so widely, with over 44 million views online, describes the significance of connection:

> Connection is why we're here; it is what gives purpose and meaning to our lives. The power that connection holds in our lives was confirmed when the main concern about connection emerged as the fear of disconnection; the fear that something we have done or failed to do, something about who we are or where we come from, has made us unlovable and unworthy of connection.[18]

Social kinship

Genetic relatedness is intrinsic to the genes but does not necessarily confer a meaningful kinship connection with other persons. Moreover, kinship results from social elements such as marriage and adoption. These give rise to the strong bonds of mutual belonging. With the advent of new reproductive technologies, the tension between social and biological kinship has grown. For example, one of the first babies to be born via IVF and a donated embryo, Lauren Walker, commented: 'When I tell people about my story, I always say my "real parents", and my "biological parents". What makes you a real parent is your ability to love and cherish your child.'[19]

The use of donated sperm and eggs is increasingly being used by couples in fertility clinics. Many children resulting from such donation are now asking to know the identity of their biological parent. For them, the biological element is important in the construction of their identity.

Tensions may also arise between different biological elements. In gestational surrogacy, a woman carries and delivers a genetically unrelated child for another couple or person who will be the child's legal parents. However, gestating a child may be seen by others as important for creating kinship. The physical process of carrying the baby in her womb gives the woman both a biological and cultural claim of deep relatedness to the child. She may even consider the child as her own thereby supporting the construction of her identity.[20] These examples demonstrate that the understanding of kinship cannot be reduced to genes alone.

Moral responsibility

Not only is there usually a connection between family members but this connection brings certain obligations and responsibilities. In particular, a remarkable bond seems to exist between human parents and children; not simply an association or connection between parents and children but a bond that elicits responsibility and care which may be upheld by the law. Parental responsibility is a legal requirement that parents care for and protect their children. Parents must provide for and decide for the child in the realms of health, welfare and education.[21]

Adoptive parents may take on the parental role because the biological parents cannot look after the child. The state permits these new parents to legally adopt the child to become their own. However, most countries now recognize the importance of both the social and biological nature of parent–child relationships. Adopted children are thus considered in every way to be the equal of the biological children of the adoptive parents.[22]

Having examined the different concepts within kinship we will return to the topic of identity and the way this is influenced by kinship.

Identity through relationship

A sense of personal identity is formed by the way persons understand their relatedness to others. This includes their knowledge of ancestry, but also of other living family members. Aspects of social identity can be expressed through the concept of closeness and include notions of belonging, of being nurtured by each other. As a result, individuals usually regard these ancestors as being a single community and 'cemented' together. It is as if one large communion between the child and his or her ancestors was present – ancestors who are all the causes of each other's existences down the ages.[23] As Zerubavel indicates:

> In fact, the very same ties that connect us to our ancestors also connect us to our relatives, with whom we share them, and the extent to which we are related to those 'relatives' is indeed a function of our mutual distance from the common ancestors from whom we co-descend. The more recent those ancestors, the 'closer' we are.[24]

This biological closeness is also shown in the way some families who have used donor insemination, consider half-siblings as part of their family.[25,26] In some form, all these existences come into a kind of communion in which there are deep relationships of unconditional acceptance but also responsibility. Moreover, this communion does not only exist between parents and their child but with grandparents, siblings, cousins and other family members. For example, biological ancestry remains the single most important factor in America for the federal recognition of an individual as a Native American. It also plays a crucial role in whether a person is considered a member of a particular Native American tribal nation conferring certain rights, privileges and, in some circumstances, financial wealth.[27]

Identity and posthumans

Posthumans will derive their origins in part from the parents who generated them. This connection could be minimal, merely a statement of fact, or it could be meaningful –

and lead to a sense of significance, value and worth. In part, this will be determined by the nature, needs and wishes of the posthuman, but also by the response of the parent. What if posthumans are so sophisticated they have no material need of us? Will they yet still yearn for a sense of connection, to be valued by those who made them?

To understand the possible relationships between posthuman children and their parents, can we learn from different forms of families? Although the analogy is limited, can we draw any useful inferences?

Genealogical bewilderment

Genealogical bewilderment refers to identity problems that may be experienced by children who do not know their biological parents.[28] In the 1950s, the psychologists Erich Wellisch and H. J. Sants described a disorientation experience in children following closed adoption (where information of the biological parents was withheld). Knowledge of biological parents was important to establish a sense of identity and in turn security and stable mental health. If this were lost by adoption or as described more recently, by assisted technology,[29] then identity, security and mental health could suffer. However, although this experience undoubtedly did occur, a simple cause and effect is not clear. Age at adoption, strong positive attachments with adopted parents, reasons for adoption could all be possible confounders. It has been suggested that this may also occur with new family structures. For example, a yearning seems to exist to have a connection with birth parents. Commenting on the search for sperm donors, the journalist Ashley Fetters comments:

> There's a name for that feeling – that curiosity, that sense of a missing piece, that anxiety that some dormant aspect of themselves might one day show up and have no traceable root . . . , the psychologists . . . called [it] 'genealogical bewilderment'.[30]

Similarly, posthumans may experience this disorientation because of the detachment between human parents and their new posthuman form. It may be difficult for them to communicate with or understand their more 'primitive' parents. They may feel adrift with a sense of belonging nowhere and to no one. However, this conjecture may prove to be unfounded if the warmth of parental relationship overcomes these barriers and the sense of welcome and acceptance is unconditional. Who could forget the 1982 film *E.T. the Extra Terrestrial*, directed by Steven Spielberg?[31] At first, there were the halting attempts by the extra-terrestrial 'E.T.' to speak to the children, but then an astonishing relationship developed throughout the film. Nevertheless, deep down, E.T.'s great longing was still to 'phone home'.

Kinship of generator and generated

Hypothetically, kinship may arise when a person is responsible for taking part in the bringing into existence of another person though no exchange of biological substances takes place between these two persons. Let us suppose a couple decided to bring into existence a child made of plastic, who was self-aware and who had none of their genes whatsoever. The child would still experience a sense of kinship towards those who caused him or her to exist.

Children do generally become aware that their parents' existence is the cause of their own existence; similarly, parents are aware that they are the cause of existence of the child. This means that they are all aware of their interdependence. Moreover, among other factors such as the social rearing of the child, this 'existential' mutual belonging may initiate a strong sense of relatedness in the parent–child identities.

From the perspective of a human child, a significant contribution to his or her identity has always been that he or she was procreated by other persons giving him or her an origin, a history and a place in society. A crucial aspect of the self-understanding and identity of a child is given through knowing how and who brought him or her into existence.

Implications for posthumans

What, therefore, can we infer for posthumans? Who will be their parents? The technicians who generated them or the human beings from whose biological material they were made? Will they experience a sense of genealogical bewilderment because they have no security of biological parents who are like them and can give them an account of family and belonging?

Perhaps the need for belonging and relationship will be diminished as the degree of mechanization increases. Although children born from assisted reproduction have the potential to experience genealogical bewilderment, it may be mitigated by the presence of a loving and secure family.

A recent systematic review by Psychologists Elena Illoi and Susan Golombok recommended further research but concluded: 'Compared with naturally conceived adolescents and standardized normative samples, adolescents born through all Assisted Reproductive Technologies seemed to be equally well adjusted, and to have positive parent–adolescent relationships.'[32] This may then be true also for posthumans. If human beings are supportive and kind, then perhaps this will mitigate a sense of disorientation that posthumans may feel.

Final caveat: Can we project our thinking onto posthuman thinking?

The British clinical psychologist Simon Baron-Cohen describes one of the facets of being human as the capacity to have 'theory of mind'.[33] He states: 'By theory of mind we mean being able to infer the full range of mental states (beliefs, desires, intentions, imagination, emotions, etc.) that cause action.'[34] In this respect, we can work out that someone is delighted or weary because of what they do and how they look. This is sometimes called cognitive perspective-taking, such that we can get into someone else's head and imagine their point of view, which may be different from our own.

Theory of mind is important in three senses. First, it begs the questions, 'Is it valid to project our human understanding on to posthuman persons? Can we really know how they might think in any given situation?' We might imagine that they would be troubled by being generated by humans, as a means to an end, rather than an end in themselves. Perhaps, but we have really no idea how they might feel.

Second, the theory of mind is the substrate under investigation. However, if having theory of mind is a quintessential ability of a human person, will posthuman persons possess it? Can machines be programmed to understand, in a meaningful way, how a posthuman or human companion is thinking? Will it be different to understand a posthuman friend compared to a human friend? Will they recognize when we are happy or sad, but also more subtle feelings such as disinterest or disappointment? Can social understanding be learned, such as social cues, subtleties of communication, read facial gestures and body language? Will posthumans not only have self-consciousness but understand the consciousness of others?

A third layer of empathy is to understand how others see us. Not simply reciprocity of social interaction but an understanding of how another might understand us. Truly, that is a gift that eludes many. The Scottish poet Robert Burns (1759–96) captured this when he wrote a poem 'To a Louse' on a young lady who thought all round were admiring her bonnet when instead they were watching a louse crawl out from under it.[35]

> *O, wad some Power the giftie gie us*
> *To see oursels as ithers see us!*
> *It wad frae monie a blunder free us,*
> *An' foolish notion'*

> *O would some Power the gift to give us*
> *To see ourselves as others see us!*
> *It would from many a blunder free us,*
> *And foolish ideas.*

Burns knew that there is wisdom in seeing ourselves from someone else's perspective. Will posthumans be able to understand how we see them?

Conclusion

Personal identity is fundamental to our sense of worth and value and affects our relationships, our decisions and our mental health. For most humans, identity is not only individual but social. We yearn for connection with other people and value a societal structure.

Generating new forms of person such as posthumans is not merely an exciting technical exercise but an awesome responsibility. We ought to be concerned about the effects of the way posthumans might be generated and what consequences this will have on their personal identity, sense of kinship and security. Although our understanding of how they might respond or react is speculative, it is reasonable to imagine they would source their identity and well-being in the connection to the persons who made them. They may have a sense of disorientation and loss if they do not have a connection with the humans who generated them.

Yet the honest answer is that we do not know. We can project our need for belonging, fellowship and identity, but a posthuman psyche may be significantly different from ours. Thus, the caveat to this chapter is that there are significant limitations in our understanding of how posthuman persons might think. But this reservation should not stop us trying. Working out what makes someone else 'tick' (especially if they 'tick' like robots) is the first step of treating them as we would wish to be treated ourselves. As Theodor Seuss (who won the Pulitzer prize for his contribution to children's literature in 1984) wisely commented: 'Sometimes the questions are complicated but the answers are simple.'[36] Parental unreserved love, respect, protection and responsibilities towards a posthuman child they generate should be the same as to any child.

Notes

1. Robert Macfarlane and Jackie Morris, *The Lost Words* (Penguin: Hamish Hamilton, 2017).
2. Nick Bostrom, *Transhumanist FAQ – A General Introduction – Version 2.1* (World Transhumanist Association 2003), 5, https://web.archive.org/web/20061231225013/http://www.transhumanism.org/resources/FAQv21.pdf (Accessed on 20 October 2020).
3. Grant Gillett, 'Cyborgs and Moral Identity', *Journal of Medical Ethics* 32, no. 2 (2006), 79–83.
4. Ibid.
5. Ibid.
6. Ibid.
7. Danny Miller, *What Is the Relationship Between Identities that People Construct, Express, and Consume Online and Those Offline?* (London: Government Office for Science, 2013), 2.
8. Nuffield Council on Bioethics, *Novel Techniques for the Prevention of Mitochondrial DNA Disorders: An Ethical Review* (London: Nuffield Council on Bioethics, 2012), 52.
9. Miller, *What Is the Relationship Between Identities that People Construct, Express, and Consume Online and Those Offline?*, 10.
10. Gazi Islam G., *Social Identity Theory in Encyclopaedia of Critical Psychology*, ed. Thomas Teo (New York: Springer-Verlag, 2014), 1781–3.
11. Saul McLeod, 'Social Identity Theory (Simply Psychology 2019)', https://www.simplypsychology.org/social-identity-theory.html (Accessed on 2 February 2021).
12. Collins English Dictionary. (HarperCollins) https://www.collinsdictionary.com/dictionary/english/kinship.
13. Nuffield Council on Bioethics, *Donor Conception: Ethical Aspects of Information Sharing* (London: Nuffield Council on Bioethics, 2013), 7.
14. Eviatar Zerubavel, *Ancestors & Relatives: Genealogy, Identity & Community* (Oxford and New York: Oxford University Press, 2012), 53.
15. Nuffield Council on Bioethics, *Novel Techniques for the Prevention of Mitochondrial DNA Disorders: An Ethical Review*, 71.
16. Ibid., 55.
17. Ibid., 55–6.

18. Brené Brown, *Daring Greatly How the Courage to be Vulnerable Transforms the Way We Live, Love, Parent and Lead* (Penguin Random House UK, 2012), 8.
19. Anonymous article accessed online at https://www.news.com.au/lifestyle/parenting/babies/im-a-grownup-ivf-baby-heres-what-i-want-ivf-parents-to-know/news-story/cccd62e0a698712cfe29a4c6a02afc01 (Accessed on 3 February 2021).
20. Nuffield Council on Bioethics, *Donor Conception: Ethical Aspects of Information Sharing*, 8.
21. The UK Government, 'Parental Rights and Responsibilities', https://www.gov.uk/parental-rights-responsibilities (Accessed on 3 February 2021).
22. The Adoption Act, 1976 Section 39 at https://www.legislation.gov.uk/ukpga/1976/36/section/39 (Accessed on 3 February 2021).
23. Calum MacKellar, 'The Biological Child', *Ethics and Medicine* 12, no. 3 (1996), 65–9.
24. Zerubavel, *Ancestors & Relatives: Genealogy, Identity & Community*, 8–9.
25. Kate Hilpern, 'Donor-Conception: 'I'd Got to the Bottom of a Secret'', *The Guardian*, 5 November 2011.
26. Tabitha Freeman, Vasanti Jadva, Wendy Kramer and Susan Golombok, 'Gamete Donation: Parents' Experiences of Searching for Their Child's Donor Siblings and Donor', *Human Reproduction* 24, no. 3 (2009), 505–16.
27. US Department of the Interior, 'A Guide to Tracing American Indian and Alaskan Native Ancestry', https://www.bia.gov/sites/bia.gov/files/assets/public/pdf/idc-002619.pdf (Accessed on 23 October 2020).
28. Kimberley Leighton, 'Addressing the Harms of Not Knowing One's Heredity: Lessons from Genealogical Bewilderment', *Adoption & Culture* 3 (2012), 63–107.
29. Glenn McGee, Sarah-Vaughan Brakman and Andrea D. Gurmankin, 'Gamete Donation and Anonymity: Disclosure to Children Conceived with Donor Gametes Should Not Be Optional', *Human Reproduction* 16, no. 10 (2001), 2033–6.
30. Ashley Fetters, 'Finding the Lost Generation of Sperm Donors', https://www.theatlantic.com/family/archive/2018/05/sperm-donationanonymous/560588/?utm_source=atlfb (Accessed on 2 February 2021).
31. E.T. the Extra-Terrestrial (1982) [Film] Dir. Stephen Spielberg, USA: Universal Pictures.
32. E. Illioi and S. Golombok, 'Psychological Adjustment in Adolescents', *Human Reprod Update* 21, no. 1 (2015), 84–96.
33. Andrew Whiten, 'Theory of Mind', in *Encyclopedia of Cognitive Science*, ed. Lynn Nadel (Hoboken, NJ: John Wiley and Sons, 2006).
34. Simon Baron-Cohen, 'Theory of Mind in Normal Development and Autism', *Prisme* 34 (2001), 174–83.
35. This can be found online at http://www.bbc.co.uk/arts/robertburns/works/to_a_louse/ (Accessed on 26 October 2020).
36. Theodor Seuss Geisel won the Pulitzer prize for his contribution to children's literature in 1984. This quote is attributed to him and is available online at https://www.goodreads.com/quotes/6805-sometimes-the-questions-are-complicated-and-the-answers-are-simple (Accessed on 26 October 2020).

Conclusion

Calum MacKellar and Trevor Stammers

This book has sought to address a number of different technological, philosophical, and religious features in examining whether it is possible to ethically generate transhuman and posthuman persons. Indeed, society has a responsibility to engage with, and be ready for, the momentous consequences resulting from a possible transhumanist future. As the American theologian and bioethicist Ronald Cole-Turner explains:

> We stand together at a decisive moment in our evolutionary history, a moment of uncertainty and peril, but also one of great promise. By some of the more optimistic accounts, we are creating technologies that will improve our capacities so dramatically that sooner than we think, we will no longer be human in the usual sense of that word, but transhuman or posthuman.[1]

Such a proposed transhumanist future, however, is not new; it is similar, for example, to the one suggested by Victor Frankenstein in Shelley's novel, who wanted to 'banish disease from the human frame and render man invulnerable to any but a violent death'.[2,3] More specifically, as Matt James indicates (Chapter 7, p. 112), the aim is a future in which 'Weakness, fallibility and finality are eradicated in favour of enhancement and improvement. We [will] pursue a better version of ourselves free of the strife and challenges that resist and define us, but rather which we choose to define instead.'[4]

Self-confident optimism is very much to the fore, therefore, in transhumanism. As another US theologian and bioethicist Ted Peters indicates: 'The transhumanist confidence in the advance of technology draws upon a utopian vision, a vision of future human fulfilment or even posthuman fulfilment in a kingdom where rational intelligence has transcended its previous biological imprisonment.'[5] He notes that, for transhumanists, the aim is for the information patterns in the minds of human beings to eventually escape the limitations of the body, including death. Posthuman persons will finally exist in a cosmic community where they will experience ultimate flourishing and the truly abundant life which earlier visionaries could only imagine.[6]

All this, of course, seems very promising but may be over-optimistic since significant ethical challenges remain, especially in actually bringing into existence such transhuman and posthuman persons. It is in this context that the present study has sought to highlight a number of important features which need addressing if new kinds of persons are ever to be generated in an ethical manner.

The purpose and aim of generation

Concerning the ultimate purpose and meaning of generating transhuman and posthuman persons, questions can first be asked about the kind of future being proposed. However, before doing this, it may be useful to examine how the generation of new beings has been considered in history, where the following clues, concepts and patterns may be distinguished.

Creation may bring about meaning and order

In early Greek and Roman mythology, the earth was created from a great flood which was shapeless, unorganized and lifeless. Only through creation by a certain deity was chaos replaced by order and all the elements organized in a harmonious whole.[7] This is also reflected in ancient Jewish tradition where God created from what the Hebrew characterizes as *tohu-bohu*. The word *tohu* representing an unformed nothingness or a sort of 'desert' uninhabited and uninhabitable in which references of space and time are impossible. The word *bohu* meaning a state of 'void', 'emptiness' or more exactly of 'mist'. So defined, *tohu-bohu* is a 'nothing', independent of any organized order characterized by measurements of space and time.[8] Accordingly, it was only when God created out of his love the cosmos and humanity, that meaning and order were achieved.

Similarly, in a number of ancient creation myths, the motifs of frustration, fear, and dissonance are present making it necessary for the creator to create so that order and harmony may be established;[9] through the act of creating, a sense of stability and purpose is restored.[10] Interestingly, in a number of cultures, creation narratives are also used to recall and recollect the ultimate purpose and order of human life as well as the meaning of the existence of the whole cosmos.[11] For example, the Swiss psychologist Marie-Louise von Franz (1915–98) explains that in the case of ancient Fijians:

> Whenever they are threatened by dissociation and panic and social disorder, they try to restore the creation and the whole cosmos by retelling the creation myth. They create again, as it were, the conscious order of things and then await the corresponding effect upon their souls, which would mean that they once again feel themselves to be in order.[12]

This means that when certain people groups recall their creation story and the reasons why they exist, they may be reminding themselves of the real meaning and purpose for their lives, making it possible to, once more, get on with living.[13]

Human beings have an ability to understand the conception of a creator or generator

Interestingly, human beings are the only kinds of living beings, at present, who are able to conceive and rationally understand the concept of a generator, including for example the notion of a creator such as a deity who they believe may (or may not) exist. A concept which was, once again, reflected in Frankenstein's monster who recognized that Frankenstein was his generator.[14] It has also been suggested that, unlike other animals, created human beings are able to stand erect with their eyes directed towards heaven and the stars while asking themselves why and how they have come into existence.[15]

Something from the creator or generator is often used in the act of creation or generation

In many accounts of generation, that which was brought into existence is often portrayed as a kind of replica, or rather a model image of what already exists before the generation.[16] For example, this is expressed in Gen. 1.26-27, which states: 'Then God said, "Let us make mankind in our image, in our likeness, . . ." So God created mankind in his own image, in the image of God he created them.' However, the generator may also use something physical originating in himself or herself in the generation. For instance, in old Germanic mythology, the generation of the world was shaped from parts of the primeval giant, Ymir, with one translation indicating:[17]

> Out of Ymir's flesh was the earth fashioned,
> from his gushing gore the seas,
> hilltops from his bones,
> trees from his hair,
> heavenly sky from his skull.

In other creation myths, the generator first conceives a thought in himself or herself which is then exteriorized in the generation of a new being who fills the isolation or dark void surrounding this generator.[18]

A further important element in these generation accounts is that some kind of continuity exists through cause and effect between the generator and the creature – that existence or life is somehow passed on from the ancestors to the new person being generated. For example, the North African theologian St Augustine of Hippo, when discussing the concept of 'humanness', argued that every offspring of human persons is also a human person, irrespective of his or her properties.[19,20] Thus, for him, deformed infants should never be rejected or mistreated as non-persons.[21] Similarly, the American theologian, R. Kendall Soulen explains: 'A first feature [of the human condition] is that the human family exists as a *single community of common descent*.'[22] Humanity thus becomes a single extended family which exists in a series of generations stretching back to the first parents and forward into the future.[23] He also indicates:

> God's electing work deeply engages humanity as a community of descent. For example, there is a profound connection between being a descendant of the first parents and bearing 'the image or likeness of God'. However uncertain we may be

about *what* the *imago Dei* denotes . . . , there can be no doubt about who bears it: everyone *who* is a son or daughter of Adam and Eve (cf. Gen. 5:3; 9:6).[24]

This argument, based on descent, remained very important right through to the Middle Ages and beyond.[25] It was even suggested that the mythical race of dog-heads with human bodies (a kind of transhuman race) were human descendants of Cain (the son of Adam and Eve).[26]

At this stage, it is possible to query whether the generation of a non-biological posthuman person without any recognizable human physical attributes could ever be considered as the generation of a 'human' being. Interestingly, the American futurologist, Ray Kurzweil, believes that any new human-like artificial intelligences which are brought into being would still be 'human even if they are not biological',[27] while suggesting that the term 'human-machine intelligence' should be used to highlight this fact. Indeed, Kurzweil proposes that the humanity of machine intelligence is based on the gradual development and evolution of these intelligences from beings who are undoubtedly human.[28] He indicates that there would then be 'a world that is still human but that transcends our biological roots' in which 'there will be no distinction . . . between human and machine or between physical and virtual reality'.[29]

The possibility of generating monsters

Intriguingly, when something goes wrong in the generation of new beings in many myths or stories, they are then portrayed as failures who are, at times, represented as monsters, demons or hidden ghostly powers.[30] Moreover, these fearful beings may subsequently be used as a warning to those who are considering going down similar paths. A warning which may be reflected in the word 'Monster' itself, since it is believed to be derived from both the Latin *monstrare*, to show, and *monere*, to warn.[31] As the Dutch philosopher Henk van den Belt explains:

> In science and technology studies, entities that challenge the settled boundaries of nature and society are often designated as 'monsters'. Like the creations of synthetic biology, Victor Frankenstein's creature was a prime example of a 'monster' in this particular sense. Whenever culturally sanctioned boundaries are breached by such 'monsters', researchers are quickly accused of playing God or of treading in Frankenstein's footsteps.[32]

He adds:

> Shelley's 'monster' is something new in world literature, a being which disturbs the very categories by which we make logical sense of the world: reality and fantasy, being and non-being, life and death, natural and constructed, organic and artificial, animate and inanimate.
>
> Victor will continue to produce a series of nominations for his creature (including 'fiend', 'abortion', 'daemon', 'spectre', 'vampire', 'devil', 'vile insect', 'detested form' and

so on) because, as Shelley well knew, there are no authentic names for a being who questions the very logical categories created by human language.[33]

The French biologist François Jacob (1920–2013) further explains: 'Each monster is the result of iniquity and bears the witness to a certain disorder: an act (or even an intention) not in conformity with the order of the world. Physical or moral, each divergence from nature produces an unnatural fruit. Nature, too, has its morality.'[34] This leads into the next important notion of what is *natural* and how this relates, at times, to accusations of *playing God*.

The concept of the natural and playing God

One important objection to the possible generation of transhuman or posthuman persons is that such an endeavour may interrupt the natural way personal life comes into being. In other words, a serious conflict may exist between what takes place by natural means and what may be considered unnatural or artificial. As the British science writer Philip Ball explains:

> It is my contention here that all the current debates about . . . bioethics and biotechnology generally, regardless of whether they have any direct link to the creation of artificial humans, cannot be interpreted without understanding the cultural history of that idea and its relation to themes of 'naturalness'. Only by examining the old myths, legends and stories and the ways that they have been modified and mutated by the ages can we grasp the fears and preconceptions that teem beneath the surface of these discussions.[35]

Accordingly, it may be the transgression of the natural and how this is understood in a culture, that is most concerning to many – a natural that has traditionally been seen as being created by God in an ordered way and which reserves the generation of life to him. For example, Ball explains that in order to address a rumour that female witches could transform themselves into animals, a tenth-century Christian Church document entitled *Canon episcopi*, which was probably the work of a German Benedictine abbot called Regino of Prüm (d. 915), stated: [36]

> Whoever therefore believes any created thing to be able to be made or to be changed into better or worse or transmuted into another shape or likeness, except by the Creator, who made all things, and by whom all are made, is without doubt an infidel and worse than a pagan.[37]

Thus, a deep sense of unease often exists when the order or limit of Nature is challenged, especially in the generation of new life – an ill-defined apprehension frequently characterized by the equally ill-defined expression of playing God.[38] The American philosopher and jurist, Ronald Dworkin (1931–2013), notes:

> Playing God is thought to be wrong in itself, quite apart from any bad consequences it will have. . . . But it is unclear what the injunction really means – unclear what playing God is, and what exactly is wrong with it.[39]

Because of this, it may be difficult to see how the expression of playing God can give any real substance to the transhuman debate from a theological perspective.[40] That is to say, many of the contemporary concerns about the generation of new kinds of life, often expressed with the metaphor of playing God, may have little or no connection to specific religious traditions or beliefs. But the 'playing God' idiom may not just point to an improper appropriation of the role of God but may reflect other non-religious concerns which may be difficult to characterize. It is, therefore, important to unpack some of these anxieties in order to clarify the relevant concerns which they express.

Playing God and the order of Nature

The first concern inferred in the expression of playing God is related to what may be recognized as the 'order of Nature' reflecting the states and processes found in Nature and unmodified by humanity, which, it is suggested, should not be challenged or undermined. As a result, anything which can be seen as 'unnatural' (or even, perhaps unusual) is condemned. More specifically, the playing God objection may suggest a position that any interference with what is given by Nature is suspect. As a result, an intervention in nature will only be considered ethical if the 'natural' state or procedure is maintained.

Playing God and the limits of Nature

In the context of the previous concept of a 'natural order', it is also suggested that such an order may include specific limits. As the Australian ethicist Clive Hamilton indicates: 'Playing God entails humans crossing a boundary to a domain of control or causation that is beyond their rightful place.'[41] Adding:

> To cross successfully would require mortals to possess a degree of omniscience and omnipotence that has always been preserved for God or the great processes of Nature that are rightfully beyond human interference.[42]

However, going beyond the limits of what is possible naturally has always been the aim of transhumanism and posthumanism, as reflected by the very words used to characterize such positions. It is also reflected (as seen in the introduction) in the early Greek legend of Prometheus when he stole fire from the sun to give to human beings – a fire which was supposed to be the sole preserve of Zeus and the other gods, and which lay beyond the limits of humanity.

From this perspective, a possible objection to the generation of transhuman and posthumans persons is that such a procedure represents an inappropriate interference with Nature and the limits of the natural, especially in the manner in which such a generation brings life into existence. However, it is worth noting that human beings have sought throughout their history to improve their natural state through, for example, the use of tools and technology, which are not 'natural' as such.

Playing God and the resulting risks

Another aspect of the playing God argument suggests that it is inappropriate to trespass into or challenge what should be the sole remit of God or Nature, especially when possible consequences cannot be completely controlled. Dworkin notes:

> Playing God is indeed playing with fire. But that is what we mortals have done ever since Prometheus, the patron saint of dangerous discovery. We play with fire and accept the consequences, because the alternative is an irresponsible cowardice in the face of the unknown.[43]

But such a brash and polarized position may not always be seen as acceptable, and the playing God objection may highlight the possible risks that may exist in crossing certain natural limits. It may reflect the belief that the natural way of undertaking a procedure should not be changed because of possible unexpected and unpredictable negative consequences that could arise which may develop beyond the control of humanity.

Further, this playing God objection supposes that the balanced equilibrium of Nature should be respected, not least because any deviation from this may have unforeseen, poorly understood, and potentially irreversible outcomes – that natural processes are more reliable and robust when they are not interfered with by human beings. The position that the old 'natural' way is seen as safer would then question the possible risks and uncertainty associated to bringing into existence transhuman and posthuman persons.

Playing God and human pride

Another aspect of the playing God accusation recognizes that humanity may be affected by a sense of false belief in its own abilities while insisting on its right to use them without properly understanding their limitations. Thus, accusations of playing God reflect a charge of human pride, arrogance, hubris, as well as an overreaching, and defiance of limits as Trevor Stammers outlines in the introduction of his chapter (Chapter 8). Those who refrain from playing God, on the other hand, are considered to reflect a certain humility in recognizing human finitude and fallibility. In this respect, Ted Peters suggests that the analogy of playing God may have its origins in the story of Prometheus.[44] He indicates:

> We should note that, in the secularization of the ancient Promethean myth, nature has replaced Zeus as the determiner of what is sacred. Whether Zeus or nature, many believe that the mandate of this myth is to restrain human scientific or technological intervention from trespassing into the domain of the sacred. That

sacred for modern civilization is nature. Trespassing nature's sacred domain will result in retaliation, in monstrous violence, we are warned. So goes the logic of the commandment, 'Thou shalt not play god.'[45]

He also explains in the same vein:

[W]e today associate Prometheus with hubris, pride, overstepping our limits, crossing into forbidden territory, and violating the sacred. The antidote to Promethean recklessness is humility, caution, and sound judgment. Sometimes when we fear Promethean overreach, we put up an ethical stop sign that reads, 'Thou shalt not play god.' Victor Frankenstein's sin was to play god, to attempt to create life out of non-life.[46]

Mary Shelley herself mentioned in the introduction to her novel *Frankenstein; or The Modern Prometheus* that taking on the role of God, inappropriately, may be dangerous indicating: 'Frightful must it be; for supremely frightful would be the effect of any human endeavour to mock the stupendous mechanism of the Creator of the world.'[47,48]

Furthermore, a temptation may exist to become a god by being able to control and bring into existence personal life. The American journalist Paul Greenberg explains:

The temptation to create human life artificially goes back to Mary Shelley's 'Frankenstein' . . . Man's first temptation in the Garden comes when the serpent assures Adam and Eve that they need only eat the forbidden fruit, and 'ye shall be as gods' [Gen. 3.5]. . . . There's always a good purpose. For there is no evil man cannot justify, especially if we were set on it all along.[49]

Consequently, a concern exists that humanity might refuse to accept, in humility, the limitations and the finite nature of human life. But again, it is worth remembering that humanity has always sought to challenge the limitations of the natural order through the use of science, technology and medicine which cannot always be seen as unethical.

Refusing to play God may also reflect an acceptance that human beings have not, until now, generally controlled the future characteristics of their children but humbly accepted, instead, the result of the natural lottery. By this argument, resisting the desire to interfere with the natural way of generating new beings would reflect a surrendering of any control over them while encouraging human beings to accept their offspring unconditionally. Leon Kass explains concerning the expression playing God:

By it is meant one or more of the following: man, or some men, are becoming creators of life . . . ; they stand in judgment of each being's worthiness to live or die . . . not on moral grounds, as is said of God's judgement, but on somatic and genetic ones; they also hold out the promise of salvation from our genetic sins and defects ([through] gene therapy and genetic engineering).[50]

Thus, the pride in being able to generate and control personal life like a god may be important. Moreover, human beings tend to forget how limited and prone to mistakes they have always been. They may forget that they are but dust in a cosmos where science alone gives no meaning. Because of this, American Christian ethicist Paul Ramsey suggested: 'Men ought not to play God before they learn to be men, and after they have learned to be men they will not play God.'[51]

Playing God and religious concerns

For some of the major world faiths, such as Judaism, Christianity and Islam, the previous secular arguments expressed in the concept of playing God are usually considered to be relevant. However, additional concerns may exist, which intimate that any interference with the (good) natural state is immoral because it was given by God through Nature. As the UK-based theologian Michael Burdett explains, 'playing God appeals to divinely ordained orders of creation', adding:

> Proponents of this position will often hold to some form of natural law. God's intentions and directions for human beings, other creatures, and the rest of creation are at least in part visible in the way God has created the world. Having been ordained by God, these natural laws are not meant to be broken and doing so is an affront to the moral order.[52]

Accordingly, it is suggested that the natural law concept enables ethical principles to be determined from reason and experience as well as from directions presented by the order of nature given by God in creation.[53] The American philosopher Francis Beckwith further explains: 'This means that the natural law participates in the eternal law—that is, the order of creation in the mind of God – because the natural law is made for rational creatures with a nature ordered toward certain ends.'[54] It follows that, for many in certain faith traditions, it is important to follow the directions of natural law and not breach the natural state given by God.[55] As Ball indicates:

> Because in Judaic, Christian and Islamic tradition nature was under God's jurisdiction and guidance, what happened 'naturally' was the result of God's will and therefore was good by definition. This principle is embodied in the ancient notion of 'natural law', an inherently theistic idea. For Thomas Aquinas, natural law stemmed from a faith in a rationalistic yet teleological universe in which everything has a part to play. He invoked an 'eternal law' by which all creation is ordered, and considered natural law to be the way humans participate in this plan.[56]

However, it is not always clear how the playing God expression is actually understood by those with a religious faith. For example, God may have intended humanity to play God from the very beginning. Thus, in the same way as God created his human children in the garden of Eden, human beings were always meant to procreate their own children (and so, in a way, play at being God). The American theologian, Jacob Shatzer, indicates: 'Maybe our lives, as those made in the image of God, should be lives of "playing" at being like God.'[57] He adds:

> If Christianity means following Christ, imitating Christ, 'playing at' being Christ, 'playing God' can be reoriented. This 'playing' is not a 'power play' as our world has come to think of power – it is not exercising our knowledge and strength in remaking ourselves. Rather, it is humble play, accepting limitations and flourishing within them, following Christ in his suffering. This humble 'playing God' can impact the ... overall stance on posthumanism.[58]

Thus, it may only be when humans cheat at the game of playing God, as in the inappropriate generation of transhuman and posthuman persons, that ethical concerns arise. This is because such a development would be considered unnatural by those who believe in natural laws of generation given by the order of God's creation. As the American based bioethicists Nigel Cameron and Amy DeBaets explain:

> In our attempt to serve as our own creator we are revealed as usurpers, capable only of manufacture. That Faustian bargain is the only one on offer. The task of creator is personal to God, and his election of the interpersonal mystery of human sexuality as the context for procreation preserves his creatorhood absolutely.[59]

In other words, concern exists that the generation of new kinds of persons may violate the divine prerogative of bringing personal life into existence and may be tantamount to playing God in an inappropriate way. Marcus Rockoff explains: 'The motif of the "artificial man" primarily focuses on the human desire to become his own creator. This happens by imitated divine creation, even without or against god's will, in a magical-mystical, mechanical-electronic or biological-chemical way.'[60]

Generating transhuman and posthuman persons in Judaism, Christianity and Islam

Before considering the manner in which the generation of transhuman and posthuman persons might take place, it may be necessary and useful for society, including those with different faiths, to ask *why* this endeavour should be contemplated in the first place. Accordingly, it may be appropriate to question the motivations of those who want to generate such new kinds of persons in the future. Cole-Turner suggests that, even in their differences, some of the most prominent worldviews seem to agree that human beings need improvement, adding:

> By whatever path we take, we yearn to have better lives or to become better people, to work in better institutions and live in better societies, while building a better world. Ordinary lives are inadequate. But what exactly do we mean by 'better'? How do we define better people or better worlds? Does a better human have a better human body, or will this one do? Must a truly better human leave behind a merely human body entirely in order to become fully human? Or does the best human have no body at all?[61]

The vulnerability and limitation of new kinds of persons

Interestingly, as Trevor Stammers indicates (Chapter 8), physical bodies will always be necessary for persons to exist even if they are reduced to, for example, silicon or radio waves being propagated though the cosmos. Indeed, for human beings, but also transhuman and posthuman persons, to actually exist at all, requires a physical support in the dimensions of time and space. Thus, even though posthumanity may be uneasy, not just with the human biological body, but with embodiment in general,[62] posthumans will never be totally disembodied. Posthumanists cannot escape from what they may consider to be the shackles of embodiment and the limitations of physics.

Moreover, a noteworthy recurrent theme in this book is the critical importance for humanity to actually remain vulnerable and limited. A frailty arising from the shortcomings of the human body. For example, many adherents of Judaism, Christianity and Islam believe that human beings have been created by God in the way he always intended them to be. The US-based Muslim scholar Hamid Mavani indicates: 'The Qur'an points out that God created humans in the best mold . . . and inspired within them the divine spirit.'[63] Moreover, the body was never seen as something bad. As the theologian Stephen Garner in New Zealand explains:

> Christianity emphasizes human beings as intentionally created embodied creatures. . . . In so doing, Christianity puts embodiment firmly on the discussion table, reinforcing the notion that human beings are finite, created creatures.[64]

In other words, God could have created supermen and superwomen right from the beginning but intentionally created, instead, incredibly vulnerable and weak embodied human beings. Indeed, it is difficult to not recognize how desperately helpless, frail and needy human beings are, especially when they are infants or very old. [65,66] As R. Kendall Soulen explains:

> This aspect of the human condition is an often overlooked part of what it means to speak of the human being as *finite, limited,* and *vulnerable*. Like seasons of grass, humans exist in a sequence of quickly passing generations. Our character as 'begotten' creatures encompasses the fact of our conception and birth on the one hand, our possible begetting and inevitable death on the other.[67]

This is also noted by Mehrunisha Suleman in her chapter (Chapter 11, p. 172):

> The word for womb, rahm, in Arabic originates from the same root as Rahmah or mercy/compassion. . . . The Islamic worldview it thus centred on relatedness and co-dependency that evokes compassion, acceptance, a duty to care and protect. . . . Furthermore, if we bring into existence beings that are resilient, independent, invulnerable to aging, disease, or the environment what does that mean in terms of their ability to form relationships that are built on mutual need and trust that form society?[68]

This means that, if vulnerability, weakness and neediness disappear through transhumanism, a world devoid of compassion, empathy and sacrificial love would emerge. James Eglinton highlights this dilemma, from a Christian perspective, when discussing Herman Bavinck's concerns that real dangers exist when children accept a Nietzschean culture, where the *Übermensch* (overlord) dominates from both a physical and psychological perspective over the weak who are now seen as a problem to be removed or taken away.[69] Eglinton explains (Chapter 6, p. 101):

> As the sad history of the twentieth century indicates, every *Übermensch* needs to determine his *Üntermensch* [underling]. Nietzsche had nothing good to say about weakness. For him, there was no virtue to be found in it, and those foolish enough to do so ... deserved scorn. Conversely, the Christian notion of humanity advanced by Bavinck portrayed an invulnerable God as embracing vulnerability, finitude and weakness in the incarnation of Christ ... The Son of God became *Mensch*, a human, *homo vulnerabilis*.[70]

He adds: 'A Christian theological account of 'being human' is shaped by the perfect human, Jesus Christ, perfect in love and willingly vulnerable. Significantly, that view ties together the embrace of vulnerability with the capacity to love.'[71] Being able to freely love in vulnerability, moreover, entails a capacity to be moral and make decisions. The German philosopher Jürgen Habermas (quoted by Christian Hölzchen in Chapter 4, p. 68) puts it thus: 'I conceive of moral behaviour as a constructive response to the dependencies rooted in the incompleteness of our organic makeup and in the persistent frailty (most felt in the phases of childhood, illness, and old age) of our bodily existence.'[72] Habermas then explains why the very existence of moral values are necessary to protect the vulnerability of human beings.[73] Morality then becomes central to being human.'[74] St John Chrysostom (347–407), who was Archbishop of Constantinople, explains, 'for a man is not merely whosoever has hands and feet of a man, nor whosoever is rational only, but whosoever practices piety and virtue with boldness'.[75] This idea is also reflected by the 2002 International Theological Commission of the Catholic Church which concluded:

> Changing the genetic identity of man as a human person through the production of an infrahuman being is radically immoral. The use of genetic modification to yield a superhuman or being with essentially new spiritual faculties is unthinkable, given that the spiritual life principle of man – forming the matter into the body of the human person – is not a product of human hands and is not subject to genetic engineering. ... A man can only truly improve by realizing more fully the image of God in him.[76]

In this regard, it is possible to question whether the generation of transhuman or posthuman persons could ever be considered as a form of co-creation with God. The metaphor of human persons being considered as 'created co-creators' was especially developed by the US theologian Philip Hefner and has proved influential in examining human technological agency. As such, the 'created' element of the metaphor affirms the creaturehood of human beings as created, dependent and limited, while emphasizing the qualitative difference between creator and creature. The 'co-creator' element, on the other hand, reflects the calling of human beings to be creative agents within the natural world. Thus, for Hefner, God created humanity to be a kind of partner with him in the purposeful creative process in the world.[77]

However, many Christians are uncomfortable with the use of the term 'co-creation', especially in the context of generating persons. This is because, among other reasons, they prefer to see the creation of human persons as God's sole prerogative.[78,79] In other words, concern exists that in using the expression human persons may seek to promote themselves, in an inappropriate way, to the position of creator next to God.[80] Nigel Cameron and Amy DeBaets explain:

> [S]ome writers have coined the term 'co-Creator' in an effort to acknowledge the enormity of the human claim to (re)shape human nature, and yet dignify it with a designation that, as it were, seeks to bridge the chasm between what is proper to God and what is proper to humankind.[81]

Thus, by claiming that human beings may be considered as 'co-creators' with God, concerns exist as to a potential hubris and arrogance related to human agency's role in creation.[82] As Garner explains, 'emphasizing the capacity to be co-creators together with the transhumanist desire to transcend the flesh may lead to a denial of human dependence upon God'.[83] This may mean that human beings are not called to be created co-creators of transhuman or posthuman persons but are called, instead, to be created procreators of human persons.

In summary, even though the transhumanist may ask how humanity can become better physically, mentally or psychologically, the moral person may ask how humanity can become better morally and how individuals can better interact with each other.[84] Moreover, from the faith perspectives of Judaism, Christianity and Islam, to be a moral person is to be a living being whose nature and destiny is always incomplete apart from God.

The ethics of generating transhuman and posthuman persons in Judaism, Christianity and Islam

In Judaism, Christianity and Islam, concerns also exist about the manner in which the generation of transhuman and posthuman persons may take place. This is because, within these faiths, the aim is not to become transhuman or posthuman but true-human with the help of God. In Christianity, for example, the perfect image of God is given by Jesus Christ who, while remaining God, became physically human (through the incarnation). The Christian philosopher and physician Tristram Engelhardt (1941–2018) argued:

> One may not alter the general character of human biological nature and the human body so that the body of humans becomes different from the body assumed by

Christ, who in the incarnation took on our form. The general human form and character are sanctified both by creation and by the incarnation.[85]

He further explains that, though many human beings are already receiving artificial implants to replace disordered body parts: 'Humans must recognizably continue to possess the biological humanity taken on by Christ.'[86] Similarly, Cameron and DeBaets defend the human archetype indicating:

> [I]t is plain that all efforts at the enhancement of human nature – with enhancement defined in terms of a break with the human analogy – are theologically excluded since they have the effect of reshaping that human nature that is both God given and God taken. The exemplar of *Homo sapiens* is the glorified Jesus Christ.[87]

This means that though human bodies may be 'fixed' or some of their parts replaced with nonhuman elements in the context of therapy, for Christians no ambiguity should ever exist as to whether such 'repaired' human persons remain part of the human species. However, if a procedure is used to significantly enhance a body beyond what is considered to be human, then the procedure could be considered as suspect. This is especially relevant if uncertainty then arises whether the new being should be considered as a person. Hölzchen indicates: 'Do not generate beings whose ethical personhood can be doubted.' Among other reasons this is because if new living beings are generated, whose personhood is uncertain, then the very understanding of personhood and the ethical framework of society may be threatened (Chapter 4, p. 71).

Most of those from the Judaic, Christian and Islamic traditions also believe that God ordered the generation of plants, animals and humans always after their own kind. As indicated in Gen. 1.21,[88] 'So God created the great creatures of the sea and every living and moving thing with which the water teems, according to their kinds, and every winged bird according to its kind. And God saw that it was good.' Thus, order and species integrity are ultimately defined by God rather than simply by arbitrary forces. The American mathematician and philosopher Nobert Wiener, who developed the concept of cybernetics, indicated in the context of generating new kinds of robotic beings:

> For the idea that God's supposed creation of man and the animals, the begetting of living beings according to their kind, and the possible reproduction of machines are all part of the same order of phenomena *is* emotionally disturbing. [89]

Similarly, the fusion of human-nonhuman genomes may be perceived as running counter to the sacredness of human life and humanity created in the image of God.[90] In 2007, Bishop Elio Sgreccia, president of the Vatican's Pontifical Academy for Life, stated that 'the creation of an animal-human being represents one of the most serious violations of a barrier in nature giving rise to a comprehensive moral condemnation'.[91] It has also been argued that the generation of human-nonhuman embryos is an offence against a Christian view of human generation by confusing what is, or is not, human as well as who is, or is not, made in the image of God and thus to be considered as a neighbour.[92]

In addition, many in Judaism, Christianity, and Islam might use a passage in the book of Lev. 20.15-16,[93] as the basis for opposing any sexual relationship between nonhuman animals and human beings including with the aim of generating human-nonhuman transhuman persons. These verses indicate:

> If a man has sexual relations with an animal, he must be put to death, and you must kill the animal.

> If a woman approaches an animal to have sexual relations with it, kill both the woman and the animal. They must be put to death; their blood will be on their own heads.

This may reflect a condemnation of any acts in which human persons give of themselves in an embodied manner to a nonhuman animal, thereby degrading their special status.

Finally, many persons with or without a faith would be extremely concerned about the unethical and irresponsible generation of transhuman and posthuman persons because the resulting creatures may not be welcomed into existence in an appropriate way. This would especially be the case if they are produced or even manufactured without compassion and any consideration as to their well-being.

The challenge of generating transhuman and posthuman persons ethically

Ever since the dawn of human history, the manner in which children have been generated and the motivation for such an endeavour have been especially important ethically. For example, some children have been brought into existence in a very positive manner by loving parents, but others have been generated in a very unethical way such as in the case of rape. Thus, a similar dual reality may exist for the generation of transhuman and posthuman persons.

Accordingly, it may be possible to ask what it would mean to generate new kinds of persons ethically. Obviously, a number of answers could be given which have been explored in this study but, for many in society, the only appropriate way to bring transhuman and posthuman persons into existence may well be through the archetypal and traditional (normative) manner of procreation. This generally implies that two persons of complementary gender generate offspring in the context of their exclusive, selfless, unconditional and faithful embodied love for each other. A love and acceptance which then expands into and towards the offspring. It is then expected that these offspring will recognize that they are not, for instance, some kind of experimental object generated by hundreds of self-confident engineers who do not care about their welfare. Instead, they would be welcomed and accepted by their procreative parents into a society which recognizes and affirms their inherent value and worth. They will know that they have a rightful place in this society where they can fully flourish. But the question then remains how it would ever be possible to ethically generate transhuman and posthuman persons through procreation.

Notes

1. Ronald Cole-Turner, 'Afterword – Concluding Reflections: Yearning for Enhancement', in *Transhumanism and the Body*, eds. Calvin Mercer and Derek F. Maher (New York: Palgrave Macmillan, 2014), 174–91 (p. 175).
2. David H. Guston, Ed Finn and Jason Scott Robert, eds. *Mary Shelley, Frankenstein, Annotated for Scientists, Engineers, and Creators of All Kinds* (Cambridge, MA: The MIT Press, 2017), 23.
3. For a discussion about Prometheus in the context of Transhumanism and Posthumanism, see: Trijsje Franssen, 'Prometheus: Performer or Transformer', in *Post- and Transhumanism: An Introduction*, eds. Robert Ranisch and Stefan Lorenz Sorgner (Frankfurt am Main: Peter Lang, 2014), 73–82.
4. Matt James, Chapter 7.
5. Ted Peters, 'Playing God with Frankenstein', *Theology and Science* 16, no. 2 (2018): 145–50 (p. 147).
6. Peters, 'Playing God with Frankenstein', 147.
7. Michelle McLaughlin, *Creation Myths and Tales of Origin* (Texas: McLaughlin Group, 2013), 24.
8. Alain Houziaux, *Le Tohu-bohu, le Serpent et le bon Dieu* (Paris: Presses de la Renaissance, 1997), 37–8.
9. Marie-Louise von Franz, *Creation Myths*, revised ed. (Boston, MA: Shambhala Publications, 1995), 211.
10. This is also reflected with Victor Frankenstein, who, in his isolation and fanatical work, generated his monster with the belief that, by doing so, he would be accepted and valued by his peers.
11. von Franz, *Creation Myths*, 1.
12. von Franz, *Creation Myths*, 23.
13. von Franz, *Creation Myths*, 24.
14. The same was true with the replicants in the film *Blade Runner*.
15. McLaughlin, *Creation Myths and Tales of Origin*, 25.
16. von Franz, *Creation Myths*, 48–9.
17. von Franz, *Creation Myths*, 156.
18. von Franz, *Creation Myths*, 186, 203.
19. Augustin, *De Civitate Dei*, 16, 8.
20. Yechiel Michael Barilan, *Human Dignity, Human Rights, and Responsibility* (Cambridge, MA: MIT Press, 2012), 76.
21. Barilan, *Human Dignity, Human Rights, and Responsibility*, 74–5.
22. R. Kendall Soulen, 'Cruising towards Bethlehem: Human Dignity and the New Eugenics', in *God and Human Dignity*, eds. R. Kendall Soulen and Linda Woodhead (Grand Rapids, MI: William B. Eerdmans Publishing Company, 2006), 107 (emphasis original).
23. Soulen, 'Cruising towards Bethlehem: Human Dignity and the New Eugenics', 107 (emphasis original).
24. Soulen, 'Cruising towards Bethlehem: Human Dignity and the New Eugenics', 107 (emphasis original).
25. Barilan, *Human Dignity, Human Rights, and Responsibility*, 75.
26. As Yechiel Michael Barilan explains: 'Augustine's descendance principle carries further ramifications. By exorcizing from anthropology hybrid, chimeric,

metamorphosing, and similarly ambiguous creatures, Augustine humanized moral anthropology and founded it on human sexuality. By no other means than the sexual union of a man and a woman can somebody acquire special moral status of human dignity', See: Barilan, *Human Dignity, Human Rights, and Responsibility*, 76.
27 Ray Kurzweil, *The Singularity Is Near: When Humans Transcend Biology* (New York: Viking-Penguin Books, 2005), 30.
28 Nicholas Agar, *Humanity's End: Why We Should Reject Radical Enhancement* (Cambridge, MA: MIT Press, 2010), 53.
29 Kurzweil, *The Singularity Is Near: When Humans Transcend Biology*, 9.
30 von Franz, *Creation Myths*, 271.
31 Philip Ball, *Unnatural: The Heretical Idea of Making People* (London: The Bodley Head, 2011), 22.
32 Henk van den Belt, 'Playing God in Frankenstein's Footsteps: Synthetic Biology and the Meaning of Life', *Nanoethics* 3, no. 3 (2009): 257–68.
33 van den Belt, 'Playing God in Frankenstein's Footsteps: Synthetic Biology and the Meaning of Life', footnote 3.
34 François Jacob, *The Logic of Life and The Possible and the Actual* (London: Penguin, 1989), 27, Quoted in Ball, *Unnatural: The Heretical Idea of Making People*, 23.
35 Ball, *Unnatural: The Heretical Idea of Making People*, 319.
36 Ball, *Unnatural: The Heretical Idea of Making People*, 46.
37 Quoted William R. Newman, *Promethean Ambitions: Alchemy and the Quest to Perfect Nature* (Chicago: University of Chicago Press, 2004), 56, quoted in Ball, *Unnatural: The Heretical Idea of Making People*, 46.
38 For a discussion, see: Ted Peters, *Playing God: Genetic Determinism and Human Freedom*, 2nd ed. (London: Routledge, 2003 [1996]).
39 Ronald Dworkin, 'Playing God', *Prospect*, 20 May 1999.
40 Philip Ball, '"Playing God" is Meaningless, Dangerous Cliché', *Prospect Magazine*, 24 May 2010.
41 Clive Hamilton, *Earthmasters: The Dawn of the Age of Climate Engineering* (New Haven, CT: Yale University Press, 2013), 178. Quoted in John Weckert, 'Playing God, What is the Problem?' in *The Ethics of Human Enhancement*, eds. Steve Clarke and Julian Savulescu et al. (Oxford: Oxford University Press, 2016), 87–99 (p. 87).
42 Hamilton, *Earthmasters: The Dawn of the Age of Climate Engineering*, quoted in John Weckert, 'Playing God, What is the Problem?', 87–99 (p. 87).
43 Dworkin, 'Playing God', 20 May 1999.
44 Ted Peters, 'Are We Playing God with Nanoenhancement?', in *Nanotechnology: The Ethical and Social Implications of Nanotechnology*, eds. Fritz Allhoff, Patrick Lin, James Moor and John Weckert (Hobken, NJ: Wiley, 2007), 173–83.
45 Peters, 'Playing God with Frankenstein', 145–50 (p. 148).
46 Peters, 'Playing God with Frankenstein', 145.
47 Introduction to Frankenstein (1831), in Guston, Finn and Robert, eds. *Mary Shelley, Frankenstein, Annotated for Scientists, Engineers, and Creators of All Kinds*, 192.
48 van den Belt also explains: '*Frankenstein wanted to play God and was as severely punished for his transgression as Prometheus, who had stolen fire from the gods.*' See: van den Belt, 'Playing God in Frankenstein's Footsteps: Synthetic Biology and the Meaning of Life'.
49 Paul Greenberg, 'Dr. Frankenstein Plods On', *Jewish World Review*, 23 January 2008, quoted in Ball, *Unnatural: The Heretical Idea of Making People*, 319.

50. Leon R. Kass, *Life, Liberty and the Defense of Dignity: The Challenge for Bioethics* (California, San Francisco: Encounter Books, 2002), 129.
51. Paul Ramsey, *Fabricated Man* (New Haven, CT: Yale University Press, 1970), 138.
52. Michael Burdett, *Technology and the Rise of Transhumanism* (Cambridge: Gove Books Ltd, 2014), 12.
53. Scott B. Rae, *Brave New Families: Biblical Ethics and Reproductive Technologies* (Grand Rapids, MI: Baker Books, 1996), 38.
54. Francis J. Beckwith, 'Natural Law, Catholicism, and the Protestant Critique: Why We Are Really Not That Far Apart', *Christian Bioethics* 25, no. 2 (2019): 154–68 (p. 156).
55. For a discussion from a Roman Catholic perspective, see for example: Brian Patrick Green, 'Transhumanism and Catholic Natural Law: Changing Human Nature and Changing Moral Norms', in *Religion and Transhumanism: The Unknown Future of Human Enhancement*, eds. Calvin Mercer and Tracy Trothen (Santa Barbara, CA: Praeger, 2015), 201–15.
56. Ball, *Unnatural: The Heretical Idea of Making People*, 26.
57. Jacob Shatzer, 'A Limited Image? Practitioners, Patients, and Playing God', *Ethics & Medicine* 34, no. 1 (2018): 21–9 (p. 21).
58. Shatzer, 'A Limited Image? Practitioners, Patients, and Playing God', 26.
59. Nigel M. de S. Cameron and Amy Michelle DeBaets, 'Germline Gene Modification and the Human Condition before God', in *Design and Destiny: Jewish and Christian Perspectives on Human Germline Modification*, ed. Ronald Cole-Turner (Cambridge, MA: The MIT Press, 2008), 108.
60. Marcus Rockoff, 'Literature', in *Post- and Transhumanism: An Introduction*, eds. Robert Ranisch and Stefan Lorenz Sorgner (Frankfurt am Main: Peter Lang, 2014), 251–70 (p. 256).
61. Cole-Turner, 'Afterword – Concluding Reflections: Yearning for Enhancement', 174–91 (p. 174).
62. Michael Wee, Chapter 10.
63. Hamid Mavani, 'Islam – God' s Deputy: Islam and Transhumanism', in *Transhumanism and the Body*, eds. Mercer and Maher, 68–83 (p. 78).
64. Stephen Garner, 'Christian Theology and Transhumanism: The "Created Co-creator" and Bioethical Principles', in *Religion and Transhumanism*, eds. Calvin Mercer and Tracy J. Trothen (Santa Barbara, CA: Praeger, 2015), 230–43 (p. 234).
65. In this regard, Blaise Pascal (1623–62) indicated: 'Man's greatness is great in that he knows his misery; a tree does not recognize its misery. So it is miserable to recognize one's misery, but it is greatness to know of one's misery.' Blaise Pascal, Pensées sur la religion et sur quelques autres sujets, 114–397.

    'La grandeur de l'homme est grande en ce qu'il se connaît misérable; un arbre ne se connaît pas misérable. C'est donc être misérable que de (se) connaître misérable, mais c'est être grand que de connaître qu'on est misérable.' Translated by Calum MacKellar.
66. Even in the procreative act itself (sexual relationship), a profound expression exists of vulnerability and deep need of the other in love.
67. Soulen, 'Cruising towards Bethlehem: Human Dignity and the New Eugenics', 107 (emphasis original).
68. Mehrunisha Suleman, Chapter 11, p. 172.
69. James Eglinton, Chapter 6, p. 101.
70. James Eglinton, Chapter 6, p. 101.
71. James Eglinton, Chapter 6, p. 102.
72. Jürgen Habermas, *The Future of Human Nature*, trans. William Rehg, Max Pensky and Hella Beister (Cambridge: Polity, 2003), 33.

73 Habermas, *The Future of Human Nature*, 33.
74 Donal P. O'Mathuna indicates: 'Attempting to remover the trials and difficulties of life by genetic enhancement might derail the very ways in which God wants to shape our characters.' See: Donal P. O'Mathuna, 'Genetic Technology, Enhancement, and Christian Values', *The National Catholic Bioethics Quaterly* 2, no. 2 (2002): 277–95 (p. 283), Quoted in Ted Peters, *Perfect Human or Trans-Human*, in *Future Perfect?*, eds. Celia Deane-Drummond and Peter Manley Scott (London: T&T Clark, 2010), 15–32 (p. 23).
75 John Chrysostom, 'Instructions to Catechumens', in *Nicene and Post-Nicene Fathers*, ed. Philip Schaff (New York: Christian Literature Society, 1889), 165.
76 International Theological Commission, *Communion and Stewardship: Human Persons Created in the Image of God* (The Vatican, 2002), paragraph 91.
77 Garner, 'Christian Theology and Transhumanism: The "Created Co-creator" and Bioethical Principles', 230–43 (p. 232).
78 Dennis L. Durst, 'Uses of Biblical, Theological, and Religious Rhetoric by Cloning Advocates: A Critique', *Ethics & Medicine* 24, no. 1 (2008): 19–28.
79 Neil Messer, *Respecting Life: Theology and Bioethics* (London: SCM Press, 2011), 139.
80 van den Belt, 'Playing God in Frankenstein's Footsteps: Synthetic Biology and the Meaning of Life', 257–68.
81 Cameron and DeBaets, 'Germline Gene Modification and the Human Condition before God', 93–118 (p. 109).
82 Garner, 'Christian Theology and Transhumanism: The "Created Co-creator" and Bioethical Principles', 230–43 (p. 232 and p. 237).
83 Garner, 'Christian Theology and Transhumanism: The "Created Co-creator" and Bioethical Principles', 235.
84 Interestingly, Bostrom also indicates: 'If there is value in being human, it does not comes [sic] from being "normal" or "natural," but from having within us the raw material for being humane: compassion, as sense of humour, curiosity, the wish to be a better person.' Nick Bostrom, 'Introduction – The Transhumanist FAQ: A General Introduction', in *Transhumanism and the Body*, eds. Mercer and Maher, 1–17 (p. 13).
85 Hugo Tristram Engelhardt, Jr., 'A Traditional Christian Reflection on Reengineering Human Nature', in *Design and Destiny: Jewish and Christian Perspectives on Human Germline Modification*, ed. Cole-Turner, 85.
86 Engelhardt, Jr., 'A Traditional Christian Reflection on Reengineering Human Nature', 85.
87 Cameron and DeBaets, 'Germline Gene Modification and the Human Condition before God', 105. For a more developed discussion of human nature from a Christian perspective, see: Gerald McKenny, Biotechnology, Human Nature, and Christian Ethics, (Cambridge: Cambridge University Press, 2018).
88 See also Gen. 1:11–12 and 24–5.
89 Norbert Wiener, *God and Golem, Inc.: A Comment on Certain Points where Cybernetics Impinges on Religion* (Cambridge, MA: The MIT Press, 1964), 47 (emphasis original).
90 Calum MacKellar and David A. Jones, eds., *Chimera's Children: Ethical, Philosophical and Religious Perspectives on Human-nonhuman Experimentation* (London: Continuum, 2012), 135–9.
91 Jean-Yves Nau Nau, 'Cellules souches: le Royaume-Uni autorise des chimères d'humain et d'animal', *Le Monde*, 22 May 2007, (passages quoted translated by Calum MacKellar).
92 Nicholas Tonti-Filippini, et al., 'Ethics and Human-animal Transgenesis', *National Catholic Bioethics Quarterly* 6, no. 4 (2006): 689–704 (p. 704).
93 See also Lev. 18.23.

Appendix

Scottish Council on Human Bioethics recommendations on the generation of transhuman and posthuman persons

The following recommendations were agreed by the Scottish Council on Human Bioethics (SCHB) and represent the first example of guidelines from a European ethics council on the topic of the generation of transhuman and posthuman persons.

Because council members had different views concerning the strengths and weaknesses of the arguments in this book, it is not possible to describe the manner in which the recommendations were decided. The recommendations do, however, represent a general consensus of council members.

Generating transhuman and posthuman persons

The SCHB accepts that an ethical generation of transhuman or posthuman persons can only take place if those brought into existence are considered to have the same inherent value and worth as all other existing persons. This would enable these new persons to have a positive regard for themselves while recognizing that they have a place in society which is affirmed by others.

Accordingly, the generation of such new persons should be the result of the exclusive, unconditional and faithful embodied love between two original persons of complementary gender. For this reason, the SCHB believes that it is very unlikely that the ethical generation of transhuman and posthuman persons could ever take place. In this respect, the SCHB supports the following provisions:

Generating transhuman and posthuman persons

- Transhuman and posthuman persons should only be generated from living beings with full inherent dignity, value and worth.
- Persons of sufficient maturity should have the right to found a family, according to the national laws governing the exercise of this right.[1]
- Transhuman and posthuman persons should be generated from a selfless, unconditional and faithful relationship between the generators.

- Transhuman and posthuman persons should be generated from the complementary male–female relationship of the generators.
- Transhuman and posthuman persons should be generated from the exclusive relationship of the generators.
- Transhuman and posthuman persons should only be generated from the bodies of the generators.
- An intervention seeking to modify the human genome should only be undertaken for preventive, diagnostic or therapeutic purposes and only if its aim is not to introduce any modification in the genome of any descendants.[2]
- The use of generation procedures should not be allowed for the purpose of choosing a future transhuman or posthuman person's sex.[3]
- The principle that the generators of transhuman and posthuman persons have common responsibilities for the upbringing and development of the generated persons should be recognized.[4]
- The generation of transhuman and posthuman persons for research purposes should be prohibited.[5]

The moral status of generated transhuman and posthuman persons

- All generated transhuman and posthuman persons should be recognized as being free and equal in dignity and rights.[6]
- No discrimination should take place between human, transhuman or posthuman persons.[7]
- The interests and welfare of transhuman and posthuman persons should prevail over the sole interest of society or science.[8]
- Generated transhuman or posthuman persons should be protected against all forms of discrimination or punishment on the basis of the status, activities, expressed opinions, or beliefs of their generators.[9]
- Generated transhuman and posthuman persons should be given such protection and care as is necessary for their well-being.[10]
- Generated transhuman and posthuman persons should have the right to a name, an identity and as far as possible, the right to know and be cared for by their generators.[11]
- Generated transhuman and posthuman persons should not be separated from their generators against their will except if exceptional circumstances apply, such as for their protection and welfare.[12]
- Generated transhuman and posthuman persons who are separated from their generators should have the right to personal relations and direct contact with their generators on a regular basis, except if it is contrary to these generated persons' best interests.[13]
- Generated transhuman and posthuman persons should be protected from economic exploitation and from performing any work that is likely to be

hazardous or to interfere with their education, or to be harmful to their health or physical, mental, spiritual, moral or social development.[14]
- No generated transhuman and posthuman persons should be subjected to torture or other cruel, inhuman or degrading treatment or punishment.[15]

Public discussion

- The fundamental questions raised by the generation of transhuman and posthuman persons should be the subject of appropriate public discussion in the light, in particular, of relevant medical, social, economic, ethical and legal implications.[16]

Notes

1. This reflects Article 12 of the European Convention on Human Rights.
2. This reflects Article 13 of the European Convention on Human Rights and Biomedicine.
3. This reflects Article 14 of the European Convention on Human Rights and Biomedicine.
4. This reflects Article 18 (1) of the United Nations Convention on the Rights of the Child.
5. This reflects Article 18 (2) of the European Convention on Human Rights and Biomedicine.
6. This reflects Article 1 of the Universal Declaration of Human Rights.
7. This reflects Article 14 of the European Convention on Human Rights. In other words, no 'personist' discrimination between human, transhuman or posthuman persons should take place.
8. This reflects Article 2 of the European Convention on Human Rights and Biomedicine.
9. This reflects Article 2 (2) of the United Nations Convention on the Rights of the Child.
10. This reflects Article 3 (2) of the United Nations Convention on the Rights of the Child.
11. This reflects Article 7 (1) of the United Nations Convention on the Rights of the Child.
12. This reflects Article 9 (1) of the United Nations Convention on the Rights of the Child.
13. This reflects Article 9 (3) of the United Nations Convention on the Rights of the Child.
14. This reflects Article 32 (1) of the United Nations Convention on the Rights of the Child.
15. This reflects Article 37 of the United Nations Convention on the Rights of the Child.
16. This reflects Article 28 of the European Convention on Human Rights and Biomedicine.

Index

Abu Bakr ar Razi 168
Abu Hamid al-Ghazali 164
Adam 135, 136, 149, 153, 164, 170, 171, 210, 214
adnei-ha-sadeh 141
Alcmaeon (of Croton) 22
al-Farabi 170
Ali 160
al-Kindi 170
Allen, Colin 118, 122
Allenby, Braden R. 109
Almond, Brenda 200
Amara's Law 87
Anderson, Hans Christian 199
android 3, 4, 9, 11, 85, 86
angel 11, 24, 26, 52–4, 150, 170
Anscombe, Elizabeth 151, 152
Anthropocene 159
anthropoeia 9, 10
Aquinas, Thomas (Saint) 12, 24–6, 39, 53, 146, 147, 150, 152, 215
Aristotle 22, 33, 36, 150, 155
Artificial Evil 11, 119, 120, 126
Artificial Intelligence 11, 32, 62, 85, 103, 118, 139, 159, 210
Athanasius (of Alexandria) 149
Augustine (of Hippo, Saint) 23, 50, 119, 153, 209
Avicenna 7

Baal Shem Tov 140
Ball, Philip 8–10, 211, 215
bar nash de-tur 141
Baron-Cohen, Simon 203
Bavinck, Herman 11, 93–103
Bear, Elizabeth 193
Beckwith, Francis 215
Benjamin, Walter 155
ben Joseph bar Ḥama, Abba (Rava) (Rabbi) 134–8, 140, 142
biohacker 82, 83

Black, Daniel 123
blastocyst complementation 81
Bleich, J. David 135, 139
Boethius 23, 24, 26, 103
Bostrom, Nick 2, 3, 5, 32, 85, 110, 112, 159
Boyle, Matthew 36–9
brain-machine interface 11, 83, 84
Bristow, Peter 186
Brown, Brené 200
Bunyan, John 116
Burdett, Michael 215
Burns, Robert 204
Burrell, David 164

Cain 210
Calvinism 93–7
Cameron, Nigel 216, 219, 220
Čapek, Karel 8
Cassam, Quassim 20
categorical imperative 11, 62, 63, 70
chimera 78, 80, 81
Chinese Room 86
Chrysostom, John (Saint) 218
Cicero 22, 23, 66
Clark, Andrew 110
Cochlear implants 83
Cole-Turner, Ronald 207, 216
Condic, Maureen 149, 150
Condic, Samuel 149, 150
Conrad, Michael Georg 95
Coutrot, Jean 112
Crispr-Cas9 system 78–80
cyborg 4, 6, 32, 42, 85, 110, 197

Danto, Arthur 20, 21
Darwin, Charles 33, 96, 98, 99, 112
DeBaets, Amy Michelle 216, 219, 220
de Buffon, Georges-Louis Leclerc (Comte) 190
deep brain stimulation 83

Defence Advancement Research Project
    Agency (US)   83
de Grey, Aubrey   114
Dennett, Daniel   26
Descartes, René   50, 111, 151
designer babies   78, 145
devil   7, 191, 210
Dick, Philip K.   9
Dionysius (of Thrax)   21
donor conception   148
Dorff, Elliott (Rabbi)   141, 142
dulphanim   141
Dummett, Michael   41
Dworkin, Ronald   211, 213

Eden   215
Eidels, Shmuel   138
Einstein, Albert   43
Emden, Jacob   137, 139
Empedocles   22
Engelhardt, Tristram   219
enlightenment   3, 50, 62, 63, 65, 67
Esfandiary, Fereidoun M. (FM-2030)   3
eugenics   65, 94, 99
euthanasia   65
Eutyches   23
Eve   149, 153, 210, 214
excarnation   102

Faust   7, 216
Fetters, Ashley   202
Finnis, John   154
Floridi, Luciano   119–21
Ford, Norman   20
Frankenstein, Victor   8, 56, 141, 154, 185,
    190–3, 207, 209, 210, 214
Franssen, Trijsje   7
Fuller, Steve   5, 113

Gaius   21
Galatea   7, 9
Galton, Francis   99
Garner, Stephen   217, 219
gender   12, 64, 86, 146, 182, 184–6, 190,
    191, 221, 227
genealogical bewilderment   12, 148,
    202, 203
gene therapy   79, 214
genome editing   11, 78, 79, 87

Gillett, Grant   197, 198
Gnosticism   187, 188
golem   8, 12, 133–42
Golombok, Susan   203
Greenberg, Paul   214
Gretzky, Wayne   106
Grimm, Joseph   140

Habermas, Jürgen   68, 218
Haikonen, Pentti   86
Halakhic literature   136, 137, 139
Halevi, Gabriel   125
Hamilton, Clive   212
Haraway, Donna   4
Harmanus   7
Hassan, Ihab   4
Hayles, N. Katherine   4, 6, 111
He, Jiankui   79
Hefner, Philip   218, 219
Heidegger, Martin   11, 107–14
Heraclitus   22
Himmelreich, Johannes   125
Hobbes, Thomas   1, 42
Homer   22
homo dominus   11, 101, 103
Homo sapiens   2, 39, 77, 87, 113,
    183, 220
homo vulnerabilis   11, 101, 103, 218
homunculus   7, 8
Horace   21
Horwitz, Isaiah (Rabbi)   138
Human Fertilisation and Embryology Act
    2008 (UK)   82
humanism   4, 5, 62
Hume, David   25
Hurlbut, J. Benjamin   48
Husserl, Edmund   111
Huxley, Julian   1, 2, 112, 113
hybrid   11, 78, 80–2

Ibn Miskawayh   170
Idel, Moshe   136
Illoi, Elena   203
incarnation   23, 67, 101, 102, 218–20
International Theological Commission
    (Catholic Church)   218
intracortical microstimulation   83
Irenaeus (Saint, Bishop)   188
Islamic World League   166

Jacob, François 211
Johnston, Josephine 192
Jonas, Hans 72
Joy, Bill 118

Kant, Immanuel 11, 25, 26, 62, 63, 66, 69, 70
Kaplan, David 35
Kass, Leon 9, 182, 187, 189, 214
Kekes, John 119
Kenny, Anthony (Sir) 151
Kuhse, Helga 20
Kurzweil, Raymond 5, 102, 118, 210
Kuyper, Abraham 93–5

Leiner, Gersom Hanokh (Rabbi) 137, 138
Lewis, Clive S. 102, 106, 116, 154
Lindeboom, Lucas 95
Locke, John 10, 19, 20, 25, 26, 50
Loew ben Bezalel, Judah (Rabbi) 8, 133, 140–2
Loike, John 138, 139, 141

McCorduck, Pamela 118
MacKellar, Calum 124
Magus, Simon 7
Mavani, Hamid 167, 168, 217
Mehlman, Maxwell 183
Meilaender, Gilbert 181, 182, 184, 190, 192
Midrash Tanchuma 139
Minsky, Marvin 118
modernity 49, 56, 70
Molyneux, William 19
monster 141, 154, 185, 191–3, 209–11
Moral Turing Test 121, 122
Moravec, Hans 5, 118
Muhammad (Prophet) 160, 170, 171
Multatuli 95, 101
Musk, Elon 84, 85

natural order 152, 156, 166, 168, 212, 214
Neanderthals 183
Nestorius 23
Neuralink 84
Nevins, Daniel 139
Nicene Creed 148, 149
Nietzsche, Friedrich 11, 93–103, 218

Nuffield Council on Bioethics 198, 200
Nyholm, Sven 125

Oderberg, David 41
Oksenberg Rorty, Amélie 19
Ord, Toby 110
Ovid 7

Panaetius (of Rhodes) 22
Paracelsus 8
Parfit, Derek 19
Paul (Apostle) 68
Pearson, Karl 99
Perconti, Pietro 34–6
Perry, John 34
Peter (Apostle) 7
Peters, Ted 207, 213
phenomenology 26, 68, 70, 111
pig 71, 79–81
Pilate, Pontius 96
Plato 22, 50, 168
Playing God 12, 164, 168, 210–16
Pontifical Academy for Life (Vatican) 220
preimplantation genetic diagnosis 78, 165
Prometheus 4, 6–8, 212–14
Pygmalion 7, 9

Qaliqulas 7, 8

Ramsey, Paul 187, 215
Rav Hanina 134
Rav Oshya 134
Rawls, John 66
Regino (of Prüm) 211
Renan, Ernest 95, 96
Rescher, Niklas 26
Richard (of Saint Victor) 24, 25
Robot 3, 4, 8, 83–7, 110, 118, 123–6, 138, 170, 185, 186, 198, 205, 220
Rockoff, Marcus 216
Rosenberg, Yudel (Rabbi) 140
Rousseau, Jean-Jacques 50
Russell, Bertrand 36

Salaman 8
Sarewitz, Daniel 109
Savulescu, Julian 80
Scholem, Gershom 133, 136

Scott, Ridley (Sir)   9
Searle, John   86
Sefer Yetzirah   8, 134, 135, 137, 142
Seuss, Theodor   205
Sgreccia, Elio (Bishop)   220
Sharkey, Noel   125
Shatzer, Jacob   215
Shelley, Mary   8, 185, 211, 214
Sherwin, Byron (Rabbi)   141
Shi'i   160, 161
Shwerin, Byron (Rabbi)   141
Silver, Lee   187
Singer, Peter   20, 64
socio-technical imaginary   48, 54–7
Sorgner, Stefan Lorenz   5
Soulen, R. Kendall   209, 217
Sperling, Matthew   53
Spielberg, Steven   202
Stahl, Bernd   122
Stammers, Trevor   11, 213, 217
Strathern, Marilyn (Dame)   190
Strawson, Peter   26
Strong AI   85
Sunni   160, 161

Tajfel, Henri   198, 199
Talmud   12, 134, 140
Taylor, Charles   10, 11, 47–54, 57, 70
Tendler, Moshe (Rabbi)   138, 139, 141
Thomism   146
Thomson, Iain   108
Tirosh-Samuelson, Hava   3, 5

transcranial direct current stimulation (tDCS)   82
transcranial magnetic stimulation (TMS)   82
Turing, Alan   85
Turing test   85, 86, 121–3, 134
Tzvi, Hacham   137

Übermensch   11, 94, 96–101, 218
Ulrich, Werner   122

van den Belt, Henk   210
van Eeden, Frederik   96
von Franz, Marie-Louise   208
von Goethe, Johann Wolfgang   7
Vought   54–6

Wallach, Wendell   118
Warwick, Kevin   82
Washofsky, Mark (Rabbi)   141
Waters, Brent   181, 188
Weak AI   85
Welby, Justin (Archbishop)   146, 147
Wellisch, Erich   202
Wesley, John   190
Wiener, Norbert   118, 220
Wittgenstein, Ludwig   151

xenograft   80, 81

Zeira (Rabbi)   134, 137
Zerubavel, Eviatar   199, 201
Zeus   6, 7, 212, 213

Printed in the USA
CPSIA information can be obtained
at www.ICGtesting.com
LVHW011648091223
766046LV00004B/133